LANGUAGE LEARNING BEYOND THE CLASSROOM

"I am happy to see this innovative collection. ... I do not know of another volume with this focus. So, this is a very exciting venture, and I am very pleased to see it."

MaryAnn Christison, University of Utah, Department of Linguistics/Urban Institute for Teacher Education, USA

"This is a very original idea and an innovative publication, certainly in keeping with the times with its attention to autonomy, digital learning, and language learner strategies."

Paul Nation, Victoria University of Wellington, New Zealand

This volume presents case studies of language learning beyond the classroom. The studies draw on a wide range of contexts, from North and South America to Europe and the Asia-Pacific region. Each provides principled links between theory, research, and practice.

While out-of-class learning will not replace the classroom, ultimately all successful learners take control of their own learning. This book shows how teachers can help learners to bridge the gap between formal instruction and autonomous language learning. Although English is the primary focus of most chapters, there are studies on a range of other languages including Spanish and Japanese.

David Nunan is a language teacher, teacher educator, researcher, consultant, and author. He has published over 30 academic books on second language curriculum design, development and evaluation, teacher education, and research.

Jack C. Richards is an applied linguist, teacher educator, and textbook author, a specialist in the teaching of English as a second language (TESOL) who has had an active career in the Asia Pacific region (Singapore, Hong Kong, Indonesia, Hawaii) for many years. He is an honorary professor at the University of Sydney.

ESL & Applied Linguistics Professional Series
Eli Hinkel, Series Editor

Kachru/Smith • *Cultures, Contexts, and World Englishes*

McKay/Bokhosrt-Heng • *International English in Its Sociolinguistic Contexts: Towards a Socially Sensitive EIL Pedagogy*

Christison/Murray, Eds. • *Leadership in English Language Education: Theoretical Foundations and Practical Skills for Changing Times*

McCafferty/Stam, Eds. • *Gesture: Second Language Acquisition and Classroom Research*

Liu • *Idioms: Description, Comprehension, Acquisition, and Pedagogy*

Chapelle/Enright/Jamieson, Eds. • *Building a Validity Argument for the Test of English as a Foreign Language*™

Kondo–Brown/Brown, Eds. • *Teaching Chinese, Japanese, and Korean Heritage Language Students: Curriculum Needs, Materials, and Assessments*

Youmans • *Chicano-Anglo Conversations: Truth, Honesty, and Politeness*

Birch • *English L2 Reading: Getting to the Bottom, Second Edition*

Luk/Lin • *Classroom Interactions as Cross-cultural Encounters: Native Speakers in EFL Lessons*

Levy/Stockwell • *CALL Dimensions: Issues and Options in Computer Assisted Language Learning*

Nero, Ed. • *Dialects, Englishes, Creoles, and Education*

Basturkmen • *Ideas and Options in English for Specific Purposes*

Kumaravadivelu • *Understanding Language Teaching: From Method to Postmethod*

McKay • *Researching Second Language Classrooms*

Egbert/Petrie, Eds. • *CALL Research Perspectives*

Canagarajah, Ed. • *Reclaiming the Local in Language Policy and Practice*

Adamson • *Language Minority Students in American Schools: An Education in English*

Fotos/Browne, Eds. • *New Perspectives on CALL for Second Language Classrooms*

Hinkel • *Teaching Academic ESL Writing: Practical Techniques in Vocabulary and Grammar*

Hinkel/Fotos, Eds. • *New Perspectives on Grammar Teaching in Second Language Classrooms*

Hinkel • *Second Language Writers' Text: Linguistic and Rhetorical Features*

Visit **www.routledge.com/education** for additional information on titles in the ESL & Applied Linguistics Professional Series

LANGUAGE LEARNING BEYOND THE CLASSROOM

Edited by
David Nunan & Jack C. Richards

Routledge
Taylor & Francis Group

NEW YORK AND LONDON

First published 2015
by Routledge
711 Third Avenue, New York, NY 10017

and by Routledge
2 Park Square, Milton Park, Abingdon, Oxon OX14 4RN

Routledge is an imprint of the Taylor & Francis Group, an informa business

© 2015 Taylor & Francis

The right of the editor to be identified as the author of the editorial material, and of the authors for their individual chapters, has been asserted in accordance with sections 77 and 78 of the Copyright, Designs and Patents Act 1988.

Library of Congress Cataloging-in-Publication Data
  Language learning beyond the classroom / Edited by David Nunan & Jack C. Richards.
    pages ; cm. — (ESL & applied linguistics professional series)
  Includes bibliographical references and index.
  1. Language and languages—Study and teaching. 2. Reading.
  3. Educational technology. 4. Computer-assisted instruction.
  I. Nunan, David, editor. II. Richards, Jack C., editor.
  P53.75.L36   2015
  418.0071—dc23   2014015004

ISBN: 978-0-415-71314-6 (hbk)
ISBN: 978-0-415-71315-3 (pbk)
ISBN: 978-1-315-88347-2 (ebk)

Typeset in 10/12 Bembo
by codeMantra

Printed and bound by CPI Group (UK) Ltd, Croydon, CR0 4YY

CONTENTS

PREFACE

Much of the focus of research, theory, and practice in language teaching has traditionally centred on learning within the second language classroom, and how the classroom, together with teachers, learners, and learning resources can provide the necessary conditions for learning to occur. Thus the focus has been on the design of syllabuses, methods and materials, and the training of teachers in how best to exploit the classroom context as a source of appropriate input to learning and authentic language use. A complementary perspective emerged in the 1980s with the notion of learner autonomy, which shifted the focus from the teacher to the learners. This meant involving learners in decisions concerning setting objectives for learning, determining ways and means of learning, and reflecting on and evaluating what they have learned. Autonomous learning is said to make learning more personal and focused and consequently to achieve better learning outcomes since learning is based on learners' needs and preferences (Victori & Lockhart, 1995). Benson (2001) outlines five principles for achieving autonomous learning:

1. Active involvement by students in their own learning
2. Providing options and resources
3. Offering choices and decision-making opportunities
4. Supporting learners
5. Encouraging reflection

In classes that encourage autonomous learning:

*   The teacher becomes less of an instructor and more of a facilitator.
*   Students are discouraged from relying on the teacher as the main source of knowledge.
*   Students' capacity to learn for themselves is encouraged.
*   Students are encouraged to make decisions about what they learn.
*   Students' awareness of their own learning styles is encouraged.
*   Students are encouraged to develop their own learning strategies.

    This book offers an important perspective on autonomous learning by focussing on out-of-class learning and the role it can play in facilitating learning, one that provides an important complement to classroom-based learning. Contributors come from many different countries and describe approaches used both with English and other languages. The book reflects our observations of how successful language learners over the years often achieve their success: They are highly motivated; they set targets for themselves; they reflect on their learning progress; and, most importantly, they look for opportunities to learn language beyond the classroom. While opportunities for learning beyond the classroom have always been available to learners, technology and the Internet have dramatically expanded both the scope and nature of these opportunities. In this book, we focus on the diversity of opportunities and resources learners can make use of today and provide descriptions from many different contexts of how such opportunities can be planned for and implemented. Each chapter is organized in five parts: an introduction to the activity, a vignette of the activity in use, principles that derive from use of the activity, applications of the activity beyond the examples discussed, and payoffs and pitfalls. Discussion questions are provided at the end of each chapter.

The chapters are grouped into five parts that reflect the main topics addressed by the contributors, although many of the chapters also address issues found in other parts of the book.

Part I. Involving the Learner in Out-of-Class Learning

A recurring theme throughout this collection is the need to prepare learners for out-of-class learning. Day & Robb describe the power of extensive reading in language learning and how it can contribute not only to language learning but also to gains in both motivation and confidence. They describe the features of an effective out-of-class reading program. In a complementary chapter, Gilliland describes an approach to extensive listening in which learners use listening logs to document and reflect on their out-of-class listening experiences. She provides a useful set of guidelines for the effective use of listening logs. Walters presents a procedure for activating vocabulary learning outside the classroom. Kerekes describes how she tried to find opportunities for independent learning and, through trial and error, found that listening to songs and studying their lyrics provided a valuable learning opportunity, one that helped with many aspects of language learning, including pronunciation, idioms, predicting meaning from context as well as cultural knowledge. In the next chapter, Long & Huang focus on mastery of pronunciation and an approach in which the teacher directed students to resources and exercises to improve specific aspects of their pronunciation, required them to record a monthly pronunciation test and to take part in peer evaluation of each other's pronunciation. In the final chapter in this part, Chiesa & Bailey describe the use of dialogue journals, an out-of-class activity which takes the form of a written conversation in which students personalize, review, and reflect on issues and which becomes an important source of learning for both teacher and students.

Part II. Using Technology and the Internet

The chapters in this part provide examples of how technology and the Internet offer new opportunities and resources to support out-of-class learning. English is the natural language for much Web-based communication and students often feel more comfortable using English than they do using it in the classroom. New roles are required for both teacher and students and learners also need to acquire new skills and learning strategies. Although technology is an aspect of some of the chapters in other parts of the book, it takes on a central role in the accounts included in this part. Coxhead & Bytheway in their chapter describe how two on-line learning resources can be used to support vocabulary development—one a site containing conference talks and presentations including transcripts, and another an online gaming site. Chik describes how digital gameplay can enhance language learning and take the learner beyond the limits of classroom learning. In the next chapter, Righini discusses how social media resources were used to provide a means for students to authenticate themselves out of class both to encourage extensive reading and develop learner autonomy. Teachers created blogs where students could respond to news and the other readings and make podcasts based on things they read. They also created a Facebook group to share responses to readings. Beatty continues the exploration of online language-learning programs based on social media principles. Using an example from a learner of Chinese, he discusses the limitations a learner encountered when using online self-study resources, which led to an examination of social media sites that connect learners and provide a format for authentic communication and language practice. Kozar provides a further account of how the Internet and online social networking provides a replacement for pen-pal exchanges of the past—in her case, language exchange websites that link people wishing to improve their mastery of each other's language. In the final chapter in this part, Sasaki describes an activity involving tandem learning through e-mail. He shows how the activity can raise awareness, foster autonomy, and provide opportunities for authentic language use.

Part III. Learning Through Television

Watching television has long been cited by learners as a useful input to out-of-class learning. Indeed, in northern European countries, where English-language movies and TV programs are usually shown in English with subtitles, it plays a major role in young people's informal language learning. This part provides a number of accounts of how television can support out-of-class learning. Curtis gives an account of how the TV cartoon series Pokémon has many features that support learning, such as songs, rhymes, and a narrative structure, and shows how it supported the learning of a young learner. Hanf turns to the role of multi-episodic television series as a source of authentic language usage and how the use of captions and subtitles as well as the use of digital flashcards to note down important words and expressions can support viewers in TV-based learning. In their chapter, Lin & Siyanova-Chanturia show how learners can acquire authentic functional language through the use of Internet TV, which allows the delivery of traditional television to any Internet-enabled device (e.g., smartphones, tablets, personal computers) using video streaming. In a related chapter, Webb gives further support for the role of watching out-of-class television, describing "extensive viewing" as a parallel to extensive reading. He outlines strategies teachers can use to prepare students for such viewing by selecting suitable viewing materials and providing for follow-up so that the activity becomes not merely entertainment but a key component of successful language learning.

Part IV. Out-of-Class Projects

This part contains a number of examples of innovative project-based learning. Grode & Stacy describe a shadowing process in which students transcribe a short segment of a movie or TV scene and then practice reproducing it so that it sounds as close to the original as possible. In their chapter, Pontes & Shimazumi report on a project that makes use of VoiceThread©—a collaborative tool that allows users to create, comment on, and share documents, presentations, images, audio, and video files. In their project, learners prepare a short recording out of class and upload it to VoiceThread, where others can listen to it and comment on it. Mercado describes the implementation of two projects designed both to develop autonomous learning as well as facilitate extended engagement with English outside of the classroom. Calvert describes the use of field trips in an English for professional and academic purposes program, and their contribution both to language learning as well as the student's awareness of issues related to sustainability. Miller & Hafner extend the project concept by describing a digital video project in which students document a simple scientific experiment and upload it onto YouTube. They also describe the in-class activities that were needed to help guide the students through successful completion of the out-of-class project.

Part V. Interacting with Native Speakers

For many learners, interaction with native speakers or advanced language users is seen as essential to facilitate language learning. However, providing for such opportunities is not always easy to achieve. The chapters in this part provide accounts of a number of ways in which contacts with native speakers can be provided for learners. Arnold & Fonseca-Mora describe study-abroad experiences as well as immersion experiences such as "language villages" and the opportunities they provide for authentic language contact and for the development of communicative competence and cultural awareness. Macalister provides details of what learners perceive as the benefits of an extended study-abroad experience, its professional, personal, and cross-cultural benefits as well as the opportunities it provides for extended communication with native speakers. Stanley focuses more closely on the interactional strategies that speaking with native speakers require as the basis for both understanding and communication. Cadd recommends the need to build in credits for studying abroad and describes the use of tasks that require the students to interact with native speakers so that they do not spend all of their free time with fellow speakers of English. Grau & Legutke describe student-conducted interviews with native speakers in a German city and the preparation and follow-up necessary to make effective use of this approach. Thomson & Mori describe how a language program can overcome the limitations of classroom-based learning by linking learners to a community of practice—other learners, teachers, and target language speakers who participate in learning and using the language in a variety of shared practices. Lastly, Barkhuizen describes learning through home tutoring, an arrangement in which a tutor and a learner work together to meet the particular language-learning needs and goals of the learner.

Conclusions

A number of themes emerge from these accounts of learning beyond the classroom.

- Out-of-class activities provide opportunity to address some of the limitations of classroom-based learning.
- The wide-ranging benefits such opportunities provide encompass the development of language and communication skills, improvements in confidence and motivation, personal growth, and intercultural awareness.
- Out-of-class learning provides authentic language experiences and opportunities for real communication.
- There is a need to integrate classroom-based learning with out-of-classroom learning since both support each other.
- It is important to establish clear goals for out of class learning activities, to prepare students for the activities, and to provide follow-up in the classroom.
- The activities entail new roles for both teacher and learners as well as the need to develop learning and communication strategies to support out-of-class learning.
- Particularly through technology, many out-of-class activities allow learners to make use of the tools and digital resources that are a part of their everyday lives.

In summary, by providing opportunities to engage in authentic language use beyond the classroom, teachers can help learners develop autonomous learning skills and improve both their linguistic and communicative skills.

References

Benson, P. (2001). *Teaching and researching autonomy in language learning.* London: Longman.

Victori, M., & W. Lockhart. (1995). Enhancing metacognition in self-directed language learning. *System* 23(2), 223–234.

PART I

Involving the Learner in Out-of-Class Learning

PART 1

1

EXTENSIVE READING

Richard Day & Thomas Robb

Introduction and Overview

Extensive reading in the target language is an excellent vehicle for learning that language. Research has clearly demonstrated that learners who read extensively in the target language become fluent readers, improve their reading comprehension, learn new vocabulary, and thus increase their listening, speaking, and writing skills. Research has also shown that learners who read extensively increase their motivation to learn the target language and have positive attitudes toward learning the language (Day & Bamford, 1998). Since reading is an individual act that can be done by learners anywhere, any place, and any time, it is an ideal out-of-class learning opportunity. To engage in extensive reading, the only thing needed is an appropriate book.

We begin with a vignette describing the highlights of one person's engaging in extensive reading by herself to help her learn Japanese as a foreign language (Leung, 2002). We then look at what extensive reading is and briefly discuss five principles of an extensive reading approach that are relevant to an out-of-class learning opportunity. The Applications section outlines a case study illustrating how extensive reading can be done out-of-class individually. We then describe some potential problems to individual extensive reading and offer some solutions. This section includes a case study describing the *MoodleReader* program. The chapter concludes with a list of resources and discussion questions.

Vignette

The story of how Wendy learned Japanese as a foreign language by reading extensively in Japanese takes place in two stages and in two different parts of the world. She first started to read extensively while she was a graduate student in Hawaii. She took a course on second language reading and became very interested in extensive reading. Wendy wanted to take a beginning Japanese course that offered extensive reading but could not find one. So she decided to do it on her own.

For nine weeks, Wendy borrowed books from her friends and the local library to learn to read and write Japanese *hiragana*. She read books that contained mostly vocabulary that she already knew when she had studied Japanese previously. At the end of the first stage, Wendy had read 32 books, about 1,260 pages of simple Japanese text, of which 483 pages came from comic books (*manga*) and 170 pages from children's textbooks. The rest of the pages were from simple children's storybooks with an average of about 10 sentences per page.

During the first stage, Wendy read Japanese for about an hour each day. She reflected on what she learned and kept a daily journal about her experiences reading Japanese extensively.

After an interlude of about two and a half months, Wendy resumed reading extensively in Japanese. During the second stage, which lasted 11 weeks, Wendy followed the same study pattern and journal-recording procedure that she did in the first stage. In the second stage, Wendy found a Japanese friend who was willing to help her with her study for about half an hour to 1 hour each week.

In order to discover if extensive reading helped her learn vocabulary, Wendy took a vocabulary test twice during the second stage, at week 16 and week 20. The results showed that her vocabulary knowledge increased by 23.5% during this four-week period. The gain in vocabulary knowledge as assessed by Wendy's ability to use words in sentences resulted from the large linguistic input she received through extensive reading and her increased knowledge in Japanese grammar and sentence structure through self-study.

Here are some entries Wendy made in her journal about her learning vocabulary while reading:

> *Journal entry, Week 10*
> The cool thing about reading so far or perhaps I should say the rewarding part is when I am able to recognize words that I have read from other books before. Last night I took a Japanese children's book from the bookshelf and was going to show the pictures to my baby. As I scanned through the book, I realized that I could read some of the words.

> *Journal entry, Week 14*
> I used to think that *kirei* only mean "pretty" or "beautiful," but today I read something from a children's story book which used *kirei* to describe drinking water. I then realized that *kirei* could also mean "clean" or "pure."

Wendy's journal entries also demonstrate that her reading comprehension gradually improved from having a hard time decoding the *hiragana* orthography to understanding some simple children's stories.

In addition, Wendy's diary entries show how her attitude toward reading Japanese generally became more positive throughout the two stages.

> *Journal entry, Week 4*
> Yes, I think I am slowly progressing. I feel very proud of myself as I discovered that I could recognize some vocabulary I learned while reading different materials.

As Wendy's confidence in reading grew, she found herself having more tolerance of the different features and complexity of Japanese. When things got complicated, instead of thinking that Japanese was too difficult to learn, she tried to acknowledge the complexity and patiently learned to resolve one thing at a time. When she came across books that she really wanted to read, it motivated her to improve her reading proficiency so that she could truly comprehend the essence of the story.

Extensive reading promoted a positive attitude toward reading when appropriate reading materials were accessible to Wendy. Also, reading extensively helped her develop a habit of reading Japanese. From her journal entries, she wrote that she tried to read Japanese advertisements, directions on the package of children's toys, Japanese instructions on a phone card, Japanese signs everywhere, and items on the menus of a Japanese curry house near a bus stop.

Principles

Day & Bamford (2002) laid out ten principles of extensive reading for instructional purposes. Not all of these principles are relevant for an out-of-class learning opportunity. However, we believe that their first five principles should be followed when engaging in extensive reading in an out-of-class environment. Following these should help the learner in learning the target language. Let's look at these five:

> *Principle 1. The reading material is easy.* For extensive reading to be possible and for it to have the desired results, texts must be well within a learner's reading competence in the foreign language. In helping beginning readers select texts that are well within their reading comfort zone, more than one or two unknown words per page might make the text too difficult for overall understanding. Intermediate learners might use the rule of hand—no more than five difficult words per page.
>
> Wendy clearly followed this very important principle. She read material that had vocabulary she knew and that used a writing system, *hiragana*, that she found easy. She avoided selecting hard, difficult books, and reading material that did not have a lot of *hiragana*.

Principle 2. A variety of reading material on a wide range of topics must be available. The success of extensive reading depends largely on getting students to read. Research clearly demonstrates that we learn to read by reading. And the more we read, the better readers we become.

Without easy and interesting materials, it is impossible for a beginning reader to learn to read. Wendy understood this, and borrowed books from her friends and from the local public library.

Principle 3. Learners choose what they want to read. The principle of freedom of choice means that learners can select texts as they do when they read in their first language. That is, they can choose books they know that they can understand and enjoy or learn from. And, just as in first-language reading, learners are free to stop reading anything they find too difficult, or that is not interesting.

For out-of-class learners, this principle of extensive reading is obviously appropriate. Wendy's case is a perfect example. She sought out books that she found easy and interesting.

Principle 4. Learners read as much as possible. We know that the most important element in learning to read is the amount of time spent actually reading. There is no maximum amount of reading that can be done; the more the learner reads, the better. Wendy followed this principle. Recall her journal entry from week 4: "I spent a long time reading today. I feel a lot more comfortable to read Japanese than ever before." During the first stage, Wendy reported that she read about one hour a day and read a total of 32 books. This amounts to about three and one-half books per week.

We would like to discuss one more principle of extensive reading next. The fifth principle is different from the first four because it actually describes what happens when learners read easy and interesting books for pleasure that they select themselves:

Principle 5. Reading speed is usually faster rather than slower. This is very important. When we read slowly, one word at a time, comprehension is poor. When we read word-for-word, by the time we reach the end of the sentence, we have forgotten the first part of the sentence. Comprehension is poor. We have to go back to the beginning, and read again. So learners who read a lot of easy and interesting books actually understand what they read.

Applications

An extensive reading approach is the ideal out-of-class learning experience for learners who can read in their first language.

A requirement of the out-of-class learner is that she has a minimal vocabulary of at least 100 words. This requirement allows the learner to begin reading at the most basic level. Hitosugi & Day (2004) describe university students in a second-semester Japanese course reading picture story books for children. Wendy also read children's books and was able to figure out the meaning of the words from the pictures.

Next, we offer ten suggestions from Ono, Day & Harsch (2004) for learners who engage in extensive reading in out-of-class situations. If the learner can integrate them as she reads extensively, we are confident that she will learn to read fluently, read with greater comprehension, increase her vocabulary knowledge, and enjoy reading in the new language.

1. Read, read, and read.
2. Read easy books.
3. Read interesting books.
4. Reread books that that you really like.
5. Read for overall understanding.
6. Ignore difficult words or words you don't know. Skip them and keep reading.
7. Avoid using dictionaries.
8. Expand your reading comfort zone—challenge yourself to read books that earlier you found hard to read.
9. Set reading goals and keep a reading log.
10. Enjoy, enjoy, enjoy!

Payoffs and Pitfalls

Good things happen when learners read extensively in the new language. Studies show that they not only become effective, skilled readers: they learn a lot of new words and expand their understanding of words they knew before. In addition, they write better, and their listening and speaking abilities improve. Also, perhaps the best result from numerous studies is that students develop positive attitudes toward reading and increased motivation to study the target language.

However, these benefits cannot happen without the right books for out-of-class learners to read. The biggest challenge to engaging in an extensive reading approach in out-of-class situations is finding the appropriate reading material. As we describe above, learners need to read books that are easy and interesting, and it is not always easy to find a lot of books that are both easy and interesting.

The best material is graded readers (GRs). Graded readers are highly recommended for extensive reading because the vocabulary and syntax of the texts are controlled in order to make them accessible to learners at specific ability levels. The vocabulary used in graded readers is determined primarily by frequency of occurrence (e.g., the most frequent 200 words in English).

Also, GRs have appropriate syntax, which means beginning levels have *easy* syntax while higher levels use more complex structures. In addition to appropriate vocabulary and syntax, the *length* of GRs is controlled. The lower the grade, the shorter the GR. GRs written for beginners may be 10 to 15 pages with many illustrations to help convey meaning. GRs written for advanced learners may be 80 to 100 pages with few, if any, illustrations.

Graded readers are also controlled for their degree of *complexity*. For example, the plot of a graded reader written for beginners would not be as complicated as a plot of a GR novel written for advanced learners (a level 6). In addition, in the starter graded reader, there would not be as many characters as the level 6 book.

Thanks to technology, it is now possible to access virtually any text on the Internet with some form of glossing or translation provided as an aid to comprehension.

One of the drawbacks to graded readers is that they are not widely available in languages other than English. There are some in French, German, Italian, and Spanish.

If graded reading material is not available in the target language, we suggest that out-of-class learners consider reading books written for children. For beginners, picture story books are excellent sources of material to consolidate knowledge of the writing system and high frequency vocabulary. The pictures help the beginner to understand the story. For high beginners, books written for older children could be appropriate. And for intermediate learners, books written for adolescents would do very nicely.

The challenge for adults reading such literature is that the content is immature, and the learner might feel it is too childish. But books written for children and adolescents have been used successfully by university students learning Japanese as a foreign language (see Hitosugi & Day, 2004). Recall that Wendy also read children's books.

One problem related to second-language self-instruction is the high learner drop-out rates and the issue of motivation. All too often learners become discouraged and stop trying to learn the new language by themselves. They lose their motivation to continue.

This problem may not be as severe when learners engage in extensive reading as it is with learners who attempt to learn to speak and understand the target language. Gaining proficiency in order to communicate in the new language in out-of-class situations can be challenging as it is often better done in group situations.

In extensive reading, the learner simply needs the right material. She can read an easy, interesting book anywhere at any time. The overall goal is to read for general understanding and to enjoy the book. If the learner is a reader in her first language, then she already knows that reading is magic, that reading can take her to another place, another country, and even another world. She has experienced the excitement and pleasure of being so engaged in a book that she forgets where she is and what time it is. Thus, we believe that an extensive reading approach for out-of-class learners might not be as problematic as other approaches.

A Case Study

In the first section of this chapter, we reviewed the case of a learner of Japanese who was highly motivated to practice her Japanese through a self-enforced regimen of extensive reading in Japanese. Students like this are a joy to teachers, despite the contradiction that they are perhaps the students who need us the least. A little guidance and inspiration is often all that they require.

More challenging are the weakly motivated learners, those who expect the teacher to provide not only strict guidance on what to do, but close follow-up. This is sadly the more common case, particularly in curricula where English is an unwelcome required subject.

The extensive reading (ER) program at Kyoto Sangyo University in Japan was designed to work with reluctant students. After a brief history of previous efforts, we describe how ER was implemented over the entire entering student body of over 3,000 students in 2009 using a Moodle-based "plug-in" to assess the students' reading. Finally, we suggest how such a program might be implemented in other educational environments.

Background Study

The English Department at Kyoto Sangyo has been using extensive reading since the mid-1980s. Students were initially required to read a target of 1,000 pages outside of class and were required to write a summary in a dedicated notebook at a ratio of one notebook page per 40 pages read. Around 2001, the department implemented *Accelerated Reader* (http://renlearn.com), which, according to Wikipedia, is "an assessment that determines whether a student has read a book, with more efficiency, speed, and accuracy than a book report would because it is computer-scored."

The software worked relatively well and the notebook summary requirement was abandoned. With time, however, severe limitations became apparent. Since each quiz had only ten fixed questions, answers to the quizzes started to circulate. Soon after implementation, it became apparent that we had to restrict computer access to lunchtimes, with one of the faculty monitoring the students.

Our dissatisfaction with *Accelerated Reader* spurred us on to develop our own software in 2007, using the Moodle course management system as the basis. A plug-in was developed that forced students to pace their reading since it would only allow them to take a quiz every three days. Furthermore, it restricted quiz access to books within their own reading level and gave them a maximum of 15 minutes to respond to ten randomized questions. When implemented in the 2008 school year, it was a resounding success. Student reading was spread more evenly throughout the term and students could take quizzes any time they wanted, even from home.

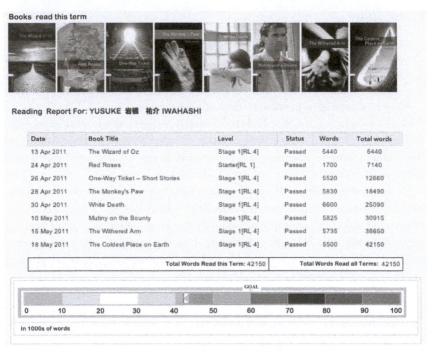

Books read this term

Reading Report For: YUSUKE 岩橋 祐介 IWAHASHI

Date	Book Title	Level	Status	Words	Total words
13 Apr 2011	The Wizard of Oz	Stage 1[RL 4]	Passed	5440	5440
24 Apr 2011	Red Roses	Starter[RL 1]	Passed	1700	7140
26 Apr 2011	One-Way Ticket – Short Stories	Stage 1[RL 4]	Passed	5520	12660
28 Apr 2011	The Monkey's Paw	Stage 1[RL 4]	Passed	5830	18490
30 Apr 2011	White Death	Stage 1[RL 4]	Passed	6600	25090
10 May 2011	Mutiny on the Bounty	Stage 1[RL 4]	Passed	5825	30915
15 May 2011	The Withered Arm	Stage 1[RL 4]	Passed	5735	36650
18 May 2011	The Coldest Place on Earth	Stage 1[RL 4]	Passed	5500	42150

Total Words Read this Term: 42150	Total Words Read all Terms: 42150

GOAL

0 10 20 30 40 50 60 70 80 90 100

In 1000s of words

FIGURE 1.1 A student's screen from the *MoodleReader* module.

Success with the English Department made us realize that we could easily implement the program over the entire first-year student body. The second author (Robb) as Chair of the General English Curriculum Committee pushed this idea forward, and in April 2009 some three thousand students started using the program. The library was extremely cooperative, purchasing and organizing by level additional graded readers for the massive influx of student-readers. This new clientele had the additional effect of boosting library patronage. Furthermore, there was a rub-off effect with the students using other library functions and facilities more than in previous years. The extensive reading collection now has around 12,000 volumes.

Implementation

As is often the case, Kyoto Sangyo relies on adjunct teachers for most of its basic skills classes. While there are clearly some dedicated professionals among them, many of these instructors have a full load of classes daily in various universities that leaves them with little time for preparation or professional development. We thus deemed it impractical to place yet another requirement upon these instructors, nor could we expect them to deal with computer access nor to appreciate the benefits of the ER approach. The curriculum committee thus decided to implement extensive reading in a manner that would minimize the burden on the individual teacher.

All instructors were provided with a set text to incorporate into their course descriptions for the following year concerning the ER requirement. A large double-sided sheet was distributed to the students in their first class that explained briefly in Japanese the benefits of the extensive reading approach, their reading requirement, where to borrow books, how to access the Moodle quiz program, and how their work would be assessed.

During the term, we monitored the quiz activity of each class and encouraged the instructors with low rates to remind their students about their ER requirement.

For the final assessment, we distributed a spreadsheet to each teacher with one column for the results of our joint final examination, another for the students' extensive reading grade, and one for the instructors to input their own class assessment, which, when input, automatically calculated the final course grades.

We thus implemented the extensive reading program without relying on "buy in" by the instructors, since it was impractical to do so prior to the introduction of the intensive reading program. Many of the instructors, however, soon discovered that extensive reading "worked," many students were doing the reading, and this apparently had an impact on their overall improvement in English. This was verified by their scores on the reading section of our joint final examination. We had given the same test to the previous year's cohort and the results revealed an extremely significant jump in scores at every ability level. (Identical placement test items were used that confirmed that both cohorts were of equal ability at the onset of their respective academic years.)

Discussion Questions

1. What are the major advantages of an extensive reading approach for the out-of-class learner?
2. What are some drawbacks? How might they be overcome?
3. The authors suggest that children's literature might be a source of reading material for adolescents and adults. Do you agree? Why or why not?
4. How might you encourage your students to read extensively outside of class?
5. The authors report that the MoodleReader was successful at a university in Japan. Do you think it would work with your students? Why or why not?

Resources

Mreader—This online system is the successor to MoodleReader mentioned in this chapter and is freely available for use by schools. See http://mreader.org for further details.

Other online testing programs—There are currently two online programs that are somewhat similar to *MoodleReader*, but targeted towards native speaker young learners, *Accelerated Reader* (http://www.renlearn.com/) and *Scholastic Reading Counts* (http://src.scholastic.com). Neither program, however, offers quizzes for graded readers and lacks specific functions that allow the program to work more effectively for second language learners.

Xreading (http://xreading.com) is targeted to second language learners although some aspects of it require payment of a fee.

Other sources of online reading—The main factors when selecting extensive reading or listening material are that the text be of a suitable level of readability for the learner and that the student can select material of personal interest.

When graded materials are not available, a side-by-side translation in the mother tongue can help make more difficult texts accessible. Another source is prescaffolded material—stories that the students are already familiar with such as fairy tales, or even books or movies already experienced in their native tongue.

Thanks to the Internet, the motivated student has a wealth of material just clicks away. In addition to "easy English" news sites such as those available on BBC, Voice of America, and the New York Times, there is a "Simple English" version of Wikipedia with close to 100,000 entries. Many *manga* series of current interest to many younger learners are available in English translation, as well as that of most major languages.

Naturally, if any material described above is intended for less motivated learners, some system will need to be established to hold them accountable for their reading be it a quiz or some form of written or oral report.

References

Day, R. R., & Bamford, J. (1998). *Extensive reading in the second language classroom*. New York: Cambridge University Press.

Hitosugi, C. & Day, R. R. (2004). Extensive reading in Japanese. *Reading in a Foreign Language 16/1*.

Leung, C.Y. (2002). Extensive reading and language learning: A diary study of a beginning learner of Japanese. *Reading in a Foreign Language*, 14(1), 66–81.

Ono, L., Day, R. R., & Harsch, K. (2004). Tips for reading extensively. *English Teaching Forum*. 42(4), 12–18.

Robb, T. (2001). Extensive reading in an EFL Environment. In J. Murphy & P. Byrd (Eds.), *Understanding the courses we teach* (pp. 281–235). Ann Arbor: University of Michigan Press.

Robb, T. (2010). Getting them to read outside of class: Let Moodle be the enforcer! *Mex TESOL Journal*, 34(2), 123–129.

Robb, T., & Kano, M. (2013). Effective extensive reading outside the classroom: A large scale experiment. *Reading in a Foreign Language*, 24(2), 234–247.

2

LISTENING LOGS FOR EXTENSIVE LISTENING PRACTICE

Betsy Gilliland

Introduction and Overview

Learning to listen in a new language takes practice and time, often more time than learners have in class. In order to improve their listening abilities, learners must do more than just listen to interesting programs—they must also think about *how* they listen and *what* they could do to improve their listening. Teachers can facilitate learners' out-of-class listening by helping them access appropriate materials and teaching them ways to reflect on their listening experiences. This chapter describes *listening logs*, a flexible activity that can be adapted for use in either second or foreign language settings to support students' development of extensive listening skills in any language.

Listening logs are an ongoing assignment through which students document their participation in out-of-class activities and reflect how such participation helped them improve their listening abilities. Listening log assignments require learners to attend a variety of authentic (real world) events, take notes on the content, and reflect on their own comprehension of each event. Teachers initiate the process in class by introducing students to a range of extensive listening strategies and modeling how to summarize and reflect on the experience. Students then choose what to attend and when to go as they document their experiences in the community.

This chapter explains how I have used listening logs to enhance intermediate and advanced level students' extensive listening proficiency. I describe introducing the assignment to a class and supporting students' participation in a range of listening experiences. I suggest ways that the listening log assignment can be adapted for students from different levels of language proficiency in both second and foreign language settings. The chapter concludes with a discussion of the benefits and drawbacks of the listening log assignment and suggestions of ways to resolve potential problems in students' participation and out-of-class learning. Finally, I review listening resources that learners can use to practice extensive listening.

Vignette

I first discovered extensive listening as an undergraduate studying abroad in Russia. After language classes focused on grammar and pronunciation, I joined my host family every evening to watch the TV news and soap operas. Some evenings, we also watched classic Soviet films. After hours of watching television, I found I could understand people talking on the street with much greater ease.

Years later, I was teaching advanced oral communication in an intensive English program at a California university. My students complained that their classmates were all international students, so they did not have contact with American English speakers, one reason they had chosen to study in the United States. These students had high TOEFL (Test of English as a Foreign Language) scores and wanted either to gain admission to degree programs in U.S. universities or to increase their English proficiency for business purposes. They said they had no trouble understanding their teachers or classmates, but could not grasp what the McDonald's cashier was saying.

My challenge as a teacher was helping my students improve their listening and speaking to the point that they could effectively participate in university classes during the following semester. Because we had limited time together, I wanted to take some of the listening out of the classroom. Based on memories of watching TV in Russia, I asked my students to document their listening practice after school hours. They kept listening logs where they summarized what they had heard, responded to the content of the program, and reflected on their listening ability.

I introduced the listening logs process during class time. We watched an episode of *Friends*, a TV show popular in my students' home countries. I played the entire episode, encouraging students to focus on how they were making sense of the characters' interactions as well as what was going on. After watching the show, we collaboratively summarized and discussed the plot. In this episode, the characters threw a baby shower, so we discussed American traditions and how they differed from what people do before someone has a baby in the students' home countries. Then we examined strategies the students had used to understand the story and whether they had encountered any new vocabulary or phrases.

This discussion modeled the process for students to follow in listening and writing listening log entries. I distributed a template (in the *Applications* section of this chapter) and asked them to submit five entries every four weeks. They could decide what to listen to and when to listen during that period. I also set some requirements to challenge them to go beyond their comfort zone: they had to document a range of different listening events, including at least one live (nonrecorded) activity such as a public lecture or a movie in a movie theater. To support the students' search for a variety of listening opportunities, I shared announcements from the local newspaper and the university campus.

Most students focused their listening log activities on TV shows, particularly those available online. Others, however, attended lectures on campus and around the city. The following reflections from their logs demonstrate their strategies for understanding some challenging events:

- One student took a guided tour of an art museum: *[T]he subject of the museum now is about politics, so it was pretty difficult to understand every art. The guide helped me to understand very well. … The guide told about the background of those arts and explained very well. … This field trip was really fun and interesting for me, so I could concentrate on looking at arts and listening to the guide. Sometime I couldn't understand what she said about the history or politics of 60 years ago.*
- Another participated in a service-learning project teaching elementary school children: *Even small kids, as long as they were native speakers in English. We still need to pay attention of what they said, and I found that sometimes it was difficult to follow that speed they speak in English. … Children couldn't use difficult vocabulary, but their speaking speeds are really fast, more than I think. Adults are good to practice our English, and they could critic our grammar at the same time. But I like children I like to talk to them. I feel so comfortable when I have chance to talk with them.*

Other students noted that they had some difficulty with the listening, reflecting on why an experience was not as easy to follow:

- A student attended a campus lecture about the death penalty followed by student questions: *I would like to try new listening log especially on tough topic in class. It is a social issue internationally and I have a concern about capital death. … I think the topic is a social problem and it is not talked in normal life. Therefore, I could not understand the most parts of lecture. There is no additional informant such as hand out and especially optical informant. Some students spoke so fast I could not understand at all.*
- Another watched a documentary on ancient Egypt: *While I listened and saw the documentary, I was so sleepy and often lost my concentration on the film. The narrator's boring voice was terrible to hear.*

After several semesters of listening logs, I surveyed my students about the process. They mentioned that listening logs had encouraged them to try new genres. Overall, their favorites were TV comedies, dramas, and feature films. Their least favorites were lectures, news, and documentaries. Many mentioned learning about American culture through television shows, and a few said they had become involved with campus activities because of the assignment. Several commented that they had noticed an improvement in their listening abilities and critical thinking skills.

Principles

The listening logs described in this chapter document *extensive listening*, that is, "listening for pleasure and without obligating the listener to keep demonstrating a satisfactory level of understanding" (Field, 2008, p. 54). Extensive listening differs from intensive listening, which focuses on brief listening texts for the purpose of making sense of a language structure or extracting exact details (Waring, 2010). The principles of extensive listening, similar to those of extensive reading (see Chapter 1 of this book), promote improved listening through access to greater quantities of listening texts (audio and video recordings and events such as lectures):

> *Principle 1. Learners need access to a wide variety of authentic listening texts.* In contrast with the slow, scripted recordings accompanying textbooks, the events students listen to outside class provide authentic input, at a natural pace, in realistic situations (Field, 2008). As my students noted in their listening logs, they watched and listened to different language styles, from spontaneous banter in a reality TV show to formal, planned analysis in an academic lecture. Students further benefit from access to the cross-cultural and social dimensions of listening.

> *Principle 2. Learners choose listening opportunities based on individual interests.* They should have some background knowledge about the topic in order to draw on prior experience to make sense of what is going on (Field, 2008). With free choice, learners show greater interest and motivation to practice listening and continue learning on their own time (Lynch, 2009). Although I did set some restrictions (such as requiring a variety of genres of TV shows and one live event), within those broad expectations, my students had options. They could select documentaries on topics about which they already had some knowledge or choose a film based on a book they had read in their home language, thus using schema from the past to help understand the present.

> *Principle 3. Listening texts should be at* "i minus 1" *level for maximum comprehension.* This means that listeners can make sense of almost everything that is being said without much effort (Vandergrift & Goh, 2012). There are many reasons to select listening texts at this level: Learners build motivation to continue practicing; they can figure out their limitations; it encourages self-efficacy; and they can focus on content rather than language (Field, 2008). One of my students noted what made comprehension possible in a situation comedy on TV: "[T]he story and joke is very understandable. Any countries' people must have the same problem. ... This story is about family, so I could understand most of the story."

Principle 4. Students should listen on a regular schedule for a minimum duration each time. In extensive listening, students should make an achievable plan and commit to practicing their listening (Vandergrift & Goh, 2012). With recorded listening texts, learners have control over when, how often, and how long they listen, as well as when, whether, and how often they repeat the recording (Field, 2008). By listening regularly, learners maintain exposure to their new language when they are not in class. My students chose when they listened and attended events with friends, making the assignment a social activity as well.

Principle 5. Learners should repeat some listening texts multiple times. "[L]istening to the same text again allows learners to become familiar with the content, vocabulary, and structure of the spoken text" (Vandergrift & Goh, 2012, p. 201). Repeated listening helps students develop bottom-up skills and learn new language beyond overall comprehension (Field, 2008). Many of my students watched recorded videos more than once to increase their understanding. I believe, however, that learners also need the challenge of live events to train their ability to use contextual cues, revise interpretations based on new input, and draw on background knowledge to make sense.

Principle 6. Learners should develop metacognitive knowledge about their own listening processes. Repeated listening only helps if leaners know ways to make sense of what they do not immediately understand (Field, 2008). Students should learn strategies to automatize the comprehension process (Goh, 2005). Teachers can help students develop strategies through awareness raising and focused practice (Vandergrift & Goh, 2012). One of my students noted her strategy for understanding Dr. Martin Luther King, Jr.'s "I Have a Dream" speech: "Actually, it is difficult to hear his voice because he uses high-level vocabularies. However, I can understand the general ideas. He spoke repeatedly some sentences such as I have a dream that one day the state. ... I have a dream that one day every valley. ... Therefore, his presentation was very strong and he made people to be persuaded and understand easily what he said even though they could not understand a lot."

Principle 7. Subtitles may help—but they may hurt. One debate is whether learners should use subtitles when watching recorded videos. Vandergrift & Goh (2012) suggest that research shows that students using subtitles had greater listening comprehension and vocabulary learning, although these results may be due to learners' dependence on reading, rather than on their improved listening abilities. Field (2008) points out that listeners using first language subtitles may not focus on the spoken language. He suggests listening several times before turning on subtitles *in the language of the video* for subsequent listening. I required my students to attend live events or movies in the theater to ensure that they listened without subtitles once in a while.

Applications

Listening logs allow intermediate and advanced learners to practice extensive listening outside the classroom. Waring (2010) suggests that extensive listening is unsuitable for beginners because they need to practice with comprehensible texts at an appropriate level for their language abilities. There are, however, real-world listening texts recorded specifically for lower-level learners, such as the BBC and VOA Learning English recordings. (See the *Resources* section of this chapter for suggestions.) In target language settings, students have opportunities to listen to unedited spoken language in many venues. In other countries, new technologies allow students to develop listening proficiency while learning about other cultures. Students need help finding these opportunities and using them to improve their listening proficiency.

A listening log entry includes these elements:

- Brief summary of the event
- Personal response to the content
- Reflection on the listening experience, including a plan for improving comprehension in the future
- New idioms, expressions, or vocabulary learned through the experience

Each element of a listening log entry advances learners' listening development. To write a summary, they must attend to main points rather than details. To respond, they must engage with the concepts, connecting background knowledge with what they heard. Reflecting on the experience promotes metacognition, pushing listeners to think about strategies they used for making meaning. Finally, listing new lexical items connects this out-of-class experience with learners' overall language learning. Teachers should provide students with guidelines for how long each section should be and how to present vocabulary words.

When listening logs are an extension of the classroom, teachers can support students' independent learning through preparation activities during class time. Teachers must introduce the principles behind extensive listening and the listening logs, including the importance of variety and risk-taking to promote language learning. Because most students want to improve their listening abilities, if they understand how the listening logs fit their own goals, they will try new genres of listening texts.

Students may need guidance in summarizing and response. In my classes, we created a model listening log entry after watching a TV show together. Teachers could model language-focused metacognitive reflection. The Metacognitive Awareness Listening Questionnaire (Vandergrift, Goh, Mareschal, & Tafaghodtari, 2006) helps students understand strategies they already use and which they could try in the future. Teachers can support students' access to listening opportunities available in their region by providing Web links to bookstores and organizations with lectures, movie theater listings, and campus events.

Lower-level students benefit from support of their listening experiences. Students could watch a film in class and discuss it instead of writing an evaluation. Students could use a language self-assessment checklist or rubric (see Wilson, 2003 for a model). Teachers could select appropriate films, shows, or podcasts for a class library or website with links and support materials (vocabulary lists, prelistening background information, etc.). They could invite guest lecturers to speak on a topic for which the students all have appropriate background knowledge and vocabulary.

Independent learners keeping listening logs will need to find events by themselves. In target-language-speaking countries, they may choose to attend public lectures, audit courses at a university, attend theatre performances, watch movies in the theater, or observe cooking demonstrations at a store. Universities host guest lectures, libraries and bookstores invite authors to read from their books, and movie theatres screen films not available on video. These learners also have access to Internet options discussed below.

Independent learners in other countries may have limited access to live events, but they can find resources on the Internet, including TED talks, streaming audio radio programs, podcasts from VOA, BBC, and NPR, movies, and TV shows. More advanced students may enjoy satire news sites such as *The Onion*. Lower-proficiency learners may focus on "English learning" podcasts and recordings for learners. See the Resources section for links.

Regardless of their location, independent learners may want to share their listening logs with "listening buddies" (Vandergrift & Goh, 2012). Buddies can watch shows together and discuss their responses and what they learned, improving their own learning and gaining new perspective on the content. Advanced students could write listening guides for lower-proficiency students, providing a preview of challenging vocabulary, or explaining cultural practices in a film or TV show. These could be published on a blog or shared in a language program.

Payoffs and Pitfalls

Listening logs can benefit learners worldwide. They facilitate learners' participation in authentic experiences attended by local native speakers where there is no adaptation for language learners. These authentic experiences also immerse learners in community events and offer an opportunity to see what local people value. Learners can thus broaden their knowledge of a country's culture and the pragmatics of the target language as it is spoken. Participating in listening log activities can further integrate students into the university or city, giving them an opportunity to get out of the classroom and learn about the community.

Listening logs also support good language-learning habits. Students develop autonomy, as they are responsible for selecting, attending, and responding to events without teacher handholding. The activities also build metacognitive listening, as students reflect on experiences and determine where comprehension broke down and how to improve. The activities further expose students to new modes of communication, from detailed academic language to casual interpersonal dialog.

Listening logs do present some challenges. My students needed support in finding and attending new events. Learners may be intimidated by events for local residents, especially events on less-familiar topics. Teachers could attend campus events with their classes, to show students how to purchase tickets and participate appropriately. Some of my students also needed support finding online resources, as they were not familiar with the options that were available in English. Teachers can create a resource website with links to recommended sites (such as those mentioned in the Resources section).

When Listening Logs are a class assignment, teachers may need to set parameters for types of events and how many of what kind are permissible. Otherwise, students may watch 10 episodes of their favorite TV show online (as a few of mine did). A few of my students copied TV and movie reviews from the Internet, rather than write their own reflections. This problem made me realize the importance of teaching students metacognition (i.e., how to pay attention to one's comprehension) and strategies for making meaning and repairing breakdowns.

Discussion Questions

1. What are some advantages and disadvantages of using the listening log assignment?
2. What strategies would you recommend to your students so they can improve their comprehension of audio texts?
3. In what ways are subtitles and repeated watching/listening beneficial? In what ways is it better to watch/listen with no subtitles?
4. Of the resources in this chapter, which are appropriate for your students? What additional resources (on the Internet and in your community) could support your students' listening log experiences?
5. How could you support your students' listening log activities?

Resources

Learners living where the target language is spoken can find live listening opportunities in local newspapers and university websites, which list lectures, author readings, guided tours, and theatre performances. Public libraries also provide information about upcoming events in the community. The following are English-language Internet-based resources. Learners of other languages may seek similar types of resources (news, television, and language-learning sites) in their target language.

Resources Adapted for Language Learners

Australia Network Learning English—http://australianetwork.com/learning-english/—Australia Network provides high quality English language learning videos that learners can use to practice their conversational English as well as find tips and advice to refresh their skills.

BBC Learning English—http://www.bbc.co.uk/worldservice/learningenglish/—This BBC website provides many tools for improving spoken English, especially for use in the personal realm and business world, the workplace, working abroad, and the like.

Voice of America (VOA) Learning English—http://learningenglish.voanews.com/—These national broadcasting sites offer audio and video programming and support materials for English learners. BBC Learning English is for intermediate level learners, Voice of America has two levels (high beginner and intermediate), and Australia Network Learning English has three levels (high beginner, intermediate, and advanced).

Breaking News English—http://www.breakingnewsenglish.com/—This website offers current news for learners. Each mp3 format story is recorded by two native English speakers with different accents (British, Canadian, American, and South African). The stories are rated *easier* or *harder* depending on the vocabulary (the audio is always the same pace). Breaking News English includes transcripts, lesson plans, and exercises for independent practice.

English Listening Lesson Library Online (ELLO)—http://www.elllo.org/—ELLLO provides dialogs and monologs recorded by ordinary people from around the world, some native and some non-native English speakers, about cultural traditions, hobbies, and general interest topics. Recordings are supported with vocabulary and comprehension exercises, plus some games.

Resources Not Adapted for Language Learners

TED Talks—http://www.ted.com/talks—*TED* (for technology, entertainment, and design) promotes "Ideas Worth Spreading." This website provides videos from 18-minute talks by celebrities, scientists, and other prominent thinkers. Many talks have been transcribed, but the site does not link to transcripts, so users must search independently.

Selected Shorts—http://www.selectedshorts.org/onair/—Professional actors read short stories by contemporary and historical authors in dramatic readings that bring stories to life. Printed versions of the stories can be found on the Internet or in books.

This I Believe—http://thisibelieve.org/—The audio podcasts on *This I Believe* are recordings of both famous and ordinary people from around the globe reading "essays describing the core values that guide their daily lives." Each recording has a complete transcript.

Lit2Go—*http://etc.usf.edu/lit2go/*—*Lit2Go* is a free collection of full-length books, stories, and poems in Mp3 format, with pdf files of the written text. Readers can sort the pieces by readability level.

References

Field, J. (2008). *Listening in the language classroom*. Cambridge, UK: Cambridge University Press.

Goh, C. C. M. (2005). Second language listening expertise. In K. Johnson (Ed.), *Expertise in second language learning and teaching* (pp. 64–84). London: Palgrave.

Lynch, T. (2009). *Teaching second language listening*. Oxford: Oxford University Press.

Vandergrift, L., & Goh, C. (2012). *Teaching and learning second language listening: Metacognition in action*. New York: Routledge.

Vandergrift, L., Goh, C. C. M., Mareschal, C. J., & Tafaghodtari, M. H. (2006). The Metacognitive awareness listening questionnaire: Development and validation. *Language Learning*, 56(3), 431–462.

Waring, R. (2010, 3 November). Extensive listening. Retrieved from http://www.robwaring.org/el/

Wilson, M. (2003). Discovery listening—improving perceptual processing. *ELT Journal*, 57(4), 335–343.

3
CARRYING VOCABULARY LEARNING OUTSIDE THE CLASSROOM

JoDee Walters

Introduction and Overview

Both second and foreign language learners have the opportunity to be exposed to a great deal of *target language* (TL) input outside the classroom. Learners in a second language environment can read signs, advertisements, books, newspapers or magazines, watch television or listen to the radio, read and listen to content on the Internet, and interact with others, face to face, on the telephone, or by e-mail, chat, or text. Foreign language learners, whose direct, face-to-face contact with native speakers of the TL may be limited, can access many of the same sources, especially on the Internet. This input contains a great deal of useful vocabulary that is meaningful to the learners. Learners who notice and try to learn that vocabulary will in turn improve their language skills in other areas, such as reading comprehension (Nation, 2001; Walters, 2006).

A vocabulary notebook, which is essentially a collection of words arranged so as to facilitate vocabulary learning, usually as an independent learning strategy, is one way for learners to keep track of the new words they encounter. It may not be an actual notebook: Words may be recorded on index cards or slips of paper, or collected on a computer or a mobile device. I will use the term *vocabulary notebook*, while recognizing that learners should collect vocabulary words in any way that makes it easy to learn the words effectively.

In this chapter, I describe how one student uses a vocabulary notebook to collect new words, and how she incorporates the notebook into her language study. I then describe some important principles underlying vocabulary notebooks. In the next section, I discuss how vocabulary notebooks can be used by language learners outside the classroom. I conclude with a discussion of problems that learners may encounter and some possible solutions.

Vignette

Marie lives and works at an English-medium university in Turkey. She has been studying Turkish for about two years, through a class provided by the university. She is always looking out for new words that she thinks will be useful. She may notice a word on a Turkish soap opera, in an advertisement, in a news article, on a billboard, or in a Facebook post. Sometimes, the meaning is clear from the context, or she looks the word up in a dictionary, or asks a friend. If the word seems useful, she records it on a blank index card, writing the Turkish word on one side, and the meaning on the other side (usually the English equivalent), along with, as accurately as possible, the sentence or phrase in which she encountered the word. Marie always carries a stack of these index cards with vocabulary words, along with some blank cards, bound together with a rubber band.

Marie spends a little time each evening adding more information to any new cards she has made, such as part of speech, and any particles accompanying the word. She also tries to write a few Turkish words that she associates with it, such as synonyms, antonyms, and collocations. Much of this information comes from an online Turkish dictionary that provides information about expressions and idioms. Finally, she writes her own original sentence using the word.

Once a week, Marie sits down with all of her vocabulary cards. She glances quickly through cards with words that she knows very well, and pays more attention to the more recent additions, picking out words that need more study. With this selection of words, she writes sentences or a paragraph using the words. Sometimes she randomly selects words and sorts them into piles, trying to think of how the words in each pile are related to one another. Finally, she selects the cards she will carry around with her, to study whenever she has time. This stack includes new words from the previous week, as well other recent additions.

At her Turkish class, Marie spends the moments before class comparing vocabulary cards with two of her classmates. When class begins, Marie asks questions about her new words. The teacher checks the information written on her cards, and also checks her sentences. Marie makes any necessary corrections and additions to her cards.

Marie reports that she has always used index cards when studying a new language, although she now puts more information on the cards. In the past, she simply used them to test herself on her new vocabulary words. She began using the cards with more complex activities at the urging of her Turkish teacher. She thinks that this strategy makes her more alert to words in her environment, but that it is easy to be overwhelmed by the number of new words there are. She says the hardest thing is being selective about which words to record; her solution is to carry only a limited number of blank cards around with her!

Principles

Vocabulary notebooks should be created and used according to the principles of vocabulary learning and memory (Schmitt & Schmitt, 1995). In this section,

I present two important concepts related to vocabulary learning, and four important concepts related to memory. Taken together, these principles provide a rationale for the format of a vocabulary notebook and the way it is used:

Principle 1. Vocabulary knowledge is more than meaning knowledge. There is much more to "knowing" a word than just knowing its meaning. For example, we know its form, both spoken and written, and its parts; other words that are associated with it, such as synonyms, antonyms, and collocates; how it functions in a sentence; and finally, when it is appropriate to use the word and how frequently it occurs (Nation, 2001). A vocabulary notebook that includes only meaning is unlikely to be very effective. Above, we see Marie recording a variety of aspects of word knowledge that will help her use new words accurately.

Principle 2. Vocabulary learning is memory work. Learning vocabulary entails committing word forms and their meanings (along with the other aspects of word knowledge) to long-term memory. Marie understands this need, taking every opportunity to work on memorizing her new vocabulary words throughout the week. Vocabulary notebooks should be constructed and used so as to promote this memory work, according to what is known about how memory works.

Principle 3. Recall helps future recall. When a learner uses a target word as a stimulus to remember the definition, she is engaged in *recall*. Memory research tells us that the act of recalling a word increases the chances the word will be recalled on subsequent occasions (Baddeley, 1997). Thus, a vocabulary notebook that encourages recall will be effective in helping learners to commit new words to memory. Recall is achieved by keeping the word form separate from meaning and other aspects of word knowledge. Marie does this by writing the Turkish word on one side of the card, with the meaning and other information recorded on the other side.

Principle 4. Practice makes perfect. Words that are encountered more frequently will be better learned than those that are encountered only a few times (Nagy, Herman, & Anderson, 1985). The vocabulary notebook should be used for recycling and rehearsal of new words. Learners should cycle through their collection of words frequently to create strong associations between the words and their meanings. Because Marie's vocabulary cards are always accessible to her, she can practice and study her words frequently throughout the day.

Principle 5. Stretch it out. Expanding rehearsal is the practice of lengthening the time between rehearsals of a word. As recall becomes more successful and reliable, the length of time between exposures should be gradually increased, so that more and more time elapses between rehearsals (Baddeley, 1997). Learners should also periodically return to previously learned words, to reinforce the connections between word form and the various aspects of word knowledge. Vocabulary notebooks should be constructed so that the time between rehearsal opportunities can be varied. Marie achieves this aim by focusing on new and nearly-new words during the week, and returning to older words periodically.

Principle 6. The more you think, the better you remember. The depth of processing hypothesis states that the deeper the level of processing used in learning something, the more likely it is to be learned (Craik & Lockhart, 1972). Rote learning is considered to take place at a rather superficial level and thus does not produce strong, long-lasting memory traces. However, if the learner processes the word at a deeper level, the memory traces created may be stronger, and the word is more likely to be recalled at a later time. Marie writes sentences and paragraphs with new words and thinks purposefully about how the new words are related to each other, all of which require deeper levels of processing, helping her to create strong memory traces for these words.

Applications

The task of learning vocabulary is common to all language-learning contexts. Whatever the reason for learning a language, a certain level of vocabulary knowledge is essential, and learners recognize this. Language learners almost universally report that learning the vocabulary of the target language is a priority, and many learners use rote learning with vocabulary lists as an independent vocabulary learning strategy (Schmitt, 1997). This tendency to independently study vocabulary in a focused manner suggests that vocabulary notebooks can be used by language learners at all proficiency levels and in virtually all settings. With guidance and encouragement, learners can channel their eagerness to learn new vocabulary into a more organized and principled learning strategy.

In beginning a vocabulary notebook, three issues are important: What to put in the notebook, how to organize it, and how to use it to facilitate learning. These issues are addressed by referring to the principles discussed above.

1. *What to put in the notebook?* Many teachers have their students record the target words from classroom materials in their vocabulary notebooks. However, learners can also record the words they encounter outside the classroom. These words may be learned more effectively because they are chosen by the learners themselves, from contexts that they find interesting and worthy of attention, and thus may be more relevant to their interests.

    Of course, the meaning should be recorded in the notebook, since the aim of the notebook is to help the learner make connections between form and meaning. Meaning might be represented by the first language (L1) equivalent, a TL synonym, or a TL dictionary definition. At the early stages of language learning, the L1 translation equivalent (if one exists) may be the most helpful, but learners should be encouraged to eventually include a TL synonym (again, if one exists) fairly soon in the learning process. "Dictionary definitions," or more complicated explanations of a word's meaning, may be necessary for words without an L1 equivalent or useful TL synonym.

As discussed in the previous section, there is much more to "knowing" a word than knowing its meaning. Learners can add information about pronunciation, roots and affixes, synonyms and antonyms, and so on. An example sentence is useful for illustrating grammatical function and collocations. Information about register and frequency, and thus appropriateness, can also be included in the notebook.

Below we can see an example of a vocabulary notebook entry (recorded on an index card):

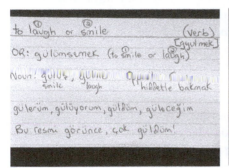 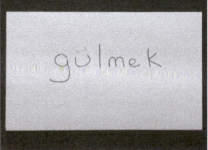

This vocabulary entry is for the Turkish word *gülmek*. The target word is written on one side of the index card, and on the other side is written its English equivalent, part of speech, pronunciation, an alternative word (synonym), words within the same word family, an antonym, some conjugations of the verb, and a sample sentence.

Not all of this information will be available upon first encountering the word, especially if it is encountered while interacting in the TL. The first action might be to record the word, what is known about its meaning, and, if possible, the sentence or phrase in which it occurred. The remaining information can be added later, either on subsequent encounters, or during a dedicated vocabulary study time.

2. *How should the notebook be organized?* A vocabulary notebook does not have to be a notebook *per se*. Vocabulary entries can be recorded on paper, index cards, a computer, or some mobile device such as a mobile phone or tablet, using a flashcard application. Whatever is used to record the entries, some decision must be made as to how they are be arranged. Learners may choose to arrange the words alphabetically, by part of speech, by topic or theme, or in order of first encounter. Perhaps the most important feature of the arrangement is the ability to move words around, and to remove them when they

have been learned. This suggests a loose-leaf arrangement, such as a loose-leaf notebook, a stack of index cards held together with a rubber band (or with a metal ring and punch holes), or an easily sorted collection on a computer, tablet, or phone. Being able to sort the words allows learners to change the arrangement of the words according to their needs.

3. *How should learners use the notebook to facilitate learning?* As stated above, the purpose of the vocabulary notebook is to help learners commit new TL words to long-term memory. Therefore, the notebook should be used in ways that reflect what we know about learning and memory.

   a. Promote recall, not just repetition. The target word should be separated from information about meaning, part of speech, associations, collocations, and so on. In this way, the learner must recall the various aspects of word knowledge when the form is presented. On paper, the word might be written on one side of the page with the meaning and other information written on the other side (i.e., the overleaf). Index cards would, like flash cards, have the target word on one side with the word information on the overleaf. Words recorded on a computer, tablet, or phone might make use of a hyperlink function to create links between the target words and their information.

   b. Recycle the words. Learners should be prepared to go through their collection of words many times, rehearsing their recall of word forms, meanings, and other aspects of word knowledge. If the vocabulary notebook is easily accessible, frequent rehearsal is easy to accomplish throughout the day, while waiting for a bus, in between classes or meetings, while eating lunch, and so on. Learners can flip through the pages of a notebook, go through a stack of index cards, or scan through entries in a document, slide-show, database, or spread-sheet arrangement.

   c. Expanding rehearsal. As recall becomes increasingly successful, the amount of time between rehearsal opportunities for the words should be gradually increased. New words in the collection should be quickly recycled, while older words should be practiced at gradually increasing intervals. Eventually, words that have been learned should be removed from the notebook, although the learner should return to them occasionally to ensure they are still known.

      This idea of expanding rehearsal means that learners must be aware of the words in their notebook, and how successful they are in recalling the words. They must also actively organize their practice sessions ahead of time, taking some time to sort through words according to how often they should be rehearsed. Learners who plan their study can take time each week to monitor their progress, and organize the words they plan to study that week.

   d. Process at a deeper level. There is no question that rote memorization is very useful for establishing a connection between form and meaning (Nation, 1982). However, for strong, long-lasting memory traces, there is no substitute for processing the words at a deeper level (Craik & Lockhart, 1972; Craik & Tulving, 1975). Learners should work with their collection of words in ways that will help them think about meaning, relationships with other words, functions in sentences, and the ways they are put together.

In the following table is a small selection of vocabulary activities that promote depth of processing. These activities can be done during a period of individual vocabulary study (or with a friend) and can be used over and over again with different collections of words. Teachers may have more ideas for good vocabulary activities that promote depth of processing.

Draw pictures to illustrate the words.	Not all words lend themselves to illustration.
Develop key word associations.	Conjure a mental image that combines the target word (form and meaning) with another word (either L1 or TL). For example, when I was learning the Japanese expression for "good morning," I envisioned a picture of my sister's house in Ohio, with a morning sun rising over it. This helped me to remember *ohayo gozaimasu*.
Write sentences using the words.	The sentence should illustrate the meaning of the word. For example, rather than *My mother is a doctor*, a sentence like *My sister was sick, but she went to the doctor and now she feels better* is more illustrative of the meaning.
Write a story using a selection of words.	Words can be chosen because they are related to a single theme or topic, or chosen randomly, as a challenge!
Make a mind map.	For a selection of words, think about how they are related to each other, and make a mind map to illustrate it. The words can be chosen because they are related, or chosen randomly, for a challenge.
Sort the collection of words into different categories.	There may be several ways the words can be sorted, and perhaps not all the words will group together, but this activity helps build connections among the words. (This activity may be done with a friend: Sort into categories and see if the friend can understand the categories.)
With a friend, make crossword puzzles for each other.	Pick a selection of words from your friend's notebook, and make a crossword puzzle for her. Use the definitions for clues. Have her make a puzzle for you with words from your notebook. Switch puzzles, and solve!
Practice adding prefixes and suffixes, to make a word family.	Choose words that are appropriate to make different forms. Check your work in a dictionary.

Payoffs and Pitfalls

Vocabulary notebooks have long been advocated as a valuable learning strategy to help learners take control of their vocabulary learning (Fowle, 2002; Laufer & Nation, 1999; Schmitt & Schmitt, 1995), and a study conducted in 2009 (Walters & Bozkurt, 2009) lent empirical support to the notion that vocabulary notebooks are beneficial for vocabulary development, finding that students who used vocabulary notebooks were more successful in learning target words from classroom materials than a parallel class that did not use vocabulary notebooks. So it seems that teachers have good reasons to encourage students to use vocabulary notebooks.

However, as with any learning strategy, learners must understand how and when to use the strategy. Vocabulary notebooks may devolve into simply a collection of words and meanings, used only for rote memorization that may not last beyond the study period. In addition, the sheer number of new words that learners are exposed to may make the task seem so overwhelming that it is quickly abandoned. Learners may need guidance and structure when first embarking on this strategy. Below are some suggestions for introducing vocabulary notebooks in the language classroom:

- Ask learners to bring in one word per week, for "vocabulary show and tell."
- Ask learners why they chose their "show and tell" word and give feedback to help them understand what kinds of words they should be alert to.
- Make a "class vocabulary notebook" to model the format, using the words the learners bring in every week. Demonstrate the kind of information to be included, and show different ways of organizing the words.
- Include target words from class materials to ensure there are words in the collection that all students are familiar with.
- Allot class time for memory work with the vocabulary notebooks. Have learners work in pairs or small groups to help each other memorize the words.
- Gradually increase the number of words learners contribute to the vocabulary notebook and shift from a class notebook to individual vocabulary notebooks.

Fowle (2002) suggests that vocabulary notebooks can enhance learner autonomy because learners can take charge of their own vocabulary learning. However, Walters & Bozkurt (2009) failed to observe this effect in their study. While the students enjoyed using the notebooks and experienced success in vocabulary learning, the majority of them reported that they would not continue to keep a vocabulary notebook if they were not required to by their teacher. This suggests that some learners may not be motivated enough to keep and use a vocabulary notebook independently. There are two possible solutions to this problem. The first has to do with the choice of words to be included in the notebook. It is important that learners should choose the words they include in their vocabulary notebooks, from contexts selected by the learners themselves, according to their interests and abilities. It is hoped that this level of personal choice and autonomy in what is included in the notebook will result in the desire to independently keep and use a vocabulary notebook.

The second possible solution involves building learners' confidence. For learners who are new to vocabulary notebooks, motivation to use the notebooks independently may depend on their level of comfort and confidence in using the notebooks. For this reason, the classroom guidance and support given in the initial stages should be continued, by incorporating the vocabulary notebooks into classroom activities. Schmitt & Schmitt (1995) provide a sample program for incorporating vocabulary notebooks into class work, an adaptation of which is described in Walters & Bozkurt (2009). The program includes allotting time for adding information to the notebook, sharing words with classmates, and using words from the notebooks in classroom activities, including activities that require depth of processing.

Discussion Questions

1. The author has stated that vocabulary notebooks can be used by language learners at any proficiency level. How do you think the notebooks of beginning and advanced learners would differ? How would their use differ?
2. How can learners be encouraged to independently keep and use vocabulary notebooks outside the classroom?
3. If learners are keeping a vocabulary notebook for words they choose themselves, can you think of some ways that they can get feedback about what they are learning?
4. The author has suggested that vocabulary notebooks might be kept on computers, tablets, or mobile phones. What kinds of programs or applications can you think of that might lend themselves to a vocabulary notebook?

Resources

For a PC, tablet or smartphone, enables learners to enter words and related information, save, categorize, and study them, and test themselves. These can be used individually, or as part of classroom study. www.vocabularynotebook.com
An application for mobile devices, allowing learners to study predetermined packs of words, as well as words entered individually. http://learnenglish. britishcouncil.org/en/apps/mywordbook-2
An online service that allows learners to copy and paste sentences from their reading, and then mark and store vocabulary words from those sentences, for studying and self-testing can be found at https://vocabnotes.com/

References

Baddeley, A. (1997). *Human memory: Theory and practice, revised edition.* East Sussex, UK: Psychology Press.

Craik, F.I.M., & Lockhart, R. S. (1972). Levels of processing: A framework for memory research. *Journal of Verbal Learning and Verbal Behavior,* 11(6), 671–684.

Craik, F.I.M., & Tulving, E. (1975). Depth of processing and the retention of words in episodic memory. *Journal of Experimental Psychology, General,* 104(3), 268–294.

Fowle, C. (2002). Vocabulary notebooks: Implementation and outcomes. *English Language Teaching Journal,* 56(4), 380–388.

Laufer, B., & Nation, P. (1999). A vocabulary-size test of controlled productive ability. *Language Testing,* 16(1), 36–55.

Nagy, W. E., Herman, P. A., & Anderson, R. C. (1985). Learning words from context. *Reading Research Quarterly,* 20(2), 233–253.

Nation, I. S. P. (1982). Beginning to learn foreign language vocabulary: A review of the research. *RELC Journal,* 13, 14–36.

Nation, I. S. P. (2001). *Learning vocabulary in another language. Cambridge Applied Linguistics Series (CALS).* Cambridge, England: Cambridge University Press.

Schmitt, N. (1997). Vocabulary learning strategies. In N. Schmitt & M. McCarthy (Eds.), *Vocabulary: Description, acquisition and pedagogy* (pp. 199–228). Cambridge: Cambridge University Press.

Schmitt, N., & Schmitt, D. (1995). Vocabulary notebooks: Theoretical underpinnings and practical suggestions. *English Language Teaching Journal,* 49(2), 133–143.

Walters, J. (2006). Methods of teaching inferring meaning from context. *RELC Journal,* 37(2), 176–190.

Walters, J., & Bozkurt, N. (2009). The effect of keeping vocabulary notebooks on vocabulary acquisition. *Language Teaching Research,* 13(4), 403–423.

4

USING SONGS AND LYRICS IN OUT-OF-CLASS LEARNING

Erika Kerekes

Introduction and Overview

There are many approaches that may help someone learning a language outside of the classroom. As we are all different in how we reach goals in life, the same applies to language learning. Experimenting with different methods while learning a language, and then settling on one that is most effective, are great ways to find out about ourselves as learners.

In this chapter, I describe my own self-study processes while learning English, and describe in detail one method that worked best for me beyond the classroom.

I begin by describing my own language-learning background, the different methods I experimented with, and why I stopped using those that seemed unsuccessful. I also discuss why.

I focused on one specific method more than others: listening to songs and lyrics, singing them, as well as translating them into Hungarian. Next, I describe how this method can be used with other English language learners by giving some practical ideas. Finally, I discuss the challenges I faced while using songs and lyrics, and possible solutions to similar problems that other learners may face while using them in their own language learning.

Vignette

It is often said that it is best to start learning a language at a very young age, the earlier the better, but I was not that lucky as a young language learner. Growing up in communist-era Hungary, I was only able to learn Russian as a compulsory foreign language. Students tend to not take school subjects seriously when they are compulsory, and we all wished to study other languages besides Russian.

I always had English in mind; first, because it sounded good to my ear, and second, because I loved singing and listening to music and wanted to understand song lyrics. The wish to learn English eventually came true with the fall of communism. When I entered college in 1989, the school gave me the choice to study English instead of Russian. This all led to wanting to be able to communicate in English and trying different things to reach that goal.

During my college years, I soon came to the realization that relying only on classroom learning would not bring me any closer to my desire to accomplish my language goals.

First, I experimented with grammar worksheets outside of the class and gave them to my teacher for correction and comments. No matter how many of them I produced, I always made the same mistakes.

I also tried listening to language tapes, but I was only passively listening and not producing any language. I could not measure if I was really accomplishing anything or not.

Another approach I tried was to read newspapers and magazine articles and translate them, but there was always more unknown vocabulary words than known, so I soon became discouraged by the fact that every time I translated an article, it remained the same difficulty level and I didn't notice much improvement.

I consider myself an analytical learner and, if I had chosen the proper level, I could have been more successful with this type of learning. According to McCarthy (1990), analytical learners are patient and reflective; they want to develop intellectually and draw on facts while learning. They want to know "important things" and to add to the world's knowledge. Lewenston (1985) presented the role of translation value in learning a second language. He found many benefits of practicing grammatical structures, explaining vocabulary items and in developing communicative competence. According to Richards & Schmidt (2002), focusing on form in language learning is valuable if attention is focused on the formal linguistic characteristics of language. Ellis (2002) goes even further in supporting a focus on form, claiming the evidence overwhelmingly supports a focus on form in second-language acquisition (SLA).

It was in my final year as a college student when I came across a learning method, even though I did not think about methods directly then, that could help me improve my language skills.

I grew up surrounded by music. My father played the bass guitar and my mother was a very good singer. When I was a child, my father often worked at home and cared for me when my mom was busy. He constantly listened to the radio with '60s and '70s music and played his favorite songs on his guitar. He noticed that while spending time with him, I mimicked all the songs in English, even though no one in my family spoke English around me. My parents and neighbors thought this remarkable. I remember my father saying, "You have a great sense for languages and by learning many you will be able to travel around the world."

He turned out to be right about his prediction. The love of music and singing also gave me the chance to join a Christian group of singers and musicians called "Continental Singers." In this group, we sang songs by famous contemporary Christian musicians that were originally written in English. Our group had to translate the lyrics into Hungarian and make them singable. I had many chances to participate in the translation. I had a noticeable interest in translating them and tried to be as accurate as possible in retaining the meaning of the lyrics. During this experience, I noticed that I paid more attention to the original versions. If I could not hear something clearly, I went back to it and listened again until I was able to understand the words. By doing this, I not only improved my language comprehension and accuracy, but also in learning common expressions that were normally used in everyday life.

Around this point, I made an important self-discovery about using language translation as a learning method. I started to have an understanding that many expressions cannot be translated word-for-word. It was perhaps the most important self-discovery. Once I could understand that I cannot find the exact translation for everything and that each situation requires a different one helped me in my language improvement. I tried to figure out the meanings by the context. One example of this is a song "Get a Life." In English it could mean that we want someone to have fun, lighten up, and do something different. In the song, however, this expression encourages people to make a difference in others' lives and do something for others. Translating this expression word-for-word would not make sense in Hungarian. The translation is *eletet kapsz*, which means "you receive life." It has nothing to do with the exact meaning of "Get a Life."

This clearly demonstrates that learning languages cannot be achieved by just learning vocabulary. Expressions need to be in context in order to comprehend them. Without an understanding of language surroundings, it is very difficult to learn steadily or achieve higher language skills.

Why Songs and Lyrics Worked for Me

Translating songs and practicing singing them helped me retain and remember vocabulary and grammar and opened the door to a more automatic language use. The facilitative power of songs is not a new finding and many researchers point towards the use of them with positive benefits when learning a language (Lens, 2001; Medina, 1993; Richards, 1969). According to Feric (2012) and previous research cited, our brain is responsible for language learning, the left lobe is 90% better at recognizing words and the right lobe 20% better at recognizing melodic patterns. High musical ability is very common among multilingual individuals. They are also better at producing language closer to a native accent. In addition, it is also true that musical people have advanced ability in perceiving and processing the rhythm as well as music in the right side of the brain and connecting it to the left side, which is responsible for processing verbal information.

Motivation is an important factor in the use of songs and lyrics, I felt more successful in translating the songs and being able to sing them with a native-like English pronunciation. I found this is very important when learning. I was self-motivated to reach my goals while enjoying the song translation. It fueled me to see how well my translations came across when we were singing them in Hungarian to different audiences.

In 1997, I applied to the Continental Singers in the United States and I had to send an audition tape in English. I was invited into the group out of many applicants. I could not only sing every day, but talk with tour members and they helped me develop my communication skills further. After this tour, I chose to apply to a two-year college where, after taking a placement test and a writing course, I was accepted into the program fully and studied with native speakers of English. In my opinion, it was also very helpful that I went to the United States with at least a basic language ability and by getting involved with the singing group I could accomplish more than I expected. Moreover, I was able to stay in school and study on courses with native speakers.

The reason for my choice to study with native English speakers was that I wanted to listen to natural, clear pronunciation by my classmates. Of course, there are benefits of studying with other ESL learners, learning about their culture and such, but then I felt the importance of listening to native pronunciation during my lessons. While studying in my English courses, our teacher often assigned poetry or song lyrics as homework with different purposes and I certainly enjoyed them during my studies. As a music major, I continued to work on song translations for my singing lessons, too. The more time I spent on song translations the more fluent I became when it was time to sing them.

Principles

Principle 1. Encourage learners to improve their English outside the classroom by engaging in activities they enjoy. When we do something that is enjoyable to us, we can noticeably master things faster and more efficiently. Language learners can find and take responsibility for their own learning by doing outside-of-class activities that are enjoyable to them. Enjoyable learning environments and activities create positive outcomes according to many researchers (Kolb, 1984; Richards & Bohlke, 2011).

Scarcella & Oxford (1992, p. 63) state that language tasks chosen by learners to "enhance their own learning" will contribute to positive self-regulating in learning. This exactly applied to my own learning: I enjoyed using songs and lyrics when studying English and by seeing positive improvements I could learn faster than with other types of methods.

Nunan (1999) puts it very well, "[I]f learners are to learn, then they have to do the learning for themselves" (p. 166).

It is easy to see that we can reach any of our learning goals faster when we enjoy what we do and do the learning for ourselves.

Principle 2. Song lyrics and poems can be used to learn pronunciation, grammar, vocabulary, idiomatic language, as well as memory recall among other things. Through songs, learners can accomplish the natural stretching of pronunciation of English speech. Practicing the natural reductions by reading the lyrics out loud helps learners in any L2 background. Songs and lyrics are also very good for context predicting such as trying to find missing vocabulary before listening to a song and checking the correctness of predictions. It can also be used by omitting "can and could, may and might" the auxiliary or other grammar terms. According to Griffee (1990), any grammar point can be deleted depending on the specific grammar point.

They are also great to teach idioms depending on the level of learning: Idioms such as "Go fly a kite" can be confusing for some English learners. These always need an explanation before listening to the actual song (Lens, 2001).

Learning songs in a second language contributes to cultural knowledge and provides opportunities to learn about similarities and differences compared to the learned language culture and our own native language' culture. It teaches human relations, customs, ethics, humor, and history, among other things.

Several features of pop songs can help second language acquisition. These songs include common short words, personal pronouns, imperatives, questions and are sung at a slower rate and words are uttered with more pauses than spoken language. There is also repetition of vocabulary and structures in songs. According to Murphey (1992), these factors help learners relate to the songs. Song lyrics also contribute to different interpretations such as poetry.

Being *learner-centered* means giving choices to our learners. One approach is to ask them about their favorite songs, especially those they cannot understand. Help them comprehend the song while reading it out loud before later trying to sing it. The opportunities are endless.

Humans are vocal learners, so for this reason the possibility of singing is given to us from birth unless one is tone deaf. Songs can also increase memory recall. Racette & Peretz (2007) stated, "[I]t is often not obvious why music should facilitate word recall, since there is more to learn in a song than in a text" (p. 242). In this study they set out to examine if music facilitates text recall. Their theory that sung words are easier to recall than spoken words turned out the other way around. Music was found to be little help for text recall. When learning a new song, the melody and lyrics are remembered separately, making singing a dual task. When learning the song right away without practicing the words causes word loss by 14%. This suggests that learning lyrics first is probably more beneficial when learning languages as well and supports memory recall over the melody.

Ginsborg (2002) found that expert singers do not take more time than novice singers to practice words and melodies together when learning a new song; however, professional singers practice the words before singing it in support of better memory recall.

Applications

We will now give piratical suggestions for using songs and lyrics in language learning:

Grammatical points can be taught using songs and lyrics. First, the teacher chooses a grammatical point, then a song that contains the specific grammatical point. Then the teacher provides students with the lyrics with the grammar item deleted. Then have learners listen to the song and try to fill in the missing items. Any grammar point can be deleted such as past tense in this example:

This little piggy ... to market, etc.

The above example is for beginner, younger learners of English, but grammatical points can be made more difficult with advanced students (e.g., by choosing not only simple past tense, but irregular past tense verbs if the focus is past tense).

Learners can do the same on their own by finding "songs and lyrics" websites provided in the Resources section of this chapter and find songs according to their grammar practice needs. Many of the song lyrics are accompanied by music, so learners can listen and practice the grammar focus area using these websites.

If the focus is on pronunciation, then, we can print out song lyrics depending on the pronunciation area. For example, Japanese learners often meet with problems pronouncing "r" and "l" or "b" and "v" sounds. There are many songs to choose from when it comes to different sounds, but for these specific sounds, there is a song called "Blessing in Disguise" by Ashton, Becker, & Dente on the album *Along the Road* (the link to the song is found in the Resources section). Using this song, learners can practice these troubled sounds: "r" and "l." This is a longer song, suitable for intermediate or advanced learners. It is a good idea to go over the song by listening to it or having it read out loud by the teacher. Then, ask students to highlight the practice sounds, in this example "r" and "l." Once students are familiar with the lyrics and its meaning, have them read it for a few minutes alone and then together in chorus. In this case, even shy learners will be braver.

As for self-practice, individual learners can do the same at home by printing out specific lyrics that interest them and that are not too difficult. Listen to the song a few times first and try to understand the lyrics or the message of the song. Then practice it reading it out loud. For more practice, it is a good idea to record it as well, then listen to the recording and try to address any problems that occurred.

The same song is also excellent for learning idioms starting with the title "Blessing in Disguise."

The teacher should start by explaining the meaning of this idiom, so learners have a clear idea of its meaning. Next, ask learners to come up with their own ideas using this expression to check whether they truly understand the meaning. See the following example:

1. *Today's idiom: Blessing in disguise*
2. *Meaning:* When we have something positive that happened to us, but we do not notice it right away, we experience a ***blessing in disguise***.

   Try to include the above idiom in a sentence of your choice where you could use it or relate it to your own experience in the past.

   _____
   _____
   _____
   _____

3

Now, draw a picture of your sentence to try to help you remember this idiom.

We can also give our learners a vocabulary list including about 15–20 words. This activity works in small groups with 4–5 learners. They can try to create their own song and lyrics with the list of words. They can add more words if needed, but ask them to try to include all of the words from the list first. If they are musically gifted, they can write the music, too. Read it as a poem for other groups to hear in the classroom. This is a communicative activity and often turns out to be very humorous. Students discuss about what to write and how to write it. Individual advanced learners can also try this alone and see if they can write a song. They can randomly select words or if there is a focus—e.g., adjectives—and then try to include different adjectives in the word list.

Payoffs and Pitfalls

I met quite a few challenges when using songs in my own language-learning process. The first challenge was that the songs I tried to translate were already given by the singing groups' program. This meant that I could not choose the level that would suit my knowledge at the time. It is important to choose the right level for learners, so they will not struggle while working on the lyrics. When choosing lyrics for beginner learners, these songs need to be short, with repetition and simple lyrics. As students progess, they can be given longer lyrics with more complicated vocabulary and expressions. Idioms always need an explanation before having learners listen to the songs. These steps will help learners gain more confidence, experience positive learning opportunities, and not discourage them in their own progress.

Another challenge that I faced was that I often tried to sing the songs right away without practicing or reading out the lyrics first; and I did not analyze the vocabulary before singing the songs. Singing the words right away will lead to vocabulary loss. This means that I was not able to retain some important vocabulary in my memory efficiently. To solve this problem, first learners should always read the lyrics out loud and go over the vocabulary presented. This will lead to better memorization that a learner will easily recall while singing the songs.

Songs and lyrics may not be as sufficient when using them without having one or two focus areas. If I wanted to practice pronunciation, singing the songs enabled me to pronounce the lyrics at a slower rate with more pauses and retain the natural stretch of the language. For those who have no singing ability, they can read the lyrics out loud for similar results.

Learning idioms while translating and using songs in my learning was one of the most difficult obstacles. To help solve this problem, I went to a more knowledgeable person who could explain the context of when these expressions are used. Learners should not rely only on themselves to discover these meanings, but ask another higher-level speaker of English who can give examples and help figure them out. Idioms should never be used with beginner learners because of their difficulty, but as they progress they should be included.

Another challenge I faced is who should choose the songs when learning. When I chose a song, I tried to pick the ones that interested me, but then those songs sometimes included some difficult vocabulary and were more advanced level songs. To eliminate this problem, it is better to ask someone who is trained about how to choose songs while learning a language, so it is manageable and not frustrating. What we need to watch out for is the length of the songs, the simplicity of the lyrics, whether there are repetitions included and what the focus area is: pronunciation, grammar, memory recall, and so on. Most importantly, we have to match these with our language level if we would like to gain more success.

Discussion Questions

1.   Who in your opinion would benefit from using songs and lyrics as a learning tool?
2.   Would you be interested in using songs and lyrics in your own language learning or suggest it to learners as a self-study method? Why or why not?
3.   Do you agree that songs and lyrics have great benefits for even those who are not musically gifted?

Resources

The following are suggested teaching English as a second language (TESL) songs and links to websites where they can be accessed:

> *Blessing in Disguise Lyrics* by Susan Ashton, Margaret Becker & Christine Dente—http://www.lyricsnmusic.com/susan-ashton-christine-dente-and-michelle-tumes/blessing-in-disguise-lyrics/1936057
> *TESL Songs*—http://iteslj.org/links/TESL/Songs/
> *Jazz Chants* by Carolyn Graham—http://jazzchants.net/
> *TEFL Tunes: Songs for Teaching English Grammar*—http://tefltunes.com/grammarsongs.aspx

References

Ashton, S., Becker, M., & Dente, C. (1994). *Blessing in disguise.* Retrieved from http://www.lyricsmusic.com/susan-ashton-christine-dente-and-michelle-tumes/blessing-in-disguise-lyrics/1936057

Ellis, R. (2002). Does the form-focused instruction affect the acquisition of implicit knowledge? *Studies in Second Language Acquisition, 24*(2), 223–236.

Feric, N. (2012). *Learning English with music.* Retrieved from http://www.usingenglish.com/articles/learning-english-with-music.html

Ginsborg, J. (2002). Classical singers learning and memorizing a new song: An observational study. *Psychology of Music,* 30, 58–101.

Griffee, D.T. (1990). Hey baby! Teaching short and slow songs in the ESL classroom. *TESL Reporter, 23(4),* 3–8.

Kolb, D. A. (1984). *Experiential learning: Experience as the source of learning and development.* Englewood Cliffs, NJ: Prentice-Hall.

Lens, K. (2001). Using music in the adult ESL classroom. *Center for Applied Linguistics.* Retrieved from http://www.cal.org/caela/esl_resources/digests/music.html

Levenston, A. (1985). The place of translation in the foreign language classroom. *English Teachers' Journal,* 1985(32), 33–43.

McCarthy, B. (1990). Using the 4MAT system to bring learning styles to schools. *Educational Leadership*, 48(2), 31–36.

Medina, S. L. (1993). The effect of music on second language vocabulary acquisition. *National Network for Early Language Learning*, 6, 1–8.

Murphey, T. (1992). The discourse of pop songs. *TESOL Quarterly*, 26(4), 770–774.

Nunan, D. (1999). *Second language teaching & learning*. Boston: Heinle & Heinle.

Racette, A., & Peretz, I. (2007). Learning lyrics: to sing or not to sing? *Memory and Cognition*, 35(2), 242–253. Retrieved from http://link.springer.com/article/10.3758%2FBF03193445#page-1

Richards, J. C. (1969). Songs in language learning. *TESOL Quarterly*, 3(2), 161–174.

Richards, J. C., & Bohlke D. (2011). *Creative effective language lessons*. Cambridge: Cambridge University Press.

Richards, J. C., & Schmidt, R. (2002). *Longman dictionary of language teaching and applied linguistics* (2nd ed.). Essex: Longman Group.

Scarcella, R., & Oxford, R. (1992). *The tapestry of language learning: The individual in the communicative classroom*. Boston: Heinle & Heinle.

5

OUT-OF-CLASS PRONUNCIATION LEARNING

Are EFL Learners Ready in China?

Nana Long & Jing Huang

Introduction and Overview

As stipulated by the *National Curriculum for Teaching English Majors* (2000), English pronunciation is a compulsory course for first-year university students majoring in English in Mainland China. This arrangement is reasonable as research has exposed that English pronunciation has long been neglected in primary and secondary education in Mainland China—English teachers tend to focus on reading, vocabulary, grammar, and writing in their classroom teaching as these are the foci of examinations, especially the High School Entrance Examination and National College Entrance Examination (NCEE)[1] (Lin & Mao, 2011; Luo & Zhang, 2002). As a result, students' knowledge of English pronunciation is normally quite limited and their pronunciation is generally poor.

In spite of its importance, English pronunciation is only scheduled for one semester in most English major undergraduate programs in Mainland China. In-class, time is always too short for students to make improvements in important aspects of their pronunciation—sounds, word and sentence stress, rhythms, and intonation. If students make good use of their out-of-class time, they may gain more effective results in learning pronunciation.

In this chapter, we first introduce how the teacher (author Nana Long) of a class of 27 English majors in a Mainland China university guided her students to learn English pronunciation inside and outside the classroom by taking into account their particularities. Then we list six principles and show how and why out-of-class pronunciation learning worked for this class of students. In the next section we propose this pronunciation teaching approach to other ESL/EFL (English as a second language/English as a foreign language) formal education contexts and make recommendations on how to put it into implementation. We also further analyze the strong and weak points of this approach.

Vignette

Nana was a teacher for an English major undergraduate program at a Mainland China university. In the year 2010, she was assigned to teach pronunciation to a class of 27 English majors. In the first lesson, she was surprised to find that most students could not even recognize phonetic symbols and they had various problems in their pronunciation, although they had learned English for at least six years before entering the university. Realizing that it was impossible for the students to make much improvement if they merely relied on the limited time in class (there were only two lessons each week), Nana began to guide the students to make use of their out-of-class time. Every week she allocated specific tasks for the students to do after introducing new pronunciation knowledge and doing some practice together with them inside the classroom. She checked them in the following week to see their out-of-class learning effectiveness. Besides, she assigned the students an important role in class—judges of their peers' performance. After negotiation, most students accepted this role and reached the consensus that a qualified judge must have the ability to use pronunciation knowledge for critical evaluation. After a series of student comments, Nana would provide immediate feedback on each student's performance, including areas of improvement and problems. To avoid losing face, most students worked diligently beyond the classroom so as to perform the best they could in class.

In the middle of the semester, most students became well aware of their prominent problems and were eager to overcome them. They voluntarily registered a common email account and invited Nana to join their e-mail communication. They shared a variety of resources in this virtual space—books (including e-books and information about printed books), websites, movies, songs, cartoons, and the like. A special form of material Nana sent to the students every month was an examination paper with different types of exercises on pronunciation knowledge (consonants, vowels, word stress, sentence stress, linking and weak forms, intonation) (see Item 4 in Resources for a sample). She gave them one week for preparation and asked them to send their recordings to the common e-mail account at the prescribed time. The students took these out-of-class examinations seriously as their work would be graded by the teacher (80%) and all classmates (20%) and the results would be included in the final score of this course.

At the end of the semester, most students told Nana that their consciousness of pronunciation was raised once they listened to, spoke, read, and wrote English. They recognized the importance of pronunciation for them as English majors and decided to continue working on their particular problems even though they had no pronunciation lessons in the future. Here is some feedback Nana received from the "Teacher Evaluation System" (translations from Chinese):

STUDENT A: Thanks to the resources shared by my teacher and classmates. I picked out the audio and video materials in which the native speakers did not speak too fast and kept imitating their pronunciation. I have more confidence in myself as an English major now.

STUDENT B: We only met the teacher once each week. I contacted her frequently because I always had many questions to ask. She was patient to answer my questions and gave me much advice. I liked to communicate with some of my classmates too. Their pronunciation was so beautiful that I could not help imitating them.

STUDENT C: My classmates and I always spent quite a long time analyzing each pronunciation item on the examination papers. We also read the items to each other to seek advice. I felt good to learn together with my peers.

Principles

In this case study, the teacher and the students worked together to make out-of-class pronunciation learning possible. The following principles proved to be necessary and effective in the whole process:

Principle 1. There must be effective tools to evaluate students' out-of-class learning. Within the formal education context, most EFL learners mainly rely on classroom teaching to learn English. They tend to be dependent on their teachers as they lack knowledge in the English language and lack the capacity to take control of their learning. Therefore, language teachers should guide students to learn out of class and employ effective tools to evaluate their learning.

Taking into consideration that the students were not ready to learn out of class independently, the pronunciation teacher assigned them specific tasks to do and employed the strategy of out-of-class practice and in-class evaluation in the whole semester. Besides, she arranged monthly examinations to evaluate the students at different learning stages. These two evaluation tools not only drove the students to work diligently, but also helped the teacher adjust her teaching based on the students' learning progress.

Principle 2. Students should be empowered in class so that they will feel capable of directing their out-of-class learning. EFL learners, especially learners in East Asian countries, tend to regard the teacher as the authority "whose superior knowledge and control over classroom learning events should not be questioned" (Littlewood, 1999, p. 85). As suggested by critical pedagogy, the teacher should address issues of power relations in classroom teaching. Granting students a certain degree of freedom is conducive to a better understanding of themselves as learners.

In the pronunciation class, the teacher tried peer evaluations, which made the students reconceptualize their own roles in the classroom—they were not only *actors* in class whose performance would receive feedback, but also *judges* who were responsible for evaluating the classmates' pronunciation. Moreover, the teacher's examination strategy gave the students much freedom: She allowed them to spend one week practicing the exercises on the given examination papers in any way they liked. As the students enriched their knowledge of phonetics and developed their learning ability in the process of gaining power and freedom, they felt more capable of doing independent learning outside the classroom.

Principle 3. Identity formation is important to motivate students to learn out of class. Identity formation refers to how learners see themselves as they continuously interact with their learning context. Huang's (2011, 2013) studies reveal that first-year English majors generally experience 'loss, confusion, puzzlement' without having clear learning goals, so they are not ready for directing their own learning. But this status quo may be changed as long as they are more conscious of their English-major identity.

To highlight the students' new identity as English majors, the teacher tried to expose their problems in pronunciation and assessed them based on the requirements for English majors which are stated in the *National Curriculum for Teaching English Majors*. Many students started to set more specific learning objectives for their pronunciation and became reluctant to commit the same errors over and over again. The English-major identity constituted one of the major motivators that drove the students to learn pronunciation outside the classroom.

Principle 4. Out-of-class communication can enhance the efficiency of out-of-class learning. Compared with communication in class, teacher–student communication as well as peer communication outside the classroom has many advantages. For example there is more time: students anxiety may be reduced; the teacher's attention can be shifted from the whole class to individual students.

Coming from different regions of China and having different social–educational backgrounds, the first-year English majors had various problems in their pronunciation. Via e-mail communication the teacher helped individual students with their particular problems; working in either pairs or groups, the students did pronunciation exercises, prepared monthly examinations, sought learning resources, and shared their gains and setbacks. These types of out-of-class communication generated unexpected positive learning outcomes.

Principle 5. Sufficient and appropriate resources must be available for out-of-class pronunciation learning. To make out-of-class learning possible, EFL learners must have free access to sufficient learning resources. They can be either recommended by the teacher or shared by learners themselves.

As novice pronunciation learners, the English majors found it difficult to select appropriate learning resources. Therefore, the teacher first recommended a BBC pronunciation learning website and a book with rich pronunciation exercises (see items 1 & 5 in Resources) to them. In their out-of-class time, the students could watch the videos on the website imitating the native speaker's pronunciation; they could do the exercises in the book and follow the mp3 to tell whether there were problems in their own pronunciation. When the students knew more about English phonetics and paid more attention to it, they began to search the resources that they found useful to themselves. They applied for an e-mail account on their own initiative to share resources including the recordings of their own pronunciation. At the end of the semester, the email account became a treasure of pronunciation resources, which benefitted many students in the whole semester.

Principle 6. The number of students in the language class should be small. Class size always affects the effectiveness of EFL teaching and learning. It is normally easier for the teacher to manage small classes than big ones to pay attention to individual differences. In the pronunciation class, the teacher put more emphasis on practice than knowledge acquisition. She adopted various strategies to ensure that the students had sufficient practice and made improvements. These included weekly in-class checks, out-of-class communication, regular examinations, etc. Since there were only 27 students in her class, she found it feasible to implement these strategies. But if the number of students became larger, she would be unable to take care of all the students.

Applications

The context of this vignette is a mainland China university, and the target language learners were first-year undergraduate students majoring in English. Their pre-tertiary education was predominantly examination-oriented and their major learning goal in senior secondary school was to pass the NCEE to secure a place at a university. Many of them had been accustomed to a classroom approach characterized by teacher-centeredness, an emphasis on teacher transmission of knowledge, and student passivity in learning. Therefore, it is not realistic to expect that they could learn effectively out of class on their own as soon as they entered university. They needed to experience a period of time looking for their own goal of university education and learning to learn independently and interdependently.

We recommend the English pronunciation teaching and learning approach in this chapter to language teachers who intend to foster their students' autonomy both inside and outside the classroom, whereas the students do not have much knowledge of the course they take and they are not motivated enough to learn out of class. It is especially suitable to the students who are too dependent on their teachers. In face of this type of students, the teacher should be patient enough to develop their ability to take control of their own learning step by step (see Figure 5.1).

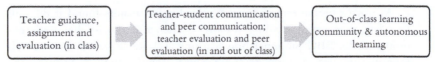

FIGURE 5.1 Process of leading students to learn beyond the classroom.

First and foremost, it is necessary for the teacher to gain a general understanding of students' language proficiency and let them have a general idea of the course, including the main content, the usefulness and importance of the course, and the teaching and learning objectives. If students lack knowledge in the given course, the teacher needs to prepare resources for them and assign them suitable out-of-class tasks. These tasks must be accompanied with timely checks and evaluations to help them learn their strong and weak points. At first the teacher may need to play the key role in evaluating students' work. But he or she can gradually try out more evaluating strategies such as self-evaluation, peer evaluation, and so on. When students are more ready to take control of their learning, the teacher can grant them more freedom to seek and exploit the resources that are suitable for themselves. An out-of-class learning community may be spontaneously built up when they fight for the same learning goal, share resources and experiences, and offer help to each other. The teacher must keep monitoring the students and communicating with them out of class to learn their progresses and needs. The teacher should be alert to those 'problematic' students who take negative attitudes toward learning, especially out-of-class learning, those who feel frustrated in the learning process, and those who are unconscious of their own problems. To find possible solutions, it is necessary to investigate the psychological and social factors that affect their learning (Benson & Nunan, 2005).

Payoffs and Pitfalls

The following positive learning outcomes may occur if in-class teaching and out-of-class learning are well integrated:

> *Knowledge enrichment.* The most obvious manifestation of this approach may be that students can gain more knowledge on a new course by learning both in and out of class than simply learning inside the classroom. In this case study, the students did not know much about English pronunciation in the initial phase. After some time, they not only gained certain pronunciation knowledge but also began to use their knowledge to analyze pronunciation exercises and evaluate their peers' performance. When the semester was over, many of them mastered the basic knowledge of pronunciation as they frequently used it in real practice.
> *Motivation enhancement.* In the EFL learning context, learners may take different attitudes towards language courses because of the contents of the

courses, the course instructors, their social–education backgrounds, and so on. In countries like Mainland China and Japan, many EFL students learn the English language for examinations (Huang, 2013; Nakata, 2011). Passing examinations may be a motivating factor for these learners, but can hardly sustain their enthusiasm for learning English in the long run. One way to motivate them to make long-term efforts is to let them always know about their progress and involve them in "communities of practice" (Lave & Wenger, 1991) where all learners work together towards the same goals. In this case study, the teacher set many challenges for the students that they had not met before, such as presenting in class every week, commenting on peers' work, working on examination papers out of class, and the like. The students set up an out-of-class learning community to meet these challenges. By working on the same exercises, commenting on each other's work, and sharing learning gains and difficulties, the students were highly motivated to improve their pronunciation.

Autonomy development. Learner autonomy is defined as "the ability to take charge of one's own learning" (Holec, 1981, p. 3). Autonomy is beneficial to learners' long-term development as autonomous language learners are expected to take responsibility for all aspects of their learning, including setting learning objectives and agendas, selecting learning materials and learning methods, monitoring the learning process, and evaluating what has been learned. However, "in formal educational contexts learners do not automatically accept responsibility for their learning" (Little, 1995, p. 176). It is unrealistic to let students totally take charge of their learning all at once if they do not feel ready. The teacher had better foster students' autonomy step by step—equipping them with necessary learning strategies, granting them freedom bit by bit, guiding them to evaluate their own learning, and so on. In this case study, the teacher gave the students certain freedom to evaluate their peers' performance and guided them for out-of-class learning by assigning them specific tasks to do. When the students became well aware of their problems in pronunciation and were eager to overcome them, they became more willing to take responsibility for their learning inside and outside the classroom. For example, they set more specific learning objectives for themselves, selected suitable learning resources for themselves, and turned to the teacher and peers for help.

In spite of the above advantages, the following factors may pose challenges for the integration of in- and out-of-class learning:

Teacher. Language teaching will fall into a swamp, if the EFL teacher simply focuses on students' language skills rather than their overall development, or if the EFL teacher is not qualified enough to conduct effective language teaching by taking into consideration students' particularities and the importance of in- and out-of-class learning. Recent developments in education highlight the importance of critical thinking, reflective learning, and self-direction in preparing students for lifelong learning. Therefore, EFL teachers cannot be simply confined to developing students' language skills and in-class teaching. They must put students at the centre and make efforts to develop their learning abilities. To meet this challenge, teachers should be able to self-direct their teaching while institutions and teacher education programs should also espouse teachers' development.

Learners. Learner differences are one challenge for adopting this approach. Since learners have their own idiosyncrasies, the EFL teacher must take into account these differences when setting teaching agendas and conducting teaching. Outside the classroom, learner differences may become more prominent—some learners may be capable of learning independently; some may lack ability and skills to learn on their own; some may be reluctant to learn the English language. Therefore, it is a big challenge for the teacher and students to work out an effective mechanism to monitor students' out-of-class learning. In addition, EFL learners may be weak in self-evaluation and peer evaluation if they have no such experience. In this case they are always dependent on the teacher's feedback. The teacher must be willing to offer them opportunities to make evaluations and provide immediate feedback on their work. To develop their own ability to evaluate, EFL learners should also take the initiative to gain knowledge, think critically, and interact with peers and teachers.

Resources. Teachers cannot always provide sufficient and suitable learning resources for students. To enhance learning effectiveness, students need to seek resources that meet their own needs and capitalize on them. Once they are drawn into a situation where resources are limited, they can communicate with teachers and peers who may recommend useful materials for them. However, teachers may not have easy access to useful resources all the time, so students should work together to design their own materials. Another problem facing students may be how to exploit the available resources. According to our experience, teacher scaffolding (teacher demonstration and advice on using resources) and peer collaboration are good solutions to this problem.

Discussion Questions

1. The authors report that the EFL learners in the case study were not ready for out-of-class English pronunciation learning in the Chinese tertiary context in terms of both knowledge and learning ability. How about the learners in your context?
2. The authors suggest integrating in-class teaching and out-of-class learning when teaching English pronunciation in the EFL educational context. Do you think it applicable in your context? Why or why not?
3. In this case study, the teacher gradually granted freedom to the students to enhance their sense of self-efficacy. Have you tried to give your students certain freedom in class? Do they enjoy it? What further actions do you take if they enjoy the given freedom or if they do not enjoy it?

4. The teacher employed several strategies (assignments, peer evaluations, examinations, e-mail communications, etc.) to either motivate or push the students to play an active role inside and outside the classroom. Have you employed any strategies, effective or ineffective, to sustain your students' efforts?

5. The students' out-of-class learning in this case study was evaluated by in-class check, peer evaluations, and teacher evaluations. How do you evaluate your students' out-of-class learning? What principles do you follow to employ these evaluation tools?

6. The authors highlight learner differences in pronunciation instruction. Do you often have instructional dialogues with your students to know more about their differences in language learning? To what extent do learner differences impact on your teaching effectiveness?

7. The authors put an emphasis on EFL learners' overall development. Do you pay attention to your students' language skills or their developments in other aspects in your language classes?

Resources

BBC provides the following learning website on English pronunciation tips. It contains videos teaching all the sounds of English as well as quizzes and some programs on pronunciation—http://www.bbc.co.uk/worldservice/learningenglish/grammar/pron/.

British Council provides an interesting pronunciation teaching and testing flash—http://www.englishonline.org.cn/zh-hans/learners/english-for-work/pronunciation-pro.

The students in this chapter also liked to imitate *Voice of America* special English at the beginning stage and later VOA standard English and BBC English. They also liked to imitate American TV programs such as *Friends* as well as American and British movies.

This is part of an examination paper designed by the pronunciation teacher:

I. Read the following phonetic symbols. (10%)

1. [θɔ:t] [sɔ:t]   2. [niə] [liə]   3. [twelv] [dwel]   4. ['mɔdlz] ['bætlz]

5. ['æŋkʃəs] ['meθədz]   6. ['ɔkjupai] [ˌɔkju'peiʃn]   7.['hɔspitl] [ˌhɔspi'tæliti]

8. ['kæriktə] ['kæriktəraiz]   9. ['mɑ:stəpi:s] ['sə:kəmstəns]   10. ['ðɛəfɔ:] ['ɛərəplein]

II. Read the following words. (10%)

1. shot short   2. breath breathe   3. famous singer   4. precious pleasure   5. wine vine
6. full fool   7. main name   8. win wing   9. gradual casual   10. dear dare

III. Read the following phrases. (10%)

1. war and peace   2. come at once   3. sing us a song   4. wonderful workers
5. to learn the verb   6. along the river   7. look into the room   8. the shoe and the goose
9. an approved school   10. enduring cruelty

References

Benson, P., & Nunan, D. (Eds.) (2005). *Learners' stories: Difference and diversity in language learning*. Cambridge: Cambridge University Press.

English Team of National Advisory Committee for Foreign Language Teaching. (2000). *Higher education institution English major English teaching curriculum*. Beijing: Foreign Language Teaching and Research Press.

Holec, H. (1981). *Autonomy and foreign language learning*. Oxford: Pergamon Press.

Huang, J. (2011). A dynamic account of autonomy, agency and identity in (T)EFL learning. In G. Murray, X. S. Gao, & T. Lamb (Eds.), *Identity, motivation and autonomy in language learning* (pp. 229–246). Multilingual Matters.

Huang, J. (2013). *Autonomy, agency and identity in foreign language learning and teaching*. Bern: Peter Lang.

Lave, J., & Wenger, E. (1991). *Situated learning: Legitimate peripheral participation*. Cambridge: Cambridge University Press.

Lin, D. J., & Mao, H. R. (2011). Speech sound, source text, sense of English and specialized reorientation: A proposal for elementary-secondary collegiate English education as a systematic continuum. *Foreign Language Learning Theory and Practice*, 2, 35–40.

Little, D. (1995). Learning as a dialogue: The dependence of learner autonomy on teacher autonomy. *System*, 23(2), 175–182.

Littlewood, W. (1999). Defining and developing autonomy in East Asian contexts. *Applied Linguistics*, 20(1), 71–94.

Luo, L. S., & Zhang, L. X. (2002). An overview of English pronunciation teaching and some suggestions for its improvement. *Foreign Languages and Their Teaching*, 10, 21–23.

Nakata, Y. (2011). Teachers' readiness for promoting learner autonomy: A study of Japanese EFL high school teachers. *Teaching and Teacher Education*, 27(5), 900–910.

Note

1 Middle School Entrance Examination and National College Entrance Examination are generally regarded as two of the most important examinations for students in Mainland China. Students' scores in the two examinations determine which types of senior secondary schools and universities they will be admitted to. In other words, students' performance in the examinations strongly affects the quality of education they will receive.

6

DIALOGUE JOURNALS

Learning for a Lifetime

David L. Chiesa & Kathleen M. Bailey

Introduction and Overview

> *In conclusion, dialogue journal writing is my favorite writing part. No matter which one is selected for my portfolio to show my attitude or writing skills, I will be glad. They are not only the efforts I put into the writing class, but also show that my teacher and best new friend has the patience to accompany me, spending my fleeting sophomore year in college. One day when I look back to those days, I will be glowing with glory to have them as part of my journey, of my life.* (Kyle, #2)

Dialogue journals are reciprocal, ongoing, written exchanges between students and teachers used consistently over time (Peyton, 1993). Many students, like Kyle, react positively to the dialogue journal assignment in our language classes. They see the dialogue journals not only as a language-learning task but as a way to grow socially, mentally, and emotionally with the support of a teacher. In essence, dialogue journals have been used to connect what students learn inside the language classroom to what they experience beyond the classroom.

In this chapter we will report on English language learners keeping dialogue journals in three contexts: (1) lower-intermediate students in a university speaking and listening course in Hong Kong; (2) high-intermediate learners in a translation class in Guizhou; and (3) those in an advanced writing class in Beijing. All the students whose dialogue journal entries are used in this chapter are identified by pseudonyms to protect their anonymity. In this chapter's vignette, we meet a language learner from China whose writing exemplifies how dialogue journals enhance language learning outside of the classroom. Dialogue journals yield this benefit because they are "organized so that communication is systematically dialogic" (Nassaji & Cumming, 2000, p. 99) between the teacher and the student.

The Applications section will show that dialogue journals may be used for many different purposes with varied ages and proficiency levels of students. The discussion in Payoffs and Pitfalls will cover students' opportunities to express their feelings and explore ideas in a low-risk environment, to receive individualized input and generate related output, and to give the teacher feedback about their grasp of the lessons. There are few "pitfalls," other than the teacher's time commitment in responding to each student, and the fact that the students may sometimes divulge serious problems in their journal entries.

Vignette

In this section we present a brief characterization of a student called "Jennifer." She enrolled in a course titled "Raising Cultural Consciousness through Language," in which the students completed three lengthy dialogue journal entries that were submitted once a month. We quote her comments and those of other students exactly as they appeared in the dialogue journals.

> *The time when I found my dad didn't love my mom was on my 10th birthday. My dad left us, no, abandoned us over four years. My mother woke me up in that early morning and handed me a note, asking to read aloud. (My mom is illiterate.) I recognized it was my father's handwriting. That note was very short but the content in it was so hurtful to my mom and me that it took me nearly 30 minutes to finish reading it. The scene of searching for my father around the city where I lived became a scar later in my heart. I could not understand the reason why my dad left without saying anything. (Jennifer, #3)*

If you were to meet Jennifer, who seemed happy and strong, you would not guess she came from a dysfunctional home, struggled in her identity, and was physically and emotionally abused as a child. Yet she wrote, "I had experienced much physical violence before, from my elementary school to senior high. The physical punishment from my elementary math teacher is the most unforgettable one, not only physically but emotionally" (Jennifer, #3). Her childhood determined how she later interacted with her university classmates, co-workers, and teachers. Those experiences led her to question people's motives and to doubt her own cognitive and social abilities.

Early in the course, Jennifer decided to take action and improve interactions with people by deciding to become a team leader. In her first dialogue journal entry, she wrote, "I know being a leader is not as easy as many people think, it needs patience and good interpersonal skill, and that are what I'm not good at. But I'm learning to control my temper and to interact with people peacefully" (Jennifer, #1). Her teacher, Dave, responded, "Wonderfully written, Jennifer, you are growing as an adult by taking risks."

Through interaction with her team members, Jennifer noticed that many of her classmates were complaining about life. She decided to stop being a part of this type of conversation and began to place value on thought, reflection, and discussion.

She believed that if we "think more deeply: If we use the time that is used to complain to work harder and to think more deeply, then nobody would turn into a failure" (Jennifer, #1). She took every course topic—from the themes of education, family, and friendship to the issues of disinterest/apathy, sexual harassment, and physical violence—and used the dialogue journal as a platform for discussion. The topic of racial discrimination was important to Jennifer and she used the dialogue journals for expression and evaluation. Not only had she felt discriminated against by her Han classmates for being a member of the Tujia minority, but she also came to realize that she herself had discriminated against other people based on stereotypes and what she had been taught in school. She wrote, "And I think it's necessary for me to say a sorry to the people and nations that I misunderstood before, it was the stereotype that blinded my mind" (Jennifer, #2). Furthermore, Jennifer confronted the topics of stereotype and racism outside of class:

> One person even stopped me and asked me whether I was a Japanese. Even now, I still haven't found the reason why that Chinese man thought I was a Japanese, was it because I was talking with my foreign friends in English? But I didn't speak in Japanese, nor do I know how! It may sound funny, but I was extremely irritated at that time, I even wrote this down in my notebook to write about for my journal? (Jennifer, #2)

Jennifer only had access to a computer on the weekends in a computer café. However, she still wrote down immediate feelings in order to reflect more and write in her journal later. The racism discussion continued between Dave and Jennifer in the dialogue journals for the rest of the semester.

Jennifer wrote a personal e-mail to Dave after the last class, which discussed her feelings about the course and expressed her thanks. She was particularly happy to have learned about different cultures and to have seen interpersonal relationships in a more positive light. She wrote,

> I love writing the journals (although it took most my weekends!) Unlike the composition whose format was prescribed, I could write everything in my mind in my journal. I was amazed by your comment. You did read every word we wrote and it pushed me to think more and dig deeper in my life!! It's the freedom that the formal examination composition in China was lack of, which accounts for the reason why so many Chinese students are not good at thinking independently. It is a place where you could pour out your anger, and keep record of the good and bad moments. (e-mail)

Principles

We turn now to a discussion of the principles which underpin the use of dialogue journals with language learners. There are three main principles noted here:

> Principle 1. Teachers should respond to students' ideas and comments, not their language problems. When teachers read dialogue journals they should focus on

understanding meaning rather than fixing grammatical or spelling errors. By responding to the content, a teacher is able to create an ongoing written conversation outside of class around a student's self-initiated topics of interest. The topics Jennifer chose to write about were separate from but related to the course content, as encouraged in the dialogue journal instructions:

> The [dialogue] journal is designed to give you a place to personalize your learning, by exploring what interests you, by making connections between what you know and what you are learning, what you believe and what you are learning, and what you observe out in the real world and what you are learning.

Principle 2. Teachers should relinquish power to build interactive reciprocity. One of the characteristics of a dialogue journal is that the teacher is an active participant in the writing process. Traditional teaching practices presuppose a power imbalance whereby the teacher is the giver and student is the receiver of information. However, dialogue journals create an equal relationship, in which the teacher can learn and receive information from the student. In addition, depending on the topic, the teacher might be asked to state opinions or share life experiences. The appropriateness of the response is contingent upon what the teacher feels comfortable sharing as a participant in the conversation.

In the above vignette, Jennifer took risks and was not afraid to discuss negative facets about her life. In her dialogue journals, she posed questions to Dave about what he thought about each situation, and also asked if he could explain how he felt living as a Caucasian male in China. Dave responded honestly to Jennifer's inquiries because he believed she took risks to tell him personal information about her life.

Principle 3. Teachers should be prepared to learn about experiences that might not be discussed in class. Dialogue journals often provide a platform for further discussion outside of class on a topic raised in class. For instance, Jennifer wrote, "Another sensitive topic! Sexual Harassment. I love this topic because there's a lot I want to say" (Jennifer, #3). The class period did not provide enough time or opportunity for Jennifer to talk about her ideas on sexual harassment. The dialogue journal gave her the opportunity to explore the subject more deeply and let her say what she wanted to say on her own time.

In addition, certain topics provoke personal discussions in the dialogue journals. Teachers should be prepared for students to share private and sometimes disturbing information. When Jennifer discussed family, she explained how her father abandoned her and her mother. For some people this issue would not be easy to discuss in a classroom setting.

Applications

We believe that dialogue journals "can be employed at almost all proficiency levels and in almost all educational contexts" (Mirhosseini, 2009, p. 43). Based on a brief perusal of the literature, we can see that dialogue journals have been used with elementary school children (Nassaji & Cumming, 2000), junior high school students (Connolly, 2007), secondary school students (Ghahremani-Ghajar & Mirhosseini, 2005), college students (Chiesa, Damerow, & Bailey, 2013), and adult language learners (Sanders, 2000).

From our personal experiences, we believe the dialogue journals can be used with varied proficiency levels. For instance, Kathi's students in Hong Kong could be considered lower-intermediate users of English. Their previous classes had emphasized grammar, vocabulary, and reading. Now they were enrolled in a speaking and listening class, and the idea of speaking in class and writing a page-long journal entry every week was daunting at first. However, they gradually produced more language, apparently with less effort and, as a result, we believe that the opportunity to write in their dialogue journals was beneficial in this regard.

The dialogue journals were also utilized for an advanced academic writing course at Beijing Normal University. In that context, they helped students build their own writing voice, to practice writing fluency, and to write informally. This practice helped students establish a habit of writing outside of class because writing in class focused on formal academic prose.

We turn now to a discussion of the advantages and disadvantages of using dialogue journals with language learners.

Payoffs and Pitfalls

What are the advantages and disadvantages of using dialogue journals with foreign language learners?

Advantages for Students

Dialogue journals provide opportunities for teachers to enter students' various *zones of proximal developments* (ZPD), which is, according to Vygotsky (1978), "the distance between the actual developmental level as determined by independent problem solving and the level of potential development, as determined through problem solving under adult guidance or in collaboration with more capable peers" (p. 86). Central to understanding the ZPD is the idea that through collaboration, language learners have the opportunity to develop target language skills more effectively than do those working alone. Dialogue journals allow teachers to better understand their learners' ZPD, and to provide private, tailored input and modeling to each individual while engaging with their ideas.

When students write journal entries and receive feedback from their teacher, there are several positive outcomes. First, students have the opportunity to think critically about the questions their teacher raised when responding to their entries. Second, because of the written dialogue between the teacher and the student, the students are not working alone. Finally, the dialogic creates opportunities for the teacher to better understand the students' proficiency levels.

Dialogue journals provide a private space to interact with the teacher in a non-face-to-face context—hence the potential for face-threatening situations is minimized. In our courses, this privacy gave students opportunities to explore controversial issues, disclose personal information, and express their feelings. Here is another example from, Jennifer, who is a member of the Tujia minority in China.

> *When I first told my new friends that I'm a Tujia, they ... questioned me about a lot of things, like whether I could speak Mandarin and had I ever lived in a cave. ... I felt absurd and ridiculous, if I could not speak Mandarin, how could I communicate with them in Chinese, if I was a caveman, where does the computer come from? ... Such stereotype is laughable but also hurtful.* (Jennifer, #2)

In a foreign language context, dialogue journals give students input and let them generate individual output in the target language compared to their English classes alone. Writing relieves the time pressure involved in trying to communicate by speaking, which entails planning and executing a message in real time while one's interlocutors are waiting. In addition, the written mode allows language learners to edit what they have said before sharing it with their readers. The teacher's responses to the learners' dialogue journal entries give students personalized comments. These comments served as both input and feedback. Making their own journal entries provided a vehicle for the students to develop their language (e.g., writing, vocabulary, and grammar) as well as their cognitive skills (through analysis).

Here is an example from one of Dave's students. The class had discussed Gee's (2005) idea that we are always and everywhere building or creating seven things through language: "identities, relationships, connections, perspectives on the distribution of social goods, significance, activities, and ... privileging certain sign systems over others" (pp. 11–13). In his course, Dave included Gee's (2005) seven building tasks as thinking devices to help guide inquiry about a cultural issue discussed in a lesson. Some students had trouble seeing the value of these ideas at first. In the following excerpt, we see a student, called "Jean," recount her emerging understanding of Gee's view:

> *I remember a word from you in your response to me in the journal: Language is MORE than communication. At first time I do not concur. To analysis the seven buildings in the conversations are ridiculous to me, let alone to believe them. ... But*

gradually, by your comments and the analysis made by our group members on seven buildings change my mind. Their creative and imagination impress me very much by giving a reasonable and sensible idea of the exact function of each building. ... Eventually, I'm convinced: language is more than communication, even more than a symbol of civilization. ... From language, we could enjoy most of the secrets of relations, culture, society, attitude, implied meanings. In my journal of functions of language, you have proved to me language has prefunding meanings besides communication. Now I totally agree. (Jean, #3)

We believe that "prefunding" is Jean's way of saying that language has profound meanings. Clearly she has experienced substantial growth in her views.

Advantages for Teachers

Some topics in the dialogue journal entries provide opportunities for naturally occurring information gaps. For example, Kathi asked her students what would happen during the Lunar New Year celebration in Hong Kong. Their subsequent entries were full of advice about where to go, what to eat, what to buy, and the meaning of new year's symbols and customs. Her students shared information about campus clubs and activities, the assignments in their other courses, and their own aspirations.

The dialogue journal entries give unique glimpses into the students' ideas, their language proficiency, their concerns, and cultural/personal backgrounds. They may also provide a private place to address those ideas and concerns. For example, some students told Kathi that they lacked confidence in their English abilities. She responded,

I agree with you that many Hong Kong students are lacking in confidence. Please tell me why. I was very surprised at the prevalence of this attitude among my students last term, and my students this term have expressed the same idea. (Kathi)

Providing regular supportive responses to our students' dialogue journal entries allowed for specific language input targeted at the individual learner's proficiency level. While we avoided explicit correction of errors, we did model the target forms in our responses to their entries. For example, one of Kathi's students wrote, "So I afraid English I think I do not have confidence. I afraid to speak." Kathi responded, "What do you do when you are afraid of something? When I am afraid, sometimes I tell my best friend that I am afraid, and he talks to me about what I am worried about." Thus, the teacher's reply to the journal entry both modeled the correct form of the copula verb and shared with the learner the fact that teachers also have fears.

In their journals, the students gave us ongoing feedback about the course, which helped us plan subsequent lessons. For instance, one of Dave's students wrote that she loved watching the film *Mean Girls*. As a result, she decided to watch more American movies about education and teenagers' lives. She said,

> *I strongly recommend you to watch the Accepted, it impressed me very much. Accepted is like a reformation of education, it is full of energetic and creativity, I like the main role's speech in the end, touching and convincible. I suppose it reveals the essence of American education. After seeing it, students may feel relaxed, teachers may think about their means of teaching, parents may understand their children.* (Arianna, #2)

Arianna's autonomous decision to watch English films illustrates another choice of how to gain language input outside of class. Dave subsequently used clips of the movie *Accepted* in class. He asked students to compare the language of this movie with that in *Mean Girls* and analyze whether and how their stereotypes of American college students were changed or reinforced.

In our experience, the dialogue journals often served as conceptual anchors for our courses. They helped us make decisions about what to do in class—where to push and where to pull. If we attend to the content of students' entries, dialogue journals can be a pivotal source of feedback.

Disadvantages for Teachers

Responding to dialogue journals can represent a substantial time commitment on the part of the teacher. In responding to 43 students' individual dialogue journal entries on a weekly basis, Kathi estimates that she spent four to six hours per week making handwritten comments. This amount of time could have been decreased considerably had she and her students word-processed their dialogue journals, as Dave's students did.

Another pitfall is that students may divulge serious problems (e.g., suicidal thoughts) that the teacher needs to deal with in some way. In fact, in the journal entries, teachers may discover some problems that they would rather not know about and/or cannot do anything about. For example, one student wrote,

> *Dave, do you believe that I've never got a real good friend? and never got loved by others except my mom? Thus there's a big mutilation in my heart that comes from my childhood: I just need to be loved, a sense of trust and safety that I never got in the past years. It's this kind of feeling that makes me doubt everything, even life itself.* (Brian, #1)

Disadvantages for Students

We are not explicitly aware of any serious disadvantages that the dialogue journals presented to the language learners in our courses. Although we sometimes suggested particular topics, the students were largely free to write about whatever they wished. No one was forced to give opinions or address uncomfortable or private issues.

We surmise that the time involved in writing may have been a problem for some students. Recall Jennifer's comment from the vignette, "although it took most my weekends." At first some students overtly complained about the large time commitment for the dialogue journals but later realized that it was beneficial. For example, Catherine wrote,

> You ask us to write a journal per week. At first, I do not know what to write. I think there's no need to rewrite what I have learned in the class. After the first month, I reviewed my journals and at that time, I suddenly realize I have gained a lot and I already have my own opinion compared with I used to do. (Catherine, #1)

Some disadvantages for students included the number of pages required. Although some of Kathi's lower-intermediate students initially struggled to write a page in English, a few students in Beijing thought that three pages a week was too minimal.

Discussion Questions

1. What is the optimal length and frequency of dialogue journal entries?
2. What should a teacher do if a student divulges serious problems (e.g., suicidal thoughts)?
3. What is the most efficient and effective way to respond to dialogue journal entries?
4. Could teachers use dialogue journals with class sizes over 25, 50, or 100 students? If so, how could responding to students' dialogue entries with large classes best be managed?
5. How can a teacher utilize dialogue journals to help students study for language examinations?

Resources

The *International Research Foundation for English Language Education* provides free downloadable reference lists on several topics, including one on dialogue journals. Visit www.tirfonline.org/resources/references and scroll down the alphabetized list.

References

Chiesa, D., Damerow, R., & Bailey, K. M. (2013). The use of dialogue journals with university EFL students: A sociocultural perspective. *The Journal of English Language and Pedagogy*, 6, 1–16.

Connolly, S. (2007). Peer-to-peer dialogue journal writing by Japanese junior high school EFL students. (Doctoral Dissertation, Temple University, 2007). *Dissertation Abstracts International*, 67, 3351.

Gee, J. P. (2005). *An introduction to discourse analysis: Theory and method* (2nd ed.). New York: Routledge.

Ghahremani-Ghajar, S., & Mirhosseini, S. A. (2005). English class or speaking about every-thing class: Dialogue journal writing as a critical literacy practice in an Iranian high school. *Language, Culture and Curriculum*, 18(3), 286–299.

Mirhosseini, S-A. (2009). For our learn of English: Dialogue journal writing in EFL educa-tion. *Prospect, An Australian Journal of TESOL*, 24(1), 40–48.

Nassaji, H., & Cumming, A. (2000). What's in a ZPD? A case study of a young ESL stu-dent and teacher interacting through dialogue journals. *Language Teaching Research*, 4(2), 95–121.

Peyton, J. K. (1993). *Dialogue journals: Interactive writing to develop language and literacy.* Retrieved from http://www.cal.org/resources/digest/peyton01.html

Sanders, K. M. (2000). The successful use of dialogue journals in the adult ESL classroom: A practitioner's view. In G. Brauer (Ed.), *Writing across languages* (pp. 41–52). Stamford, CT: Ablex Publishing Corporation.

Vygotsky, L. S. (1978). *Mind in society: The development of higher psychological processes.* Cambridge, MA: Harvard University Press.

PART II

Using Technology and the Internet

7

LEARNING VOCABULARY USING TWO MASSIVE ONLINE RESOURCES

You Will Not Blink

Averil Coxhead & Julie Bytheway

Introduction and Overview

TED Talks and *massively multiplayer online role-playing games* (MMORPGs) are two out-of-class online opportunities for language learning. In our discussions with English as a second language learners in the Netherlands and in Aotearoa/New Zealand over the last few years, it became clear that the students who played MMORPGs seemed to know words that other students did not know. That observation led us to consider how might TED Talks and MMORPGs be used for out-of-class learning, particularly when it comes to vocabulary.

The 'TED' in TED Talks (http://www.TED.com/talks) is for Technology, Entertainment, and Design. Experts at TED conferences give presentations that are recorded and loaded onto the TED Talks website. On this site, teachers and learners will find a very wide range of high interest talks on a wide range of subjects by a large numbers of speakers. There are also transcripts for and translations of the talks. Listeners can exchange opinions about talks with other listeners by posting messages.

MMORPGs are online games where thousands of players, simultaneously and in real time, interact to complete collaborative tasks. The whole aim of digital game play is to reach the next level, or "level-up." Gamers support each other to master the game and language required to play.

Both TED Talks and MMORPGs attract huge numbers of viewers and players. The most popular TED recording (Ken Robinson, How schools kill creativity, 2006) has over 25 million views (as of March 2014) and the most popular MMORPG, World of Warcraft®, (Blizzard, 2012) had over 12 million subscribers (as of November 2012). Both TED Talks and MMORPGs contain readily available, highly motivating material that is constantly changing. Although these resources were not specifically created for language learning, they offer learners an extraordinary out-of-classroom vocabulary learning environment.

In this chapter, we outline some key principles of effective vocabulary learning that integrate parts of TED Talks and MMORPGs. We provide practical suggestions on the use of TED Talks and MMORPGs to support vocabulary learning. We end the chapter by addressing several challenges and solutions for teachers and learners who are focussing on vocabulary using these two online resources.

Vignette

Linda teaches English for Academic Purposes to intermediate level learners. Her students seem to use the same vocabulary all the time in their writing and speaking, and Linda is worried that they don't seem to know many words overall. The classroom listening opportunities seem limited to higher level lectures on academic subjects that aren't very interesting to her class or contain very difficult vocabulary that they don't understand. Another problem is that her students don't interact much in English outside class, which means they have limited opportunities to practise their language and gain confidence. Other teachers are using TED Talks in class, but Linda's classroom schedule is packed tight already. What online activities might be available for Linda's students for independent study and how can she evaluate whether these activities can promote vocabulary learning for her students? Let's look at TED Talks and MMORPGs and how they might help Linda with her dilemma. The two main questions we will address are: (1) How do these two online environments provide such rich conditions for vocabulary learning? And (2) how do they relate to Nation's Four Strands (2007) of meaning-focused input, meaning-focused output, language-focused learning, and fluency?

Principles

The following are the principles of vocabulary learning—their conditions and strands.

> *Principle 1. Strive for large amounts of input.* Both TED Talks and MMORPGs provide a large amount of meaning-focussed input for language learners (Nation, 2007). That is, the learners are focussed mainly on understanding the message as they listen and read and are exposed to a range of vocabulary. The input in these environments can be both written and spoken. As well as the recorded talks on video, the TED Talks website includes many transcripts. The TED Talk input is varied, with talks from many different subject areas such as design, entertainment, technology, global issues, and business. In MMORPGs, the input is live audio conversation with other players through headphones, and also visual texts, such as live typed chat and in-game texts and pop-up information.
>
> Players usually have multiple texts showing on their screens and are continually opening and closing tabs to access, show, and hide information and settings.

They need to quickly prioritise what language they need to understand as well as locate and read what they need to help them play the games.

There is an interesting element of control of the input for the learners in TED Talks and MMORPGs. In TED Talks, learners can listen before or after reading a transcript in English or perhaps their first language or choose short talks on familiar topics before moving on to more difficult topics. Language learners in MMORPGs sometimes purposefully remove output opportunities to focus on input opportunities. For example, one player in a study by Bytheway (2011) described disconnecting his microphone and pretending that it was broken so that he did not have to speak and instead could just listen to his team's conversation. This means players can use the advantages of the virtual environment and technology to decrease the complexity of the learning task.

One way to ensure you get better at something is to spend plenty of time doing it. And for learning vocabulary, more time encountering and using words can only be a good thing. TED Talks vary in length, from 3–18 minutes. This means when learners don't have much time for independent listening practice, they could just focus on short talks that are not so conceptually challenging, such as Ric Elias talking about "three things I learned while my plane crashed."

For MMORPGs, time is a key focus. The average gamer plays 22 hours per week, but many gamers play more than 30 hours (Williams, Yee, & Caplan, 2008). Do not be alarmed at these hours. Many people watch TV for similar hours each week. Studies show that gamers are replacing TV watching with game play hours (Williams et al., 2008), which could be seen as replacing informal language learning with passive media with interactive media.

Principle 2. Look for opportunities for repetition and noticing language in use. Both TED Talks and MMORPGs provide opportunities to meet vocabulary items multiple times and to notice language in use. Repetition, extended practice and "overlearning" (that is, practising new skills until they become fast and automatic) are an essential part of MMORPG gameplay (McGonigal, 2011). The repetitive nature of game play is conducive to players noticing and prioritizing words that reoccur. One learner described how he learned words from the in-game repetition. He said, "[I] learn by game | because this words appears a lot of times | I seen them again and again and again (Bytheway, 2011). Another strategy players used was to purposefully read other players live typed chat conversations and notice language-in-use, as seen in this excerpt from an interview with a second language player:

[S]ometime I just learn from people chatting together | I watch their chat like | this guy's a beginner this guy's the pros | and they chatting together and this guy ask them oh how does this word mean and how you do something bla bla bla | I just like an observer | and watch the chatting groups | I learn a lot from that (Bytheway, 2011)

With TED Talks, higher frequency words occur very often. The first 4,000+ proper nouns cover 95% of a corpus of TED Talks by Coxhead & Walls (2012) (to reach 98%, the listeners need to know 8,000–9,000 words plus proper nouns). This means that TED Talks contain a large number of high frequency words and these words will be repeated often throughout different talks. By choosing a subject area, such as design, learners can narrow their listening to allow for repetition of vocabulary (Schmitt & Carter, 2000), which is similar to listening to television shows on related contexts (Rodgers & Webb, 2011). Learners might, for example, listen to Markus Fischer talking about a robot that flies like a bird, and then David Hanson discussing robots that "show emotion."

Below is the opening section of David Hansen's TED Talk (available at http://www.ted.com/talks/a_robot_that_flies_like_a_bird.html). We have marked up the words in the text according to Nation's British National Corpus frequency lists (see Nation, 2006). Words in normal type are in the first 1,000 words, words in *italics* are in the second 1,000 words, words in **bold** are in the 6,000 words, and words underlined with a broken line are in the 7,000 words. Proper nouns have been underlined with an unbroken line.

I'm Dr. David Hanson, and I build **robots** with character. And by that, I mean that I develop **robots** that are characters, but also **robots** that will *eventually* come to empathize with you. So we're starting with a *variety* of *technologies* that have converged into these conversational character **robots** that can see faces, make eye contact with you, make a full range of facial expressions, understand *speech* and begin to *model* how you're feeling and who you are, and build a relationship with you.

This example illustrates the vocabulary learners need to know to follow this text, and shows that the first 2,000 words cover most of the words in the text. Key words, such as **robot**, are repeated several times in the text. Remember that each talk has video, as well as text, and the speakers often use visuals or models during their talks, which will support learners with listening and vocabulary.

Principle 3. Take advantage of opportunities for meaning focused output. Meaning-focussed output means that learners are using language in writing or speaking. In TED Talks, learners can comment on what they have heard, post questions, and discuss ideas through comment boxes at the end of each talk. These activities can be connected to the language classroom if learners are listening to and commenting on or discussing some of the same talks. In MMORPGs, players must interact in speaking and writing to form teams, complete complex collaborative tasks, trade items, and maintain social and business-like relationships (Mäyrä, 2008). Gamers also interact with the online gaming community through blogs, wikis and social media.

Principle 4. Ensure there is plenty of fluency practice. One of Nation's Four Strands (2007, p. 6) is fluency. In this strand, the focus is not on learning new vocabulary items, but working with material that is already very familiar and on the messages that are being conveyed. After learners have listened to a TED Talk once, they can always go back and listen again. Once the language and the ideas are under the learner's control, listening to the same talk again provides fluency practice. It also means, from a vocabulary perspective, that the learners will encounter words again.

MMORPGs players feel a great sense of urgency to both play the game and learn words in order to play the game. So much is happening simultaneously. Players use the keyboard and mouse to control camera angle, character movement, select and use various skills and weapons, access inventories and other pop-up tabs and chat; meanwhile they are quickly reading information available on their screens and often also listening and speaking through headphones and microphone to team chat. This focus on fast communication results in creative non-standard language, including *leetspeak*. Leetspeek is a nonstandard, often abbreviated, form of spelling that includes numeral and other characters, for example, *leet* can also be spelled *1337* and *l33t*. The acceptance of flexible spelling is part of leetspeak and encourages creativity. Players readily accept nonstandard language because they attribute language mistakes to typing speed and creativity rather than language competence (Bytheway, 2011). Interestingly, this low learning anxiety and high risk-taking learning behaviour is also used with more standard forms of language such as the specialised terms and high frequency words. The creative approach to language appears to be extended to a creative approach to language learning too. The in-game sense of urgency forces players to prioritise fluency. Nation (2007, p. 6) lists pressure to perform as an element of the fluency strand.

Applications

We think TED Talks and MMORPGs are more suited to intermediate and above language learners who are in their late teens or older. One of the challenges of TED Talks is the vocabulary load of the talks. As noted, Coxhead & Walls (2012) found that learners need a vocabulary size of 8,000–9,000 word families plus proper nouns to cover up to 98% of the words in the talks. That means that for every 100 words, two will be unknown. Currently, 98% is suggested as the level of coverage needed for listening without support from the teacher (Hu & Nation, 2000). If learners have a vocabulary size of around 4,000 word families plus proper nouns, they should be able to work with TED Talks with support, such as the pictures, transcripts, translations, and subtitles. Analyses of the vocabulary needed to play MMORPGs in English are not yet available, to the best of our knowledge.

Talking about using these resources with learners. The Internet is increasingly available to large numbers of language learners worldwide. It is important that we help learners to take advantage of the English in the real and digital worlds around them to help them learn vocabulary out of class. Teachers could encourage learners to purposefully experiment with MMORPG as vocabulary learning environments outside classrooms and get learners to share their MMORPG learning experiences inside classroom. They could also make MMORPG players aware of how they can transfer their in-game language skills and language-learning strategies to other contexts. For example, gamers could be encouraged to treat other passive texts like television and online texts like texts in MMORPGs. Learners and teachers could discuss how their in-game vocabulary learning strategies could work while watching videos, such as TED, and while reading texts, such as online wikis. Teachers can ask players how they notice and select words for learning within TED Talks and MMORPGs and probe them to be specific in their answers.

Encouraging interaction and language use. One out-of-class activity with TED Talks that might encourage interaction is to set up a class wiki where learners post their recommendations to classmates for TED Talks to listen to, along with comments and questions for discussion based on the talks. Learners could also start a listening log where they record what they have listened to, key points, and comments or reflections. They can also record how long and how often they are listening in their log books, and use that information to reflect on the amount of listening practice they are getting. The learners could also include key words they have picked up from the TED Talks in their discussion to help them gain mastery of the lexical items they have encountered. This activity would fit into Nation's meaning-focused input and meaning-focused output strands, whereby learners are focused on familiar things and are communicating their ideas to another person (see Nation, 2007. p. 5)

Activities for TED Talks and MMORPGs-based vocabulary learning. If you would like your learners to concentrate on the language-focused learning strand from Nation (2007), you could consider the following activities. Below is an adaptation of an idea from Karenne Joy Sylvester (n.d.) from her blog on speaking activities using TED Talks. It's called "Vocabulary Collection" and here are her instructions:

Give students a piece of paper with the numbers 1–10 written on it. While watching, any video you've chosen, ask them to either write ten words they found most interesting, ten words they didn't understand, or ten words which they think would summarize the story.

After watching, encourage students to share the words they've collected and to tell each other why these words were the ones they recorded.

To make this classroom activity into an out-of-class activity, you could ask your learners to start a vocabulary log of their own TED Talks. In their vocabulary log books, they can record any new information they have gained about words they already know or partially know from the TED Talks, including collocations or phrases using these words that they have not heard before. They can also log new words that they encounter in a TED Talk, and note key aspects of the words such as meaning, spelling, and pronunciation.

Teachers might be concerned about the kinds of vocabulary learners might encounter in MMORPGs. To play MMORPGs, players must be able to understand high frequency words that are used the same way as they are in everyday usage, such as *return* and *instead*. They will also encounter specialised terms (for example, *subtlety* and *afflicting*), and *Leetspeak* (e.g., *18r n00b*). However, because of the wide range of language mixed together, gamers may need help distinguishing register and appropriate use in out of game contexts. As an in-class activity, students could brainstorm vocabulary they have learned in games and sort these words into other contexts where they could use this language, for example, business letters, small talk, exam writing, and speaking tasks.

Payoffs and Pitfalls

We see some major pay offs with TED Talks and MMORPGs and vocabulary learning. Both are highly involving environments that demand focus and are driven by people's motivation to listen or play. Learners do not need to manage motivation in MMORPGs because a play context is intrinsically motivating. Similarly, TED Talks provide a wide range of listening opportunities with different topics, speakers, styles, visual support, and length of scripts. For vocabulary learning, both environments promise high levels of possible engagement, input, output, and practice.

That said, it is important to acknowledge that TED Talks and MMORPGs set up two very different types of learning environments. One, or none, may appeal to some learners but not others because of different learning styles or interests. Also, teachers need to be careful that enforcing or encouraging games does not destroy the qualities of play that make them so engaging (Squire, 2005). Quality of play, such as being voluntary and purposeless, may be lost when games are included in or recommended by formal learning institutions. Remember that both TED Talks and MMORPGs are available online at any time. However, while TED Talks are free, MMORPGs have subscription costs of up to USD 25 per month, depending on the game.

The effects of digital games are often portrayed negatively by the media (Mäyrä, 2008). Games can be addictive. Some players find it difficult to draw the line on acceptable playing time and players describe seeking help to quit their addiction (Bytheway, 2011). Academic arguments about the effects of digital games on violent behaviour are ongoing and unresolved.

Another possible pitfall with MMORPGs could be that learners might see the learning and interaction with regard to vocabulary learning as more meaningful than in classrooms. As one MMORPG player/language learner said,

> classroom is more official| you will not learn a lot of new exciting words where it means [something]| I think we need it because of the visual | we don't have moving stuff | we just read from the book | and um teacher is talking | and yeah just write it down | this is not exciting at all | [games] keep you focused at that attention | it's like [during] the game itself | you will not blink | you try to prevent from blinking or looking away because it's exciting | things are moving | yeah every second means something | but in the classroom | just from the books you can turn away | look away | it's no big deal (Bytheway, 2011)

How can we, as classroom teachers, ever compete with that? This is the essence of outside classroom learning: Learners are in control, they prefer meaning-focused communication tasks, and set their own tasks to understand meaning-focused input and express themselves through meaning-focused output. By encouraging your learners to find real vocabulary learning opportunities outside your classroom through TED Talks and MMORPGs, we might find that learners surprise us all with what's out there in both real and digital worlds.

Discussion Questions

1. How might MMORPGs and TED Talks fit into the out-of-class vocabulary learning experiences of your students? If possible, go online and listen to a TED Talk or try a free demonstration of an MMORPG so you experience them for yourself.
2. What mobile digital games are your learners currently playing? Which mobile game is super hot right now? How could the "super-hot" game be used for language learning? Revisit this question in six months and see what might have changed.
3. Learners find online resources such as TED videos and MMORPGs extremely motivating partially because they offer control, choice and opportunities for meaning-focused communication. Which of your well-used classroom activities can you adapt so that learners are offered more control, choice and opportunities for meaning-focused communication? How can you specifically adapt these classroom learning activities?
4. Learners appear to be aware of the vocabulary learning strategies they use in online videos and games. How can we help learners identify their online vocabulary learning strategies and transfer these strategies to other learning contexts, including classroom contexts?
5. List all the specific online and mobile resources you used within the last month. Sort all the resources you used into overlapping groups, using a Venn

diagram with three sets, of those that can provide language learners opportunities for meaning-focused input, meaning-focused output, and fluency development. Which online resources may be realistically valuable for language learning? How can you justify your opinion? Where does language-focussed learning fit in your diagram?

6. Brainstorm five to ten specific ways you have autonomously learned second language vocabulary using online videos or games. Negotiating with a small group, rank these vocabulary learning strategies in order of effectiveness. How does the online environment impact on your vocabulary learning?

7. Digital games are often portrayed negatively by the media. How would you explain the positive effects of games for language learning to your students, their parents, and your school management team?

8. In this chapter, we note some disadvantages of MMORPGs and TED Talks. Which disadvantage do you consider to be the most difficult to overcome and what might an out-of-class learner in your context do to overcome it?

Resources

For *TED Talks*, go to the main website at http://www.ted.com/talks.

For an introduction to *MMORPGs*, see http://en.wikipedia.org/wiki/Massively_multiplayer_online_role-playing_game.

To test your learners' vocabulary size, check out http://my.vocabularysize.com/.

References

Blizzard Entertainment (Producer). (2012). *World of warcraft.*

Bytheway, J. (2011). *Vocabulary learning strategies in Massively Multiplayer Online Role-Playing Games.* (Master's thesis). Retrieved from the Research Archive of Victoria University of Wellington, New Zealand, http://researcharchive.vuw.ac.nz/xmlui/handle/10063/1727.

Coxhead, A., & Walls, R. (2012). TED Talks, vocabulary, and listening for EAP. *TESOLANZ Journal,* 20, 55–67.

Hu, M., & Nation, I.S.P. (2000). Vocabulary density and reading comprehension. *Reading in a Foreign Language,* 13(1), 403–430.

Mäyrä, F. (2008). *An introduction to game studies: Games in culture.* Los Angeles: Sage.

McGonigal, J. (2011). *Reality is broken: Why games make us better and how they change the world.* London: Johnathan Cape.

Nation, I.S.P. (2006). How large a vocabulary is needed for reading and listening? *Canadian Modern Language Review,* 63(1), 59–82.

Nation, I.S.P. (2007). The four strands. *Innovation in Language Learning and Teaching,* 1(1), 1–12.

Robinson, K. (2006, February). *How schools kill creativity.* Paper presented at TED Conference, Monterey, CA. Retrieved from http://www.ted.com/talks/ken_robinson_says_schools_kill_creativity.html

Rodgers, M., & Webb. S. (2011). Narrow viewing: The vocabulary in related television programs. *TESOL Quarterly,* 45(4), 689–717.

Schmitt, N., & Carter, R. (2000). The lexical advantages of narrow reading for second language learners. *TESOL Journal*, 9(1), 4–9.

Squire, K. (2005). Changing the game: What happens when video games enter the classroom? *Innovate*, 1(6).

Sylvester, K. (n.d.). *10 Speaking English Activities using TED.com*. Retrieved from http://kalinago.blogspot.com.au/2011/09/10-speaking-english-activities-using.html

Williams, D., Yee, N., & Caplan, S. E. (2008). Who plays, how much, and why? Debunking the stereotypical gamer profile. *Journal of Computer-Mediated Communication*, 13, 999–1018.

8

"I DON'T KNOW HOW TO TALK BASKETBALL BEFORE PLAYING NBA 2K10"

Using Digital Games for Out-of-Class Language Learning

Alice Chik

Introduction and Overview

One challenge for non-native English speaking university students is using English to interact with other students socially. Socializing with newly made friends in one's first language is already a challenge, and doing it in a second or foreign language can be daunting. For many students, it might be a double burden because there are no ESL courses on these topics. For instance, where is an ESL course on fashion or football or food or wine or clubbing? Acquiring vocabulary and cultural knowledge on an everyday subject like sports or shopping allows learners to interact socially and integrate better into their new social circles. Frequently, it is not that ESL learners do not have the knowledge of sports or fashion or films, they simply do not have the foreign language vocabulary to talk about these topics (Miller & Peirson-Smith, 2014).

Learners can acquire vocabulary on specific topics by reading magazines or books, or by watching TV and films. Reading has traditionally been associated with vocabulary acquisition, but it is not necessarily easy for learners to retain the vocabulary. Yet, learning vocabulary from reading or listening is all receptive learning and some learners may not find it to be a good learning method (Nation, 2008). And many learners may think acquiring vocabulary through reading and listening is not enough to help them produce the spoken form. One way that many ESL learners found to be useful for language learning, surprisingly, is through digital gaming.

In this chapter, we look at the principles for ESL learning through digital gaming. A vignette from a Chinese university student will be used to demonstrate the ways digital gameplay can enhance ESL, especially on topics usually not covered in regular language courses. We then discuss reasons why digital gaming can be a positive game changer for individualized learning, and look at the potential drawback. Finally, we provide some discussion questions and resources for readers who are interested in pursuing this approach further.

Vignette

I met Edmond from a research project on second language learning through digital gaming. Edmond was a Mainland Chinese student studying electronic engineering in an English-medium university in Hong Kong. In China, his English lessons in school emphasized reading and writing over speaking and listening. As a Mainland Chinese and an engineering student, he felt that his spoken English was not as fluent as his peers and he wanted to make himself more presentable in English. He took several non-required English for academic purposes classes at the language centre, and took all the opportunities to speak in English. He did find the lessons useful for academic purposes. Yet, Edmond found that it was more difficult to talk about everyday topics, like sports, in English.

Edmond lived in the student hall and had plenty of opportunity to interact with other residing international students socially. As an enthusiastic basketball player, Edmond did not fully understand basketball terminology and players' names in English. He wanted to improve his basketball vocabulary so he could interact without feeling inadequate in after game conversation. Edmond thought of using English-subtitled sports programs for vocabulary learning, but access to live English basketball TV programs in the student hall was limited. Taking the advice from a gaming friend, Edmond started playing digital basketball games on his PC. He enjoyed the in-game audio commentaries and jokes and read all the instructions dutifully. Transferring the learning strategies acquired from school, Edmond used an electronic dictionary and kept a vocabulary book. Even though the audio commentaries and on-screen texts were repetitive, he worked hard to memorize the terminology. He also thought the repetition necessary for learning the basketball vocabulary and names of basketball players. At the same time, he searched for gaming strategies from online discussion forums. He found a number of Chinese and English forums and blogs discussing different sports games, but the more popular Chinese forums specialized in football game series. As Edmond combed through online communities, he connected with other gamers using sports games to learn English to better enjoy live sports TV programs. After playing digital basketball games for more than six months, Edmond found it a lot easier to understand the conversation with his international team players.

Principles

In this chapter, digital games refer to all types of games played on PC, handheld and dedicated game consoles, tablet computers, and smart phones. The basic division for games includes educational-oriented and pleasure-oriented games, or frequently called commercial over-the-shelf (COTS) games. Educational games are mainly used only in classroom contexts and are not popular among gamers in out-of-class contexts. The use of educational games in out-of-class learning may be more popular among young learners when parents have greater control of the gameplay. In this chapter, we only discuss ESL learning through COTS game playing. The discussion of educational games in out-of-class learning is beyond the scope of this chapter.

Some of the most popular digital games are released by American and Japanese game developers in English or Japanese. One clarification should be made about languages and digital games. While many of the most popular COTS games claim to support multiple languages other than English, this concept of multilingualism is only very loosely defined. For most COTS games, the original in-game texts and game menus are in English, but German, Spanish or Chinese subtitles may be provided in the bilingual versions. In other instances, only the game box and instructions were translated, but the in-game texts and menus are in English. In yet one more example, the in-game menu is translated, but the in-game dialogues are still in English with or without subtitles. The extent of translation depends on a number of factors, such as game genre, the size of the game developer, targeted market, publication timeline, and the like. From all this confusion about bilingual or multilingual versions, one point we can establish is that many gamers are exposed to English-language in-game texts. It is simply a matter of degree.

Principle 1. Emphasize in-game interaction to maximize learning opportunities for ESL learners. There are three domains for ESL learning through digital gaming: online gaming interaction, in-game texts consumption, and game-related texts production. In much of the game-related ESL research, it is found that online gaming interaction is one of the most fruitful areas for ESL learning and use. First, massively multiplayer online role-playing games (MMORPGs) can cater to millions of players in their gameworlds, and one good example is the popular *World of Warcraft* (WoW). As soon as gamers log into the MMORPGs, they can play with gamers from various linguistic and cultural backgrounds in collaborative or competitive gameplay. In these globalized gameworlds, the shared goal is completing game tasks and English becomes the *de facto* gaming language. Other than MMORPGs, many console games now provide an online multiplayer mode for players to connect with others. *Grand Theft Auto V* is normally played in a single-player setting, but includes an online gameplay option for up to 16 players. Thorne (2008) analyzed the in-game chat between an American and Ukrainian *WoW* player, and the interaction happened in Russian, Latin, and English. English use was often the social action needed for gameplay in these multilingual gameworlds. However, in a study on a modded online gaming environment with Thai university students, Reinders & Wattana (2012) found that less experienced gamers and students who were less confident in their communication skills found it distracting to engage in voice- or text-based chat during gameplay.

Principle 2. Encourage ESL learners to read in-game texts to enhance reading and gaming experiences. Second, in-game texts provide popular reading materials for gamers. In-game texts are texts that gamers encounter while playing games. Contrary to popular belief that there are no (or not many) 'words' in digital games, many contemporary digital games are 'word-heavy' with rolling on-screen texts or dialogues between game characters. These in-game texts are among the most popular reading materials by young people (Williamson, 2009). While the game menu in *Grand Theft Auto V* is available in Spanish (and nine other languages), in-game dialogues are delivered in English with Spanish subtitles. This means many ESL learners are essentially reading and listening to English texts while playing games. Piirainen-Marsh & Tainio (2009) found that when playing English-language fantasy-adventure games at home, though the Finnish-speaking gamers were chatting in Finnish, they repeated the English phrases and dialogues used by game characters.

Principle 3. Guide ESL learners to utilize game-external websites and communities to harness learning opportunities. Contemporary digital games are also complex texts, and many gamers require additional help in order to advance their gameplay. In the past, gamers might have to rely on their immediate gaming to get gaming advice. Now, more gamers are soliciting help from online communities. Many gamers produce game-related texts including walkthroughs, video tutorials, fan art, and fan fictions. These game-related texts are frequently produced in English and are distributed on interest-driven online forums and websites. Sykes & Reinhardt (2013) argue that good games not only engage players in playing the games, but also encourage players to read and write about them in interest-driven websites. Popular Japanese-made role-playing games like *Kingdom Heart* attracted a lot of players to write about the characters, and currently there are more than 70,000 fan fictions about *Kingdom Heart* on FanFiction.net. These fan fictions vary in length from less than 1,000 to more than 100,000 words, in fact, there are 391 fan fictions on *Kingdom Heart* that are longer than 100,000 words. These fan fictions reimagined new alternate game characters and plots, or provided background stories to existing game plots (see Thomas, 2007 for a more detailed discussion of fan fictions). Of course, not all game-related texts were produced in English, many more gamers are moving back and forth between first- and foreign language versions of game-related walkthroughs and instructions to maximize their gameplay advancement (Chik, 2012).

Principle 4. Highlight useful vocabulary learning strategies to ESL learners to sustain autonomous learning. Gamers do not generally only play games once, they play on a regular basis. Other than constant exposure, another way of linking the SLA learning through digital gaming is the strategies for vocabulary learning.

Nation (2008) proposes the four main strategies for vocabulary learning are: guessing from context, learn to use word cards, use word parts, and use dictionary. Gee (2012) argues that "games associate words with images, actions, goals and dialogue, not just with definitions or other words" (p. xiv), thus making guessing new words from context more probable when gaming. Many gamers also *need* to learn the language used in games in order to advance their gameplay. This connects language learning through digital gaming to the hypothesis by Hulstijn & Laufer (2001) on learners' engagement with vocabulary: need, search, and evaluation. Because gamers *need* to understand vocabulary items in order to complete game tasks, they may *search* for the meaning by using dictionary or in-game visual cues, and finally they *evaluate* the cues and definitions in relation to the game contexts. And Schmitt (2008) listed some recurring factors that facilitate vocabulary learning, including frequency of exposure, noticing, intention to learn, a requirement to learn, and a need to learn the lexical items. When reviewing this list, these are all the activities that ESL gamers frequently engage in during their gameplay. Even when simply observing other gamers to play in a game, learners may actually be learning more lexical items than the player as shown in a study on playing and observing music digital games among Japanese university students (deHaan, Reed, & Kuwada, 2010).

Applications

In this section, we will see how to use digital games for ESL learning. To begin with, someone who is already open to and comfortable with playing digital games is more likely to view learning through digital gaming positively. Home entertainment games are distributed and played on different platforms, and there are four basic divisions: PC, dedicated game consoles (e.g., PlayStation 3®, Xbox 360®, and Wii U®), handheld game consoles (e.g., Nintendo 3DS® and PlayStation Vita®), and tablet computers (through game applications, or apps). Most MMORPGs are played on PCs (e.g., *Star Wars: The Old Republic*), but popular COTS are mostly played on game consoles (e.g., the *FIFA* series). Most multiplayer games will require Internet connection, and of course, multiplayer mode can also be achieved by using multiple console handheld controls.

Many MMORPGs operate on a freemium model, that means the basic play is free, but additional game items are charged. However, the more popular MMORPGs require monthly subscription for gameplay, and usually the minimal period of subscription is 30 days or a month. Most MMORPGs require the download and installation of the game software, and each game may have specific hardware and software requirements, for instance, the version of operating system or sound card. If a player wants to enjoy in-game chatting, then a basic functioning microphone and speakers will be required. A headset type of speaker-headphone will work best.

Gamers source, exchange, or ask for game walkthroughs and strategies on game-external discussion forums and websites. Just like regular discussion forums, most of these game-dedicated forums or websites require membership registration, but most are free of charge. To produce text or multimedia walkthroughs, different equipment will be needed. The basic word-processing software will suffice for composing text-based walkthroughs, however, a video camera will be required to produce multimedia walkthroughs. Many gamers also use screen capture software to record gameplay and audio commentary. These video walkthroughs usually show gaming in action and the gamer-instructors provide audio commentary behind the camera. These video instructions and walkthroughs can easily be found on media sharing websites (e.g., YouTube.com) or game-dedicated websites (e.g., IGN.com). For gamers interested in creating fan arts, the genres range from simple drawing to mashup, special software will be required (see Lowood & Nitsche, 2011 for more details).

Edmond's story illustrates that learning through digital gaming is especially good for learners who are looking for vocabulary enhancement beyond the regular vocabulary classes. Different from using pop songs or films, all games engage players in completing tasks. Many ESL gamers also experience the inevitable situation that in order to enjoy the games more, they have to improve their language proficiency. When this happens, gamers actively turn incidental learning into intentional learning. When Edmond recorded a project video of playing real-time strategy game with his friend, the same friend who suggested using sports games to learn basketball English, the video showed both of them repeating after game characters and discussing the meaning of words used in games. The two gamers also stuck a bilingual glossary next to the computer monitor as convenient help. So it can be said that playing games with others can enhance the learning process and also the strategies used.

According to university gamers and online discussants, when encountering new lexical items, they reacted by using one or more the following strategies:

1. Ask a nearby gaming partner for help
2. Guess from context or visual cue
3. Pause gameplay to use an electronic or online dictionary
4. Pause gameplay to jot down the lexical items
5. Ignore the new lexical items

Many of the participants confirmed that the first two strategies were used when they were younger and were gaming with older siblings or family members. Strategy 5 of ignoring new lexical items was generally not advised because gamers might pay by losing out in gameplay later. However, gamers were more divided on strategies 3 and 4. Depending on the type of games being played, pausing gameplay may not be an option. Edmond commented that it was virtually impossible to pause the gameplay while engaging in real-time strategy games because he was playing against other gamers, and timely interaction was a given for satisfactory gameplay. So one solution was using screen capture software to retain visual records of the in-game texts (usually as .jpg files) so he could revisit the visual files later.

As gamers advance further in their games, many compiled bilingual word lists as autonomous learning. Many online discussants mentioned the cross-comparison of the word lists among friends in their immediate social circles in the early days of the Internet use when online discussion forums or bulletin boards were not as popular. Now, when encountering new lexical items gamers are more likely to search for bilingual word lists or definitions online before they compile their own. This is also a more sensible strategy as eager, dedicated, and experienced gamers are contributing bilingual walkthroughs and word lists in a matter of hours after the official releases of popular titles.

Payoffs and Pitfalls

Contemporary gameplay is both fun and hard work. Gamers invest hours and endless energy to advance their gameplay, and at the same time learn multimodal reading skills, cooperative and collaborative skills (Gee, 2003). The combination of leisure and learning provides an avenue for interest-driven learning. Gamers are motivated to learn the lexical items to advance their gameplay or enhance their gaming pleasure. From Edmond's case, we also see the connection between different leisure activities in young people's social lives. The need for 'basketball English' prompted the playing of sports games, which in turn enriched basketball-related vocabulary acquisition. With the extreme popularity of some digital game series, it is not difficult to envision learners using such materials to learn English. The two biggest selling digital games of 2013 were *Grand Theft Auto V* and *FIFA 14*, the former an action-adventure game and the later a soccer simulation game. Both were the latest releases from firmly established brands and provide different affordances to ESL gamers. Online discussants frequently commented on the authenticity of the 'street English' used in *Grand Theft Auto (GTA)* series. The game supports a number of European and Asian languages, but the in-game dialogues are still delivered in English (or gangsta English). The more family-friendly *FIFA 14* only supports European languages and commentaries are delivered in English. The link to the immensely popular football watching culture in East Asia makes *FIFA* one of the most popular soccer game series. When the game does not support Asian languages, Asian players have to play the games in English.

Learning vocabulary from games is not without its limitation. The choice of game genre can severely limit the acquisition of vocabulary. In plot-driven games, such as *L.A. Noire & Heavy Rain*, there are a lot of in-game dialogues. These crime-themed games provide a rich learning environment for learning language related to law and order. In action–driven games, like *GTA*, the game characters use a lot of slang and inappropriate language. Is there any use to learn those? Some ESL learners may value the opportunity to learn the 'street language' not taught in the classrooms. It is also found that confidence gained from expertise in a specific area of language use can motivate learners to transfer the confidence to other domains. I once invited an undergraduate gamer to present his language learning experience to a group of MA TESOL students, with many being English teachers in local secondary schools. In 45 minutes, he eloquently presented different game genres and the language learning affordances, and explained how he acquired an expert knowledge in medieval weaponry and war tactics. At the end of his presentation, several teachers questioned the value of knowing medieval warfare in Hong Kong. The gamer acknowledged the limitation of such expertise. But then he went on to explain that he had the confidence to talk for 45 minutes in English on this topic and on other academic topics in university because he knew that he could teach himself to acquire the type of English required to communicate with a specific audience. Perhaps it is true that an expertise in sports or strategy vocabulary has no direct relation to daily communication, but the process of acquiring such an expertise is the booster that many learners needed to sustain their ESL learning.

Another pitfall is the lack of progress and structure in language learning. ESL learning can happen from textual or social interaction within the gaming environments, but instructional and advisory roles taken up by gamers were less researched. In gaming communities, it is not difficult to find gaming strategies and language learning advice from online sources. In turn, many more gamers provided these strategies and advice to younger or novice gamers. A simple search will yield abundant online forum discussion threads, YouTube videos, and gaming blog posts advising gamers on using English-language games for learning or translated game-related texts to help non-native English-speaking gamers. Though these resources were available, it could be argued that there was no structured instruction for learning as gamers were moving from games to games.

Discussion Questions

1. Do you play digital games on a regular basis? Why? Why not?
2. Do you think learners can learn through playing games?
3. What do you think about teachers using non-educational commercial games as supplementary learning materials or activities? Would it work in your context?
4. What are some of the challenges of using commercial games for language learning?
5. Do you see a future with commercial games as complementary learning materials?

Resources

J. M. Sykes & J. Reinhardt, *Language at Play: Digital Games in Second and Foreign Language Teaching and Learning* (Boston: Pearson, 2013). Sykes & Reinhardt provide a comprehensive discussion of second and foreign language learning and teaching and digital games. They used SLA learning principles, for example, goals, interaction, feedback, context, and motivation to discuss the ways digital gaming can benefit language learning.

Games to Teach (http://games2teach.wordpress.com/) is a website maintained by Jonathon Reinhardt (University of Arizona) and Julie Sykes (University of Oregon) to disseminate information and resources for developing digital game-mediated foreign language literacies.

"Digital Gaming and Language Learning: Autonomy and Community," a paper by Alice Chik in *Language Learning & Technology* 18, no. 2 (2014), can be accessed at http://llt.msu.edu/issues/June2014/chik.pdf. It provides a theoretical framework for understanding EFL learning through digital gameplay in out-of-class contexts.

References

Chik, A. (2012). Digital gameplay for autonomous foreign language learning: Gamers' and language teachers' perspectives. In H. Reinders (Ed.), *Digital games in language learning and teaching* (pp. 95–114). London: Palgrave Macmillan.

Chik, A. (2014). Digital gaming and language learning: Autonomy and community. *Language Learning & Technology*, 18(2). Retrieved from http://llt.msu.edu/issues/June2014/chik.pdf.

deHaan, J., Reed, W.M., & Kuwada, K. (2010). The effect of interactivity withy a music video game on second language vocabulary recall. *Language Learning and Technology*, 14(2), 74–94.

Gee, J. P. (2003). *What video games have to teach us about learning and literacy*. New York: Palgrave.

Gee, J. P. (2012). Foreword. In H. Reinders (Ed.), *Digital games in language learning and teaching* (pp. xii–xiv). London: Palgrave Macmillan.

Hulstijn, J., & Laufer, B. (2001). Some empirical evidence for the involvement load hypothesis in vocabulary acquisition. *Language Learning*, 51(3), 539–558.

Lowood, H., & Nitsche, M. (2011). (Ed.). *The machinima reader*. Cambridge, MA: MIT Press.

Miller, L., & Peirson-Smith, A. (2014). Football for all, organic living, and MK culture: Teaching popular culture by turning theory into practice. In P. Benson & A. Chik (Eds.), *Popular culture, pedagogy and teacher education*. London: Routledge.

Nation, I.S.P. (2008). *Teaching vocabulary: Strategies and techniques*. Boston: Heinle Cengage Learning.

Piirainen-Marsh, A., & Tainio, L. (2009). Other-repetition as a resource for participation in the activity of playing a video-game. *The Modern Language Journal*, 93(2), 153–169.

Reinders, H., & Wattana, S. (2012). Talk to me! Games and students' willingness to communicate. In H. Reinders (Ed.), *Digital games in language learning and teaching* (pp. 156 – 188). London: Palgrave Macmillan.

84 Alice Chik

Schmitt, N. (2008). Review article: Instructed second language vocabulary learning. *Language Teaching Research*, 12(3), 329–363.

Sykes, J. M., & Reinhardt, J. (2013). *Language at play: Digital games in second and foreign language teaching and learning.* Boston: Pearson.

Thomas, A. (2007). *Youth online: Identity and literacy in the digital age.* New York: Peter Lang.

Thorne, S. L. (2008). Transcultural communication in open Internet enironments and massively multiplayer online games. In S.S. Magnan (Ed.), *Mediating discourse online* (pp. 305–327). Amsterdam: John Benjamins.

Williamson, B. (2009). *Computer games, schools, and young people: A report for educators on using games for learning.* Bristol, UK: Futurelab.

9

THE USE OF SOCIAL MEDIA RESOURCES IN ADVANCED LEVEL CLASSES

Maria do Carmo Righini

Introduction and Overview

The new courses for advanced level groups at Cultura Inglesa São Paulo—a non-profit organization with branches spread throughout the state of São Paulo, with approximately 70,000 students and 500 teachers—were designed to look modern and appealing to both adolescents and young adults at college, as well as professionals.

Our challenges were mainly two. Firstly, to offer a course program that could move students out of their comfort zone by arousing their interest in the reading of authentic news texts, with more complex language on multifaceted contexts, such as politics, diplomacy, finance, health systems, and modern scientific research. Secondly, to challenge long ingrained beliefs about language teaching and learning in both communities of teachers and students, by structuring the syllabus in a more lexical rather than a grammatical view of language. Nevertheless, we were convinced that that was the way to go if we were to prioritize communicative competence and learner autonomy in a critical thinking environment, all of them key concepts of a language course that aimed at developing twenty-first-century skills.

It was in that context that the decision to officially introduce the use of social media tools as a key feature of the advanced courses came about. They would greatly enhance the course by offering students the opportunity and the means to collaborate and "go public," express themselves with more authenticity through well-known online resources: blog, voice-recording capable websites, and Facebook.

This chapter describes five projects carried out during one year with different groups of advanced learners of English and will discuss the outcomes based on reports made by the teachers involved in the projects, according to the following criteria: students' adherence to the projects, students' contributions, in terms of language and discourse competence displayed, and teachers' and students' testimonials.

Vignette

The introduction of social media tools as an integral part of the course structure was initially seen as a very powerful means to support students' development in three main aspects: encouraging extensive reading, intensifying exposure and noticing of content-related lexis, and developing learner autonomy strategies.

Therefore, an attractive extensive reading programme of news articles from the electronic media related to the syllabus was created and teachers were encouraged to create a blog where students would upload comments on their chosen news article and comment on their peers' posts.

We believed the blog would add a positive motivational factor to the activity of reading and learners would feel naturally encouraged to post comments making use of the newly acquired lexis from classroom practice activities. Contrary to our initial expectations, however, blogging and collaboration online were seen as too time consuming and challenging. Even in the groups in which the initiative did go ahead, students did not work on more than two or three articles in a whole term.

So teachers from different branches started experimenting with different blog formats and other social media tools, such as voice-recording capable websites (Voxopop and Voicethread) and Facebook.

In the following, we look into five cases of use of social media tools in advanced level groups, described according to their objectives, procedures, and outcomes. These cases will be discussed further in the section "Payoffs and Pitfalls."

Case 1: Blogger. The use of a blog platform with a group of advanced level CEF C1 students
    This was a project carried out by myself in CI Pinheiros, São Paulo.
Objective: Encourage the reading of authentic news articles, offer an opportunity for students to express their own ideas on a given current affair topic, encourage peer collaboration, by having students comment on each other's posts, and ultimately develop learner autonomy.
Procedure: The teacher posted a brief comment on the topic of the article, with the link to the text attached, and invited students to read and post their comments. The teacher's "launching" post aimed at facilitating students' approach to the news article and also providing a neat and attractive site where students could upload their own comments and initiate a discussion online.
Outcome: Very few students contributed with comments. In a class of 20, only three of them uploaded their posts on only three of the news articles

suggested. However, when asked, more than 60% of them reported having read the article on the blog, and appreciated the fact that the link was available to them in an online environment rather than on a list of web links in a separate document.

Case 2: Voxopop. The use of voice recording capable media with a group of advanced level CEF C1 students

This was a project carried out by Dennis Marcondes D'Angelo, teacher at CI Guarulhos, São Paulo.

Objective: Offer an opportunity for students to engage in the planning and production of a long-run oral text, rehearse its delivery, receive feedback on their oral performance—pronunciation, lexical choice and task achievement—work towards peer collaboration, by having students comment on each other's posts and, ultimately, develop learner autonomy.

Procedure: The teacher assigned students a task in which they had to produce a podcast on a topic of their choice. They recorded it and sent the link to the teacher, who responded with his recorded oral feedback, using the same website. Students then redid the task, making the necessary improvements.

Outcome: Very few students contributed with comments. Students reported feeling embarrassed about having to record their voices and listening to themselves. However, after working on favourable arguments for them to record their voices and analyse the quality of their speech, the teacher reported an increase of almost 50% in participation. All the students who participated reported perceiving evidence of improvement in their oral production.

Case 3: Facebook Groups. The use of a Facebook group in an advanced level CEF C1 classroom

This was a project carried out by Luciana Luzio D'Agosto, teacher at CI Guarulhos, São Paulo.

Objective: Encourage extensive reading and peer collaboration, by offering an opportunity for students to express their ideas on the topics that they felt the inclination to share with the other members of the group.

Procedure: Students created the group and one of them was the administrator. They included the teacher as a member, whose contributions consisted of sharing the links to the assigned reading text suggested in the course programme, along with some questions for reflection. Students read in the text and answered the questions online. They went even further commenting on new lexis and interesting expressions noticed on the texts. Instead of giving their opinions, some students shared videos, and other articles related to the topics.

Outcome: Students participated intensively with relevant contributions on the topics and the ideas generated in their virtual social media environment eventually spilled over into the classroom. At the beginning of every class the teacher had to allocate a 10-minute slot for students to expand on the comments made on their Facebook group.

According to this teacher's report, this experience enhanced group cohesiveness and learner autonomy in the sense that more than 70% of the students reported that reading the texts had become more meaningful and more enjoyable.

Case 4: Facebook Groups. The use of a Facebook group in an advanced level CEF C1 classroom

This was a project carried out by Carolina Marques da Silva, teacher at CI Tatuapé, São Paulo.

Objective: Foster group cohesiveness by creating a space to bring students together, even when they are not at school, expanding the boundaries of the classroom beyond its physical walls, offering an opportunity to explore a different channel of communication between teacher and students and among the students themselves.

Procedure: This teacher did not use her personal Facebook profile, but created a secondary teacher's profile to interact with her students. She created a group on Facebook for this classroom where she was the administrator. The news feed page of the group was used to share class-related content, among other things, but never homework reminders or assignments. Information on the course programme was kept separate, in another institutional online environment. In this group, teacher and students had the same level status in the Facebook group and everybody could post and make comments alike. They shared inside jokes, comments, ideas on how to brush up their English, word lists, collocations, grammar tips, photos, interesting articles, and the like.

Outcome: The number and nature of the comments provided evidence of the level of students' engagement in this project. As this teacher reports, "the sense of community and collaboration combined with intense online interaction had a knock-on effect on the development of group cohesiveness, which contributed very favourably to language learning and teaching during the term."

Case 5: Facebook Pages. The use of Facebook Pages in an advanced level CEF C1 classroom

This was a project carried out by Vera Tuffani, teacher at CI Tatuapé, São Paulo.

Objective: Motivate students to make use of more elaborate linguistic repertoire, more appropriate to CEF C1 performance level, which she knew could only be achieved if students exposed themselves to the reading of more complex authentic texts.

Procedure: Together with the students, she agreed on the number of texts for the extensive reading assignments and on a collaborative project that would provide a focus for their language noticing and recording tasks, which would help them express their own realities in the same contexts. The platform chosen to shape and develop this project was Facebook pages. One of the students created the page and the others joined as co-administrators.

Outcome: The page turned into an open-communication area in which students felt motivated and at ease to share ideas and resources. The fact that the page was not open to the general public and that the information posted still remains undisclosed to outsiders prevented students from feeling exposed, and according to this teacher's report, students' production increased exponentially, qualitatively—by students' improvement of written production through the use of more complex sentences and appropriate lexis—and quantitatively—by the number of contributions made on the Facebook page of the project.

Principles

The importance of incorporating the use of technology and Web resources in the teaching of English can no longer be ignored. There are at least three important principles, which I would like to discuss in the light of the projects described in the previous section.

Principle 1. Co-create content with students guiding them in the framing of new communication paradigms. As observed by Teeler (2000), the content that is generated on the Web and the interactions established through its medium are predominately carried out in English and, as it will still take some time before English ceases to be the common language that unites the multilingual background of its users, it is imperative that those involved in teaching English as a second or foreign language start to find ways to understand really well the specificities of the new and diverse types of communication that are booming at a rather ungoverned rate.

Teachers can provide an invaluable contribution in this process by offering support and guidance in the creation of new and unexplored forms of communication based on what is known as established and appropriate at present. In addition, teachers can provoke students to ask questions and think critically when faced with the enormous amount of content that is generated by the minute and sent to the cyber space, by anyone anywhere.

The five cases described show that teachers may assume different roles when using social media for language-learning purposes. Teachers can act as mediators when posing questions for reflection, or more capable peers, when offering feedback on students' production (content and form) always working from within the very frame which they are helping to build, pushing students to stretch their knowledge of the world, knowledge of language, and knowledge of the use of the tool itself.

Another important aspect that deserves mention is the fact that social media websites offer an array of possibilities for user-generated content to be divulged in real time at global scale. Anybody can become an author today. By managing to produce content that is accurate, appropriate, and well structured, one can expand the reach and the impact of his message exponentially simply because it was generated in English and not, for example, in Portuguese. This fact alone heightens the relevance of investing time and endeavor on improving one's linguistic and communicative competences in English at CEF levels C1 and C2.

Principle 2. Develop a new set of skills such as collaboration, teamwork, and global awareness. Introducing social media Web tools into the English language classroom demands the development of a new spectrum of skills and strategies that go beyond simply teaching the language and promoting communicative activities in English. These are the skills of the twenty-first century, prompted by the very technology that enabled social media tools and collaborative online environment to thrive in all instances of modern life. Collaboration, teamwork, and global awareness for example, need to be promoted, structured, and expanded and they need to be built in a language course, from the start. However, the description of the cases indicates the challenging nature of developing these skills in a meaningful way in the educational context.

Acknowledging the gap between the knowledge and skills learned in schools today and the ones needed in what is foreseen to be the typical twenty-first-century community and workplace settings, a Framework for the 21st Century was put together by a coalition of business communities, education leaders, and policy makers, called P21 (Partnership for the 21st Century) to ensure readiness for the twenty-first-century challenges among the younger generations in the United States. The Partnership for the 21st Century (2002) describes the competencies that need to be developed in a blend of four areas comprising:

1. Core subjects with twenty-first-century themes
2. Learning and innovation skills, information
3. Media and technology skills
4. Life and career skills

There is a lot of potential in the use of social media tools in order to contribute to the development of key competencies in the four areas mentioned above: by raising global awareness, by developing social and cross-cultural skills, by provoking critical thinking and developing problem solving strategies, by building communication and collaboration strategies. In a world in which academic and professional opportunities grow increasingly global, where big companies operate from branches placed all over the world and the number of international collaboration projects in the areas of science, technology, and school projects boom, there is an ever higher demand for solutions to be worked out in multicultural teams, through video conference and online forums, where these skills are vital to ensure good standards of communication.

Therefore, I suggest that social media tools in English language learning should not only be encouraged, but also better framed and structured so that more teachers can make use of these tools more confidently with more positive results.

Principle 3. Develop independence, learner autonomy, and negotiation of themes and texts. By giving the teacher the possibility to hinge on intrinsic motivation and peer collaboration, the use of the social media tool has a very important contribution to make in building up learner autonomy. As observed in the descriptions of the cases, building a good rapport with the group, sharing principles and aims with the students, taking a less controlling role, and allowing for students to make more choices and decisions were crucial to a positive outcome of some of the cases. In effect, Scharle & Szabó (2000, p. 5) also state that "developing responsible attitudes in the learners entails some deviation from traditional teacher roles as well. ... Learner responsibility can only develop if you allow more room for learner involvement." However, this can also be tricky, as some learners are more accustomed to a more traditional role of the teacher as the provider. Then the whole experience of bringing social media into the classroom can be seen as a transgression and the whole initiative may backfire. Developing autonomy and self-direction sometimes needs to be a gradual process. "If we take a gradual approach then there is time for everybody to get used to the change" (p. 5).

Applications

The outcomes of the cases suggest that there is room for experimentation with social media tools with positive perspectives of enhancing learning in the ELT context. They also point to some recommendations regarding the kind of preparation needed to adapt the use of the different tools according to the profile of each group of learners.

The personal blog was one of the first social media tools to allow for user generated content to be published online with relative ease by anyone. They soon became very popular tools for sharing personal or professional information, in the format of journals or diaries of events and thoughts. According to Ward (2004) it is not difficult to realize the usefulness of blogs for the language learning mainly because all the traditional learning practices (journals, diaries, written assignments) can be easily transferred to the blog, with an important differential: the blog allows for interactivity with peers and teachers, thus reinforcing the relevance of the task, by providing a genuine audience.

However, what we could see in practice, exemplified by Case 1, is that students need to feel better empowered both linguistically and also in the use of the communication tool itself. Therefore, more guidance and allocation of classroom time to deal with the practical aspects is paramount for the success of the use of this tool in the language-learning context. These comments apply to voice recording capable sites (Voxopop, for example) and even more so, as the technicalities of recording added to the fear of exposure can be very detrimental to the whole project.

The experiments with micro-blogging (Facebook in this case), on the other hand, show that the easy access and portability of this tool make it more approachable, user friendly, and organic. The fact that the vast majority of students have a Facebook account adds familiarity and readiness to the use of the tool in the educational environment on their part.

Facebook offers different possibilities of usage that spring from two main features: the creation of *groups* (open or closed) and the creation of a *page*. However, the way the teacher prepares students to make use of these tools has an impact on how interactive, student centered, and collaborative they can be.

When using groups, it is possible to exchange files, links, information, polls, and videos very quickly. It can be very appropriate for creating a space and platform for homework and revision resources. Whenever a member contributes to the groups the others receive a notification. If students have a Facebook app on their mobile device, notifications can be pushed to their devices, making it easier for the information to reach them. Also, in closed groups, only the members will see the posts and they do not need be Facebook friends as it is possible to invite members by email.

When using pages, it is possible to create a platform for a collaborative project work based on a syllabus component. The page can be administered by the teacher or by the students and everybody takes responsibility for its construction.

There are many projects that have been carried out in schools and colleges using Facebook by The Education Foundation (2013) with the description of many projects that involved large groups and cross curriculum projects in the United Kingdom. They can be used as reference for other possibilities.

Payoffs and Pitfalls

Based on the outcomes of the cases and the evidence gathered from the teacher reports regarding the use of social media as an English language-learning tool, we can say that success in attaining genuine interaction, collaboration, and self-direction comes when learners take over the use of the resources, that is, when they are given autonomy. The cases show different levels of autonomy: some groups were created by the teacher, while others were created by the students and the teacher was just a guest. But in the most successful cases, the ones that reported more interaction and more contributions from students (mainly cases 3, 4, and 5), students were involved in the decision-making process and were given choice regarding the selection of the themes and production of content. In these cases, the social media tool offered students an opportunity to expand and maximize their exposure and interaction with content generated in English by themselves, at their own pace, away from the classroom environment, but still close to it.

The cases that were not so successful in generating the desired level of contributions and interactivity, and thus learner autonomy, failed to do so either because of complex logistics of the Web tool, which required more preparation (creating logins, authorizing students to join the group, using recording devices), or the level of challenge of the task perceived by the students was too high and they did not feel prepared. In both cases, preparation is key. Therefore, the use of these media tools should not be ruled out, but rather the courses should be designed so as to allocate time and support to guide teachers and students to make a more effective use of them.

Finally, based on the cases observed, two conditions are essential for the success of the use of social media in language teaching: (1) the teachers' belief and disposition to explore and try out the tools and (2) the amount of autonomy given to the students so they can feel truly motivated to participate actively in the discussions and on the projects.

This willingness on the teachers' part entails not only the drive to experiment with technology and social media tools with a view to teaching, but also as a user. In the case described by Bhattacharya & Chauhan (2010) regarding a social networking project with an MA ELT student in Gujarat, India, the importance of having the project managers and instructors create their blogs before guiding the participants to carry out their own projects was also seen as an essential success factor. The experiments imply that teachers who want to use social media in language teaching should produce content and interact on the social media website first. Ultimately, the twenty-first-century skills and content knowledge that we want to see developed in the educational context need to start with these skills being incorporated in training programmes for teachers so that they can cope with the demands of preparing the young generation for the twenty-first century.

Discussion Questions

1. What communicative activities can be carried out in social media forums with added value to the students?
2. What preparation would be required from you?
3. What preparation would be required from students?
4. What would be the pros and cons of using your own personal Facebook profile to interact with students?
5. What would be the challenges and gains of introducing social media as a tool to enhance language learning in your context?
6. How early in the language-learning continuum should social media tools be introduced? What anticipated difficulties might students have at lower levels?

Resources

Web links to the cases discussed in the vignette:

Case 1. Blogger—http://mac1newspinheiros.blogspot.com.br/search?updated-min=2012–01–01T00:00:00–08:00&updated-max=2013–01–01T00:00:00–08:00&max-results=5

Case 2. Voxopop—http://www.voxopop.com/topic/f2bef6c1–744e–4090–89fd-29dea2614f64
Cases 3 and 4—Facebook Groups: https://www.facebook.com/about/groups
Case 5. Facebook Pages—https://www.facebook.com/about/pages

References

Bhattacharya, A., & Chauhan, K. (2010). Augmenting learner autonomy through blogging. *ELT Journal*, 64(4): 376–384.

The Education Foundation and Facebook. (2013). *Facebook for Educators*. London. Retrieved from http://www.ednfoundation.org/wp-content/uploads/Facebookguideforeducators.pdf

Partnership for 21st Century Skills. 2002. *Framework for 21st Century Learning*. Tucson, AZ. Retrieved from http://www.p21.org/storage/documents/P21_Framework.pdf

Scharle, A., & Szabó, A. (2000). *Learner autonomy: A guide to developing learner responsibility*. Cambridge: Cambridge University Press.

Teeler, D., & Gray, P. (2000). *How to use the Internet in ELT*. Harlow, UK: Longman.

Ward, J. (2004). Blog assisted language learning (BALL): Push button publishing for the pupils. *TEFL Web Journal*, 3(1): 1–16.

10

ESSENTIALLY SOCIAL

Online Language Learning with Social Networks

Ken Beatty

Introduction and Overview

In 1884, the phrase book *English as She is Spoke* was published, based on two non-English speakers' tedious word-for-word translations of French expressions (da Fonseca & Carolino, 1884). The farcical result has much in common with many modern self-study/autonomous, language-learning materials created as alternatives to traditional teacher–student language classes. Such volumes often fail to offer a systematic approach to language teaching or learning, focus on a restricted set of competencies and, not incidentally, are created by individuals unskilled in both pedagogy and the target language. This chapter looks at the most current iteration of autonomous language learning—online language-learning programs based on social media principles.

Benson (2001) notes people have been learning languages on their own for centuries and that, "in the modern world, millions of individuals continue to learn second and foreign languages without the benefit of formal instruction" (p. 7). In the absence of formal instruction, various types of language-learning aids have become popular, including travel phrasebooks (Bunton, 2013; Dolcourt, 2008) that offer task-specific language, such as business conversations. Phrasebooks and other guides remain a common method of autonomous language learning, but each new technology, from radio and audiotapes to television has provided opportunities for additional ways to undertake individualized language learning.

This is particularly true of computer-assisted, language-learning programs (Beatty, 2010) which offer high degrees of automated interaction and individualized feedback. But autonomous learning does not exclusively mean learning in isolation; citing the example of teacher-less African school children gathering to share what they know, Godwin-Jones (2011) explains that autonomous learning often features—and benefits from—a social nature.

In recent years, a new wave of online resources has recognized the social nature of autonomous language learning through social media. The term *social media* is generally understood to refer to a set of online tools and practices with which people share personal information, ideas, and opinions for the purposes of social interaction (Cohen, 2011; Nation, n.d.). Facebook, Twitter, and blogging are all examples of social media. Social media has been adapted to enrich the language-learning experience and enfranchise learners without access to the benefits of conversation with a native speaker because they live in a unilingual society or because of prohibitive costs associated with having a target-language teacher.

Either on their own or as directed by teachers, students are using social media to improve their second-language learning. This is sometimes done in place of classroom learning or to complement it. Social media-based language-learning websites present a new model for instruction and interaction, particularly through opportunities for one-on-one tutoring in video-based encounters with native speakers. The following vignette presents a social media language-learning experience within a general language biography and is followed by notes on principles, applications, payoffs and pitfalls of the approach.

Vignette

Rachel's language biography begins with her native language, English. As a Canadian Anglophone, she was required to study French in school and then switched to Spanish, which she continued in university without lasting impact. Rachel considers herself a false beginner in both French and Spanish and resents time spent learning in a system that prioritized passing tests over communicative competence.

Rachel completed a teaching degree specializing in secondary school English and a diploma in Teaching English as a Second or Other Language (TESOL). She accepted a position in China to teach at a rural university and, before leaving Canada, began studying Chinese. Rachel's experiences studying Chinese, both at home and abroad, were varied and, because they informed her decision to eventually try online language learning, are worth mention.

Before leaving for China, Rachel was unable to find an academic program teaching Chinese but located a private tutor in the form of a retired Taiwanese military officer. These weekly classes included one other student and involved long chats over tea. Rachel soon tended to completely forget the preceding week's lessons.

She was enjoined to practice, but the other student was unavailable and no notes were provided beyond sheets of paper that the tutor gave her with characters and rough transliterations of the sounds each one made. As all the initial words were typical verbal greetings and introductions (e.g., *Hello. How are you? My name's Rachel. I'm Canadian. Goodbye.*); Rachel wondered in what context she was ever likely to write most of them. Rachel focused on the transliterations, to help her pronunciation.

On moving to China, Rachel realized that her Taiwanese tutor's *zhuyin fuhao* transliterations did not match those of the People's Republic of China's *pinyin* system of Romanization. In China, Rachel engaged a private tutor and took charge of her classes, setting the topics based on her immediate needs, such as navigating the post office and organizing local travel by bus and train. Through these lessons and the occasional coaching of helpful students, Rachel achieved a low plateau of competency in speaking and listening with reading limited to important signage and writing limited to her new Chinese name and a few random characters. Back home after a year in China, she enrolled in a night school class, but found the native Chinese teacher to be a strident martinet whose shouted, mind-numbing repetition methodology was at odds with the communicative approach Rachel had both studied and used in her own teaching practice.

Eventually, Rachel stumbled on a social media-based, language-learning website, *Livemocha*. After registering, Rachel was asked to specify her native language and the language she wanted to study; *Chinese* is qualified by the word *Mandarin*, to differentiate it from *Cantonese*, which was not offered. The next step was to determine her level of expertise in the language based on five images tied to phrases in English and Chinese.

- I'm completely new to Chinese (Mandarin).
- I know a few words and phrases.
- I can use simple sentences.
- I can have a basic conversation.
- I can talk about concepts and ideas.

After modestly choosing "I know a few words and phrases," the program then asked *Learn* or *Help Others*. Two other categories, *Study Aids* and *Classes* were captioned *coming soon*.

Rachel took the first lesson but found the initial content was about the four tones, which she already knew. She clicked on it anyway and found it disappointing; many resources on the website are created by author-teachers who volunteer or are paid for their contributions based on the number of students they attract. The images were poorly rendered illustrations and it was not apparent how they were associated with four tonal pronunciations of *ma*, a Chinese word with 86+ meanings, depending on tone and context.

Skipping down the list of lessons, Rachel found one on dinner meetings. This lesson's dialog was recorded by only one speaker and featured visual support in terms of a young child's clock and play meal, as well as a rough map of a meeting location. After listening to the audio several times, Rachel proceeded to flashcard explanations with audio and text. A sentence-level translation button offered help.

Related activities included recording one's pronunciation and writing answers. However, an English keyboard meant Rachel could only write her answers in *pinyin*; there was no computer-based opportunity to write Chinese characters.

Livemocha's lessons are not exactly free, but paid for through points that are earned or purchased. Each user is given some points on registering and can purchase more. Points can also be earned by commenting on the work of those hoping to learn the user's first language. After completing the lesson, Rachel found a final activity, *Language exchange*, based on performing a seven-turn dialog with an online volunteer partner.

However, the sentence prompts were only written in Chinese characters. Rachel was unable to read the 29 character first sentence. Rachel had not expected to memorize the characters in the simple drills, particularly as the lessons had not given her the opportunity to write the Chinese characters. In any case, Rachel also knew that each Chinese character has a particular stroke order; one should not simply randomly copy characters. Rachel turned back to start the process all over to see if she could figure out a way to reach the necessary level to memorize the sentences or read the Chinese characters in order to participate in the dialog.

At this point, Rachel could have returned to the Livemocha site to see if other teachers offered better lessons, but she was conscious of the time involved in doing so with no promise of rewards; the lessons she had undertaken were surprisingly highly rated. For Rachel, at least, such ratings were undependable.

Discussing her experiences with friends, Rachel was told of other websites associated with social media-based language learning, such as *Duolinga*, *italki* and *Verbling*. To varying degrees, all offer services similar to Livemocha. Verbling uses *chat roulette* in which learners are randomly matched rather than choosing a teacher based on a system of ratings. After five minutes of talk in one language on Verbling, one is encouraged to work in the partner's first language. The website italki similarly allows one to partner with other speakers or take lessons from teachers who are rated by users.

After a month of social media-based language learning, Rachel decided one of her objectives was to learn the writing system in a structured way. She enrolled in formal classes with a teacher whose teaching style she had researched and found to her liking, but kept using the online social media language-learning programs for practicing her speech outside of class.

Principles

The following principles focus partly on the perspective of someone interested in learning a language online but also from the perspective of someone interested in creating an online learning experience.

> *Principle 1. Conduct an appropriate needs analysis to better understand the end-user.* It is difficult to know whether the creators of a particular online social media language-learning website use a pedagogical model of instruction. As recounted by Schmidt (2010), the origins of an online language learning website may

be guided by an unusual needs analysis and an innovative way of addressing problems that arise from it:

> Shirish Nadkarni, the founder of Livemocha, was traveling with his family in Spain and was discouraged to find that years of solid marks in high school Spanish classes had not adequately equipped his teenage kids to engage in basic conversations with native speakers. Upon returning to their hotel room, the kids were glued to Facebook (sometimes asking friends how to say things in Spanish). So the thought struck him: Why not bring the powerful dynamics of online social networks to bear on practical language learning? (n.p.)

This approach shows the tendency to make use of the affordances of the computer and Internet-based practices rather than start with language learners and their needs although these were doubtlessly given some thought later in the process.

Principle 2. Make use of public goodwill in creating and delivering content. One area that has led to enormous growth of online language learning is the practice of *crowdsourcing*, inviting altruistic members of the general public to contribute their time and expertise for free. A popular example of this outside language learning is the online encyclopedia *Wikipedia*. The language website *Duolingo*, for example, says that it "will allow people to apply to serve as volunteer moderators for each language, and the startup will choose a moderator who can then choose others to help contribute to the language course" (Metz, 2013, n.p.).

Such an approach might attract some language professionals anxious to garner online experience, but one wonders whether the quality of the materials and teaching are likely to be of a high standard when no payment is offered. On the other hand, some crowdsourced websites can be highly effective because of their iterative nature, with members of the public serving as impromptu editors and adding content. In the vignette, Rachel was able to rate the materials developer and provide feedback, which might or might not be acted upon.

Principle 3. Consider a language learning model or approach. In terms of the language teaching and learning methodology, the vignette featured an example of situational language learning, an approach focused on re-creating common situations. The vignette's format of discussing a restaurant visit allows learners to role-play the use of the target language. Elsewhere, the materials feature the audio-lingual method with an emphasis on listening and repeating (Richards & Rodgers, 2001).

However, the social media aspect appears to be more in keeping with the communicative approach which Thornbury (2010) summarizes as having purposefulness, reciprocity, negotiation, synchronicity, unpredictability, and heterogeneity.

In terms of purposefulness—in which speakers are motivated by a communicative goal—social media websites that connect users through video may prescribe a particular dialog to be enacted, as is the case in the Rachel vignette, but most allow learners to engage in free conversation on topics of interest to them in which case there is reciprocity, with each speaker having to talk with another.

Negotiation—in which speakers check and repair their utterances to ensure comprehension—is also a normal outcome of free video-based conversation as is synchronicity, in that interactions happen in real time. In the Rachel vignette, the dinner conversation lacks unpredictability, but new topics can make the task more communicative. And, in terms of heterogeneity, such learner-nominated tasks allow participants the freedom to use any language and language strategies at their disposal, even though the initial exchanges are prescribed in more of an audio-lingual approach.

Like many online learning programs, several portions of the social media language learning program in Rachel's vignette show a focus on mastery-learning approaches (see Bloom, 1968), wherein students complete one or more questions successfully before being promoted to the next level. Students often enjoy the immediate feedback of these approaches and behaviorist rewards in the form of points, but whether they are effective in an online environment in helping learners systematically acquire and retain language is questionable.

Applications

There is a wide variety of language-learning programs aimed at every age from toddlers (Orensten, 2013) to adults (Beatty, 2010). But websites that feature social media language learning, where one connects with strangers, usually come with requirements that the learner be of a certain age out of concerns for privacy and the need to protect young learners against online predators. Age restrictions (widely flouted) are common in some social media websites such as *Facebook*, which has a minimum age of 13, but not others, such as *Twitter*, which has no age restriction. In any case, younger children often have their language teaching and learning choices made for them within the school system or by parents and are less likely to engage in online language learning.

Generally, social media language-learning websites tend to be for older learners and many welcoming videos, such as on Verbling, exclusively feature young adults, in part because they are likely to be more digitally savvy and more in need of learning a language for travel or work. Also, as many of the websites are commercial, they attempt to appeal to an audience willing and able to make online payments.

Advantages to learning online in general and learning a language through social media in particular include appealing to those with limited time because of family and work commitments that prevent them from attending a full-time language course or even a part time course. Learning can take place online from a laptop computer or mobile phone (Beatty, 2013).

The casual nature of the courses is perhaps better suited to helping one update one's skills or learn the basics of a new language for reasons of pure interest. As online courses often lack systematic curricula and externally validated assessments, it is unlikely they could confer academic credit or professional qualifications. However, this may change over time based on learner needs and entrepreneurial innovation.

Payoffs and Pitfalls

Payoffs

1. The attractions of online language learning are likely to be similar to those that Rachel identified in the vignette. These include affordable tailored just-in-time learning opportunities. In the vignette, Rachel's choice of learning online was partly made because she lacked access to traditional classes but, even if she had, her previous experiences included demotivating language-learning experiences that she wanted to avoid repeating.
2. For assessment-phobic learners, the lack of commitment and minimal test stress can be a reason to pursue online learning. Mastery learning approaches to assessment also mean learners can take a test over and over, rather than be definitively judged on a single effort.
3. The barter-based system of payment, in which one volunteers to help others in order to garner points to pay for courses, is an attraction for the financially limited and linguistically isolated.

Pitfalls

As one would expect with a nascent methodology, there are shortcomings, some of which may be overcome in time.

1. The effectiveness of learning in online environments is vague and not empirically tested. Social media language-learning websites tout measures unrelated to standardized language tests such as TOEFL or language standards, such as the Common European Framework of Reference for Languages. Most often, online language-learning websites' external validations are anecdotal or in terms of usage, such as *X millions of registered members in X hundreds of countries*. As registered users often pay nothing to join, the level of commitment is low and it is questionable as to how many members go on to use the service in a substantive way or complete a course of studies leading to fluency.
2. The adage *garbage in, garbage out* applies in terms of instruction. Without external accreditation (e.g., TOEFL certification), the tutor/mentor with

whom one is speaking may turn out to have poor pronunciation and be ignorant of the language—even though rating systems presumably determine the most popular tutors. But popularity does not always signal competence.

3.   Although some noncommercial online social media language-learning websites are organized by volunteers and free, the ultimate objective of many websites is economic. Because of this, many follow a trajectory that begins with offering free services, then adds paid extras in the form of higher quality lessons or access to more qualified teachers, and finally reducing the free offerings. These phases prompt other startups to begin the cycle over again. For this reason, choosing an online social media language-learning website should be done with a consideration of all the costs involved, many of which may not be apparent at the outset.

4.   A lack of offline resources is typical of many online learning websites. Learners may or may not have permission to revisit portions of a course they have already completed and may only retain their own notes. This approach works against the recycling of vocabulary and structures, as does the tendency for multiple authors to be involved in creating the learning materials leading to mismatched lessons; on completing one level, one might not encounter the same vocabulary and structures in successive levels.

5.   The demand for languages differs. If one is the speaker of a popular language such as English, there are likely thousands of members anxious to work as partners sharing their language in exchange. However, two individuals from less-popular language groups, for example, a Tibetan speaker interested in learning Swahili, would be unlikely to find an exchange partner.

Discussion Questions

1.   For what reasons might a learner choose to learn a language online?
2.   What does social media language learning do best? In what ways is it inferior to the classroom experience?
3.   In what contexts and with what learners should a teacher encourage social media language learning outside of class?
4.   The author highlights several online language-learning programs. Review one and consider how it would work with your students. If your students are young, how might a similar program serve their needs?
5.   Consider the following passage from Bunton (2013), talking about a researcher who has investigated historical phrasebooks. List three individuals you know and the varied language competencies they might aspire to in a second-language context.

I'm also interested in what it means to be competent in a language and how that has shifted with time. It's about getting away from binaries between being fluent or not fluent—you can get by in a country with just a smattering of a language. It's this smattering—what it includes and what it ignores—that is so revealing about human encounters, since it shows how different people developed different kinds of competence depending on what they wanted language to do for them (n.p.).

Resources

Social media websites for language learning
- *Busuu* language learning community—www.busuu.com
- *Conversation Exchange*—www.conversationexchange.com
- *Duolingo* free language education for the world—www.duolingo.com
- *italki*—www.italki.com
- *Livemocha*—www.livemocha.com
- *My Language Exchange*—www.mylanguageexchange.com/
- *Palabea*—www.palabea.com/
- *Verbling*—www.verbling.com/

General language learning websites
- *Byki*—www.byki.com/
- *Foreign Services Institute*—fsi-languages.yojik.eu/
- *Open Culture*—www.openculture.com/freelanguagelessons
- *Fluent in 3 Months Plus/Speak from Day 1*—http://fi3mplus.com/tedx/

Use a search engine to find a language-learning website tailored to your particular language interest. Search *(name of language) online learning*.

References

Beatty, K. (2010). *Teaching and researching: Computer-assisted language learning*, 2nd ed. London: Pearson Education.

Beatty, K. (2013). *Beyond the classroom: Mobile learning the wider world.* Washington, DC: The International Research Foundation for Language Education (TIRF).

Benson, P. (2001). *Teaching and researching autonomy in language learning.* London: Pearson Education.

Bloom, B. S. (1968). Learning for mastery. *UCLA CSEIP Evaluation Comment*, 1(2), 1–12.

Bunton, A. (2013). Comm'portez vous? What phrase books tell us about our past encounters. *University of Cambridge Research.* Retrieved from: http://www.cam.ac.uk/research/features/commportez-vous-what-phrase-books-tell-us-about-our-past-encounters#sthash.61YJy8TG.VjMllM4T.dpuf

Cohen, H. (2011). 30 social media definitions. *Actionable marketing 101.* Retrieved from: http://heidicohen.com/social-media-definition/

da Fonseca, J., & Carolino, P. (1884). *English as she is spoke, or a jest in sober earnest.* New York: D. Appleton & Co.

Dolcourt, J. (2008). Lonely planet audio phrasebooks for iPhone. *c|net/Download.com.* Retrieved from: http://download.cnet.com/8301-2007_4-9995839-12.html

Godwin-Jones, R. (2011). Emerging technologies, autonomous language learning. *Language Learning & Technology*, 15(3), 4–11.

Metz, R. (2013). Want to speak Dothraki? Duolingo Can Now Help. *MIT Technology Review*. Retrieved from: http://www.technologyreview.com/view/520001/want-to-speak-dothraki-duolingo-can-now-help/

Nation, D. (n.d.). What is social media? What are social media sites? *Computing Web Trends*. Retrieved from: http://webtrends.about.com/od/web20/a/social-media.htm

Nunan, D. (1991). *Language teaching methodology: A textbook for teachers*. London: Prentice Hall International.

Orensten, E. (2013). Language-learning tools for kids: Digital aids give toddlers an edge in Mandarin and other languages. *Cool Hunting*. Retrieved from: http://www.coolhunting.com/tech/language-learning-tools-kids.php

Richards, J. C., & Rodgers, T. S. (2001). *Approaches and methods in language teaching*. Cambridge: Cambridge University Press.

Schmidt C. (2010). Livemocha and the power of social language learning. *IH Journal of Education and Development*, 28. Retrieved from: http://ihjournal.com/livemocha-and-the-power-of-social-language-learning

Thornbury, S. (2010). *C is for communicative*. Retrieved from http://scottthornbury.wordpress.com/2010/08/15/c-is-for-communicative/

11

LANGUAGE EXCHANGE WEBSITES FOR INDEPENDENT LEARNING

Olga Kozar

Introduction and Overview

It has long been recognized that there are many benefits that language learners derive from engaging in language practice with someone fluent in the language they are learning. By communicating in an authentic context, learners become more motivated, exert more effort in learning a language, and tend to improve their intercultural skills.

One of the ways that learners can organize language practice is engaging in 'language exchange'—an arrangement similar to the "barter system"—when a person provides goods or services in exchange for other goods or services. Prior to the growth of the Internet, language exchange usually involved sending letters to "pen pals," native or fluent speakers in the target language, and to occasionally talk to them on the phone. The problem historically, however, was to find a suitable "pen pal," as it required existing contacts in different countries—something that an average learner may not have had. The advent of the Internet, by bringing millions of people together online, has revolutionized communication and offered a new means of conducting language exchange. The modern day "pen pals" take advantage of e-mail, instant audio and video-conferencing, and they no longer need to wait for weeks or months to receive messages from one another as pen pals of pre-Internet age used to do.

Language exchange websites provide language learners with a tool to find language partners, and enable them to receive feedback on their speaking or writing from someone who is a native or a fluent speaker of the target language. In exchange, learners can act as experts or teachers of their own language. However, despite vast improvements in the technical aspects of language exchange, the practice of peer language support is still fraught with challenges. Some learners struggle to find a committed partner for language exchange, while other learners are not satisfied with the quality of feedback that they receive. There may also be other concerns, such as privacy considerations or meeting someone who has a different agenda from learning a language.

In this chapter, we look at both the advantages and the potential pitfalls of language exchange practice. We meet one adult language learner from Russia who decided to participate in language exchange online, and examine her experience. We discuss reasons why language exchange websites can be beneficial for language learners, and investigate the learning options that the websites currently provide. In particular, we focus on the challenges of using the websites, ways to overcome them, and learn how language skills can be sustained and improved using language exchange websites.

Vignette

A friend of mine, Katya, is in her late 30s. A successful business analyst, she is working in an investment company in Moscow. Katya needs English for work and travel. However, despite attending regular English lessons, Katya was extremely nervous about using English. She was worried that she would not be able to adequately express herself and would appear silly or incompetent. A colleague of Katya's told her about Livemocha—the largest language exchange website (claiming 15 million users), which provides online lessons and allows users to get comments on their writing or speaking from other users. Katya was sceptical—she was not a fan of online social networking but she still decided to 'give it a shot'—after all, it was free and her colleague seemed to like it. As soon as Katya created a profile, she received an invitation to chat from a man from Turkey and then another invitation from a man in India. She felt puzzled. None of these men were learning Russian. Why did they want to chat with her? She closed the page without answering these requests. The next day Katya shared her concerns with a colleague who had recommended the website and her colleague suggested deleting a photo and gender information until Katya felt comfortable enough to chat to other users. Katya followed the advice and didn't receive any suspicious invites after that. In the following weeks, Katya slowly explored the website. First, she completed some lessons and commented on the submissions of other users who were learning Russian—her native language. When she saw that most of the comments that other users were receiving were useful and friendly, she decided to submit her own writing and a speaking task. She was pleased with the feedback she received and added some 'friends' on the website. After five months Katya decided that she was ready to participate in a 'live' chat and she really enjoyed it. By the time of writing this chapter, Katya has been on the language exchange website for over two years. Her confidence in the language use grew, and the idea of talking to foreign colleagues no longer worried her. She also became less worried about making mistakes. There were times when she felt disappointed with the quality of the feedback on her writing and speaking, or when she didn't receive any comments, but overall, her experience was positive.

Principles

What makes language exchange websites work? In this section, I highlight reasons why I believe that language exchange websites can be beneficial for learners.

Principle 1. Language exchange websites provide learners with opportunities to engage in authentic communication. Firstly, the websites provide learners with an opportunity to engage in authentic communication—the process which has been recognized as critical for successful language acquisition and development (Godwin-Jones, 2008; Sykes, Oskoz, & Thorne, 2008). When participating in the language exchange, the learners are encouraged to produce language, which many learners like Katya (from the vignette) do not have much practice in. Often it is the receptive skills (reading, listening) which learners practice outside the classroom by reading the books and magazines, watching films or listening to the radio or podcasts. Productive skills (writing and speaking) tend to 'lag behind' partly because they are very complex and require a combination of different skills, but also because many learners do not find enough opportunities to practice them outside the classroom. Exchanging messages and talking to other users in English helped Katya to practice and improve her language productive skills as well as to reduce language anxiety.

Principle 2. Language exchange websites encourage learners to become 'language experts.' Secondly, language exchange websites encourage learners to act as 'language experts' by providing feedback to other learners. This experience of "wearing a teacher's hat" can increase learners' meta-awareness of language learning (= understanding how language learning works), which, according to prior research, can make learners more efficient and effective in their own studies (Leow, 1997). By commenting on other users' submissions and being a facilitator for other learners, Katya realized that accuracy was not the most important aspect in communication—even when her language partners made mistakes in Russian (Katya's first language) it didn't make her think worse of them. This realization helped Katya to become less critical of her own mistakes and helped her communicate more fluently.

Principle 3. Language exchange websites improve intercultural skills. Another 'affordance' of language exchange is helping learners to practice and potentially improve their intercultural skills. By observing communication between users from different countries, religions, and backgrounds and by communicating with them directly, learners can become more skilled at talking to people from different cultures, which is an important and valuable skill in the modern globalized world.

Principle 4. Language exchange websites provide the infrastructure within which learners can provide and receive comments and feedback. Finally, the websites provide an 'infrastructure' for giving and receiving comments. When a learner submits a writing or speaking sample, any person who is online and willing to comment can do so. When a website has thousands or even millions of users, a learner has a good chance to receive comments. Typically, those who provide feedback on learners' submissions are rewarded with 'tokens' which can be used to pay for additional services on the website (such as paid instructional content for example). This reward system motivates users to comment on the submissions of other users.

Applications

In this section, we cover how to use the language exchange websites, and who can benefit from it. We also discuss different types of websites and the possibilities that they provide.

Basic Requirements

In order to take advantage of online language exchange, learners need to be computer-literate and have basic Internet skills. If a learner chooses to engage in audio/video conversations with language partners, they also need to have a microphone, speakers, and a webcam. Most modern-day laptops have built-in microphones, speakers, and webcam, which are usually sufficient for audio/video calls; however, it is a good idea to test them prior to initiating an audio/video call, as the microphone could be muted, speakers turned down, or Web camera set to an awkward angle.

Technical requirements	**Compulsory:** Internet access, computer and Internet literacy **Optional:** Microphone, speakers (audio calls) Microphone, speakers, and webcam (video calls)

Who Can Use the Websites?

Most people on language exchange websites are adult learners of languages who create individual profiles and use the website outside the classroom for learning and social purposes. It is worth noting that the minimum age requirement on some websites is 13 years old (e.g., Livemocha), which means that teenagers can have profiles on these websites. An in-depth discussion of potential issues associated with the use of social networking websites by adolescents is outside the scope of this chapter (for a more detailed discussion see Fleming, Greentree, Cocotti-Muller, Elias, & Morrison, 2006). It should be noted that some researchers and practitioners believe that young learners and teenagers can benefit from participating in social learning if they do so under teacher or parental supervision (Masters & Barr, 2010).

Apart from individual learners of different ages, the websites encourage classroom teachers to create "class profiles" for their learners. Some of the activities that the websites suggest for classroom learning include customizing flashcards to match school curriculum, asking students to interact with websites users on set topics, reviewing other users' work, and so on.

Who can use the websites?	Adults (independent learners) Teenagers and children under adult supervision Classroom teachers for supplementary materials

Guide to the Websites

The following section is written for learners and teachers who have not had prior experience with language exchange websites. We look at the various types of websites, typical activities that can be found, and communication options available to website users.

Different Types of Websites

Currently there seems to be two main types of language exchange websites: the ones that only provide 'matching' functionalities and do not structure users' interactions—let's call them 'free' or 'unstructured' websites, and the ones that provide a framework for interactions—let's call them 'structured' websites.

An unstructured website is essentially a database of potential language partners. When users register on an unstructured website, they need to indicate their first language and the language(s) that they would like to learn. They start by creating a personal profile with details about their interests and hobbies. Using this profile, the website enables users to find other compatible users to practice language with. They can then communicate via e-mail, instant messaging, and audio/video chat.

Learners have several options on how they can communicate with potential communication partners. Some learners feel that the easiest and the least stressful way to communicate with new 'friends' is by exchanging e-mails. E-mails are viewed as a good 'stepping stone' in language exchange, as they are asynchronous by nature (i.e., not in real time), which allows learners to compose messages in their own time. The asynchronous nature of e-mails also makes it possible to exchange messages with someone who lives in a different time zone, which increases the potential 'pool' of language partners.

Learners can also engage in real-time text messaging (instant text chat), or make an audio/video call. Text chat seems to be the most popular type of interaction on language exchange websites, as it combines the advantages of life-like conversation with the possibility to 'slow down' and process the input (Clark & Gruba, 2010).

Participating in text-chat has also been shown to improve learners' accuracy and fluency in the target language (Blake, 2009; Jepson, 2005; Yamada, 2009).

Table 11.1 Modes of Communication and Advantages

Modes of communication	Advantages
E-mails	Can be done "in your own time"; increases a potential "pool" of language partners
Text messages	Combine real-time interactions with a possibility to "slow down" and compose the replies
Audio/video conversations	Speaking practice, resembling the demands of face-to-face conversations

Overall, 'unstructured' websites might be beneficial for learners at an intermediate-advanced level who are sufficiently comfortable with their language skills to initiate and sustain the interactions.

Structured websites, on the other hand, offer learners other activities in addition to the functionality described above, such as having lessons, doing exercises, and submitting written and oral tasks for community review. Usually learners, like Katya from the vignette, do these activities in a sequential fashion, starting from having lessons, then submitting and reviewing tasks, and finally, engaging in real-time interaction.

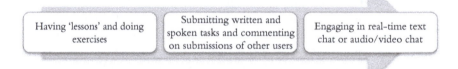

FIGURE 11.1 Typical sequence of activities on structured websites.

Following this sequence might allow learners to get familiar with the website before they engage in real-time interactions. However, following this sequence is not obligatory—a learner could potentially start from real-time interactions and then have lessons and do tasks.

More on Lessons

A typical lesson on large language exchange websites like Livemocha are designed around a particular topic (e.g., greetings, shopping, etc.), and include flashcards with new words and audio recordings of these words. The lessons tend to have a series of exercises (e.g., matching words or unscrambling a sentence for example). On successful completion of the exercises, a learner is invited to do a writing task and a spoken task. The written task and the audio recording of the spoken tasks become available for other users to comment on. Once someone comments on a learner's submission, the learner is notified via e-mail.

An important feature of Livemocha, the website used as a case-study for this chapter, is that it provides learners with instructions for the written/spoken tasks. It also provides reviewers with a framework for writing comments and some suggestions on how it could be done. Specifically, Livemocha asks reviewers to rate learners' performance on three scales (spelling, proficiency, and grammar). The website also displays tips for reviewers and encourages them to be specific, to provide examples of how the learner can use a particular word, phrase, or construction and to take advantage of Livemocha's editing features, such as italics, bold, highlighting, and the like to make corrections more visual. One might disagree with the scales used for evaluation on this website, as rating a beginner learner on the 'proficiency' scale, for example, may be considered odd. However, providing a user-friendly interface and formulating the suggestions for writing reviews are helpful.

Those users who comment on submissions receive 'tokens' which can be exchanged for paid services. 'Tokens' are not the same thing as 'points'; 'tokens' can be collected by providing feedback to other learners or can be purchased with real money. 'Points' on the other hand are earned by learners for doing exercises and are designed to help them keep track of their progress. An additional role of the 'points' is to act as a 'status marker' on the website, showing other users that a learner is a committed language learner, and has spent a considerable time on lessons and exercises.

Free/Paid Content

Large language exchange websites differentiate between free and paid lessons. The description above is based on the free content available for most languages on the Livemocha website. The websites also provide paid courses. The paid content is generally of higher quality, and, instead of vocabulary-based flashcard system, is based on a functional-notional syllabus and communicative situations. Another feature offered to the 'subscribers' is access to live group lessons conducted via videoconferencing software. As the paid features of the website might not be accessible to all the readers, they will not be reviewed in this chapter.

Payoffs and Pitfalls

There can be many rewards from participating in language exchange. Possibly the largest benefit is gained from engaging in meaningful interactions with other speakers of the target language—the process which is believed to be at the root of successful language acquisition (see for example Chapelle, 2005 for discussion). Another advantage, as reported by surveyed users and the research literature, is a considerable boost in motivation. When learners employ the target language for communication purposes, their interest in the language tends to improve, and they exert increased effort in learning this language.

Not all learners, however, find their experience on the websites useful, and discontinue their membership before they get a chance to reap benefits of the language exchange. The following section discusses the biggest challenges associated with the use of the websites along with the possible ways of overcoming these challenges.

Inadequate or Unclear Feedback

The primary reason why some learners feel disappointed with language exchange websites tends to be low quality feedback from other users. Unfortunately, occasional dissatisfaction with feedback is to be expected due to the nature of the website and the fact that anybody can give feedback (Liaw, 2011). However, there are some steps that learners could take to avoid inadequate feedback and to improve their chances of receiving useful feedback. Firstly, before submitting the writing/speaking for review, learners can formulate specific questions about their submission, for example, "Does my writing sound too formal?" or "Did I use the phrase __ correctly?," etc.). Being specific in requesting feedback increases the changes of receiving the type of feedback that you are looking for.

If a learner has received feedback that he or she is not satisfied with, the learner could contact the reviewer for more information. A good etiquette is to thank the reviewer for her or his feedback before asking the reviewer to clarify some points, such as the areas that could be improved or how the reviewer might rephrase a particular sentence. If the learner doesn't receive a satisfactory reply, an alternative is to approach another website user to review the same submission.

One more potential issue is understanding the feedback provided in the target language. If a learner has only started learning a language, then understanding feedback written in the same language could be beyond the learner's current level. Services like automatic translation (for example, Google Translate) could be partially helpful in this case. If the feedback is unclear, the author's advice is to ask for clarifications on unclear points, e.g., "Did I understand correctly that ... ?" This could be a good opportunity to negotiate the meaning, which is also an important process in language acquisition (Varonis & Gass, 1985).

Motives of Some Users

Another challenge that may arise when participating in language exchange websites is occasional social discomfort. The majority of social networking websites, including language exchange websites, tend to have users who register on the websites for entertainment purposes and disregard the rules and the etiquette of the online community. Such people have been called 'Alpha Socializers,' which describes the predominately young males who use the websites for flirting and entertainment (OfCom, 2008). The participants in one of the studies investigating the use of Livemocha, reported encounters with users who "seemed more interested in 'flirting' than in serious language exchange or peer-tutoring" (Lloyd, 2012, p. 11). Fortunately, such users are a minority; however, the encounters with them could be unpleasant.

There are several ways to safe-guard oneself from 'Alpha Socializers.' One strategy is what Katya in our vignette did after receiving several suspicious 'friendship requests'. She anonymized herself by not using her real name or a photograph. Instead, her profile was made to look gender neutral and had a photo of a book instead of a photo of a person. This measure significantly reduced the number of unwanted requests. Another commonly suggested strategy is to carefully read profiles of those users to request contact. Is the user enrolled in the learning course in the language in which you are an expert? How many contacts do they have? What is the language background of their contacts? It's important to remember that there is no obligation to connect or to chat to anybody and that any request could be ignored if it looks suspicious. Moreover, a user can be 'reported' to the website administration if their behaviour is unacceptable. The administrators usually delete or block accounts of 'reported' users.

Maintaining Motivation

Another reason why some learners discontinue using the websites is losing motivation. It can be especially true if learners have recently had a negative experience, such as low quality feedback of an 'Alpha Socializer.' Motivation is a complex feeling and it is impossible to provide easy and uniform solutions on how to maintain or improve motivation. One technique that has been reported to help with dwindling motivation is documenting positive experiences and reviewing this list on a regular basis. Another strategy is finding a friend in 'real life' who might be interested in using the same website. This strategy might work because some people become more committed to an activity and exert more effort when they can compare their experiences with a friend or a relative.

Discussion Questions

1. Would you be interested in participating in a language exchange website? Why? Why not?
2. Who, in your opinion, could benefit from participating in language exchange websites?
3. What do you think about teachers using language exchange websites for supplementing language lessons? Would it work in your context?
4. What are some of the challenges of participating in the language exchange websites? How can they be overcome?
5. Do you think that creating an 'incognito' profile—without gender or name is a good idea? Why? Why not?

Resources

"Structured" websites: instructional content + language exchange
Livemocha—http://livemocha.com/—15 million users, free and paid content; possibility to "earn" tokens to pay for paid content.

Langled—http://www.langled.com/home.php—Language courses and language exchange.

My Language Exchange—http://www.mylanguageexchange.com/—1 million members, privacy mechanism (using internal e-mails), virtual keyboards for other languages, word games, etc.

"Free" or "unstructured websites: language exchange only.

Shared Talk—http://www.sharedtalk.com/—A division of Rosetta Stone, a large website which helps finding language partners for writing and speaking.

Interpals—http://www.interpals.net/—A large website offering a database of potential "pen pals."

Conversation Exchange—http://www.conversationexchange.com/—Allows searching for a conversation partner, text chat partner, or a pen pal.

References

Blake, C. (2009). Potential of text-based Internet chats for improving oral fluency in a second language. *The Modern Language Journal*, 93(2), 227–240.

Chapelle, C. A. (2005). Interactionist SLA theory in CALL research. *CALL research perspectives*, 53–64.

Clark, C., & Gruba, P. (2010). The use of social networking sites for foreign language learning: An autoethnographic study of Livemocha. *Curriculum, technology & transformation for an unknown future. Proceedings ascilite Sydney*, 164–173.

Fleming, M. J., Greentree, S., Cocotti-Muller, D., Elias, K. A., & Morrison, S. (2006). Safety in cyberspace adolescents' safety and exposure online. *Youth & Society*, 38(2), 135–154.

Godwin-Jones, R. (2008). Emerging technologies: Web-writing 2.0: Enabling, documenting, and assessing writing online. *Language Learning & Technology*, 12(2), 7–13.

Jepson, K. (2005). Conversations-and negotiated interaction-in text and voice chat rooms. *Language Learning & Technology*, 9(3), 79–98.

Leow, R. P. (1997). Attention, awareness, and foreign language behavior. *Language Learning*, 47(3), 467–505.

Liaw, M.-L. (2011). Review of Livemocha. *Language Learning and Technology*, 15(1), 36–40.

Lloyd, E. (2012). Language learners' "willingness to communicate" through Livemocha. com. *Alsic. Apprentissage des Langues et Systèmes d'Information et de Communication*, 15(1).

Masters, J., & Barr, S. (2010). Young children online: E-learning in a social networking context. *Knowledge Management & E-Learning: An International Journal (KM&EL)*, 1(4), 295–304.

OfCom. (2008). Social networking: A quantitative and qualitative research report into attitudes, behaviours and use: Office of Communications.

Sykes, J., Oskoz, A., & Thorne, S. L. (2008). Web 2.0, synthetic immersive environments, and mobile resources for language education. *CALICO Journal*, 25(3), 528–546.

Varonis, E. M., & Gass, S. (1985). Non-native/non-native conversations: A model for negotiation of meaning. *Applied Linguistics*, 6(1), 71–90.

Yamada, M. (2009). The role of social presence in learner-centered communicative language learning using synchronous computer-mediated communication: Experimental study. *Computers & Education*, 52(4), 820–833. Retrieved from http://dx.doi.org/10.1016/j.compedu.2008.12.007

12

E-MAIL TANDEM LANGUAGE LEARNING

Akihiko Sasaki

Introduction and Overview

In the field of *second language acquisition* (SLA), it has long been acknowledged that interaction and negotiation are crucial for learning a *second/foreign language* (L2). A considerable amount of SLA research has demonstrated that less proficient L2 learners (i.e., novice) can benefit from interaction with more proficient and knowledgeable conversation partners (i.e., expert). In the course of meaningful communication, experts provide contingent modifications of novices' language in the form of recasts, repetitions, clarification requests, or overt error correction, and novice learners can, by receiving such scaffolded assistance, develop their L2 communicative ability.

In recent decades, the *computer-assisted language learning* (CALL) field has suggested that *computer-mediated communication* (CMC) allows L2 learners to engage in such meaningful interaction. Due to the availability of the Internet, learners, even those who live in *foreign language* (FL) situations, can interact with native L2 speakers (NSs) living in other regions of the world. When using *asynchronous modes of CMC* (ACMC; e.g., e-mail), in which immediate real-time response is not required, messages can be processed at any time, which is an important consideration when the communication occurs in different time zones (Beatty, 2003). Therefore, ACMC is regarded as the best fit for FL learners to have CMC-based L2 communication even outside the classroom.

This chapter presents e-mail-mediated tandem language learning (e-mail tandem) as an out-of-class L2 learning initiative. E-mail tandem is a Web-based language-learning method, in which two learners of a different *native language* (L1) use their L2 (the partner's L1) to talk about topics on their needs and interests, and offer assistance to the partner's L2 use by correcting errors and suggesting alternative expressions.

In some cases, learners use their L1 to form parts of the communication so that they have opportunities not only to produce L2 but also receive its models from their NS partners.

The unique aspect of this activity is that, unlike regular *native speaker–nonnative speaker* (NS-NNS) communication, where only one participant (i.e., NNS) benefits as a learner, tandem partners bring their own L1 knowledge and reciprocally support their partner's L2 learning. Therefore, e-mail tandem is considered to be potentially beneficial to L2 learners on *both* sides. This practice stands on the notion of collaborative learning, where each interlocutor plays an active role as an expert of his or her own L1 and provides scaffolding to assist the partner's (i.e., novice's) L2 learning. Figure 12.1 briefly illustrates how L1 and L2 messages are conveyed within e-mail tandem.

Brammerts (2003) suggested that the goals of tandem exchange encompass improving the learners' L2 communicative and linguistic abilities, as well as learning from each other's culture, knowledge, and experiences. The pedagogical benefits of e-mail tandem that past studies reported included developing learners' L2 linguistic knowledge (Edasawa & Kabata, 2007), raising cultural awareness (Woodin, 2001), increasing motivation (Ushioda, 2000), and developing language-learning skills (Braga, 2007).

Of particular interest among them is that e-mail tandem, in which students have L2 communication with a real audience and for real purposes, raises authenticity of language use (Brammerts, 2003). While communicating in L2, learners make different types of speech acts to get things done, such as posing questions, asking for help, providing suggestions. Through these acts, both learners will

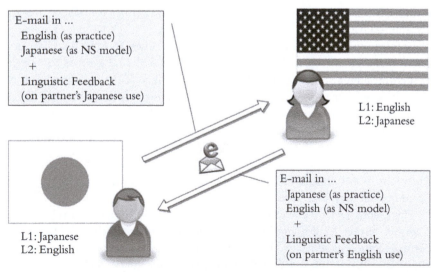

FIGURE 12.1 E-mail tandem language learning between Japanese and American students.

encounter, and eventually learn, pragmatic use of L2, which rarely occurs in most FL classrooms dictated by structural syllabuses.

Other benefits of e-mail tandem that past studies indicated are increasing learner autonomy and raising language awareness. According to Little (2003), the reciprocal nature of e-mail tandem encourages learners to help each other's learning, which enhances their autonomous attitude in the activity. Furthermore, Appel (1999) suggested that learners tend to be aware of language forms in the feedback phase. She found that correcting partner's errors and generating the explanation of the L1 rules raised her tandem learners' metalinguistic awareness, which is believed to facilitate L2 learning (van Lier, 1996).

The author, who teaches *English as a foreign language* (EFL) at a private junior high school in Japan, conducted e-mail tandem from 2003 to 2012, as an extra-curricular English learning activity. He started this project in collaboration with *Mayumi* (pseudonym) who teaches Japanese as a foreign language at a public high school in California. Every year, six to ten students on both sides voluntarily participated in the eight-week-long activity. Each of them was assigned to one partner to communicate with, and worked in out-of-class contexts, using PCs at their home and/or in the school's CALL lab.

This chapter begins with the details of the author's e-mail tandem activity. The next section will show how his students developed English skills by producing L2 and receiving feedback on their L2 use. It will also illustrate how they raised their autonomy and metalinguistic awareness through the activity. The section will be followed by the description of the principles of e-mail tandem. This chapter will then conclude with some problems within the activity and their solutions.

Vignette

The Japanese students, who participated in e-mail tandem, were all boys, EFL students, and aged 14–15 (ninth grade). The length of time they had spent learning English was two to three years, and their English proficiency was from high beginner to low intermediate. They had high potential and motivation in learning English compared to ordinary Japanese students of the same age. In fact, they achieved high success in all school English exams. However, they acknowledged that their English learning had been exclusively an accumulation of explicit L2 knowledge, and felt a strong need to use English in a realistic communicative situation. They thus voluntarily applied for the e-mail tandem activity as an extra-curricular, out-of-class learning opportunity, and had communication with the assigned partners living in the United States.

The American students that formed tandem dyads with Japanese students were both male and female and ranged in age from 14 to 17 (ninth to eleventh grade). They used English as L1, and had learned Japanese as L2 for two to five years. According to Mayumi, their Japanese proficiency was high beginner to low intermediate, which was almost identical to that of the Japanese students.

In this section, the author illustrates one Japanese student's e-mail tandem experiences, citing parts of the journal he kept during the activity.

Shogo

Shogo (pseudonym) was assigned to communicate with *Shelly* (pseudonym), who was a female tenth grader, and had learned Japanese for three years. At the outset of the tandem communication, they agreed to talk about national holidays in each other's country as a conversation topic. They also decided to use L2 mainly, but occasionally use L1, so that they can create a good balance between producing L2 and receiving its native model.

Shogo produced a lot of L2 in tandem communication by fully utilizing the English knowledge he had learned. His English writing was quite good, except for constant prepositional errors. In every e-mail reply from Shelly, Shogo found a couple of corrections on his English use. For example:

> You should write "I want to be careful <u>about</u> my past tense," but not "I want to be careful <u>to</u> my past tense."

Although he read these comments with some disappointment, Shogo was not so despondent because every corrective feedback from Shelly always came with compliments on his English in general, such as "Your English is very good" and "I'm impressed by your English skills." Later he wrote in his journal about his thoughts on Shelly's good words:

> I received a lot of compliments in her feedback, and I felt good every time I read them. I think it's an American custom to offer high praise when they give negative comments, so that their comments do not sound like refusal or rejection, but instead constructive. (English translations in this and subsequent quotations are by the author)

This was the case where Shogo experienced a pragmatic aspect of L2. It is often the case in e-mail tandem that Japanese EFL learners recognize the significance of compliments prior to negative comments by repeatedly receiving such feedback from their English-speaking partners.

One day, Shogo received a suggestion on his English:

> The sentence "I belong to the football club" could be changed to "I am a member of the football club."

At first, Shogo did not understand why his original sentence was wrong because it had no grammatical flaws. He then asked Shelly for an explanation. Later he wrote in his journal:

As I discussed with Shelly, I understood that my original sentence was a little too formal to use when speaking with friends. I had thought it was good enough to follow the grammar rules to make myself understood. But now I learned there are other rules that are beyond grammar rules.

The "other rules" he mentioned are *sociolinguistic competence*, that is, the knowledge to use the language appropriately in a given context. This was another case where authentic communication of e-mail tandem provided learners with opportunities to experience a pragmatic L2 aspect (i.e., formality).

Shogo analyzed Shelly's Japanese carefully because he wanted to reciprocate her efforts to correct his English. She wrote Japanese fairly well, with appropriate vocabulary and accurate tenses being used, but her Japanese often contained a particular error with the *-wa* and *-ga* distinction, for example:

> *Watashi-no gakko-niwa kaferteria-wa arimasu.* (There is a cafeteria in our school.)
> *Watashi-ga futsuu 6ji-ni okimasu.* (I usually get up at six.)

-wa and *-ga* are among the Japanese postpositional particles that immediately follow a noun phrase and indicate its grammatical and/or semantic roles within a sentence. Both *-wa* and *-ga* mark a subject of a sentence, but differ in that *–wa* is used to provide old information while *–ga* is for new information (e.g., Nariyama, 2002). Japanese NSs use these particles properly in context, and tend to feel awkward when encountering their misuse by Japanese NNSs. Japanese NSs are, however, seldom aware of explicit rules of their difference.

Shogo corrected Shelly's *-wa* and *-ga* errors every time he found them, but like most Japanese NSs, he had no explicit knowledge about the linguistic rules for them. He thus did not explain why they were wrong.

In the sixth week of the activity, Shogo wrote in his journal:

> In the previous reply, she wrote "How can I distinguish "-wa" and "-ga"? They both mark the subject of the sentence!" I felt she was irritated, but I couldn't answer right away. I felt guilty for not being able to solve her problem.

Since then, Shogo felt obliged to find good linguistic accounts for her, and sought them even after the eight-week activity. One day in his regular English class, where students were working on a Japanese-English translation exercise, the teacher told the students not to forget to put the indefinite article (i.e., *a*) to the first-introduced subject noun, and the definite article (i.e., *the*) to the identical subject subsequently used. Shogo wrote *a* and *the* to all the first mentioned and subsequently mentioned subject nouns, respectively, on the translation sheet. He then found that all *a*'s were associated with subject nouns followed by *-ga*, while all *the*'s were with ones followed by *-wa*. Shogo inferred that *-ga* might be used for first mention and -*wa* for subsequent mention, which corresponds to the general -*wa* and -*ga* accounts mentioned above. Shogo wrote in his journal:

> Finally! I discovered the difference between "-wa" and "-ga," which is almost like the distinction of English articles "a" and "the." I hope Shelly will be glad to know this.

As the activity period had been over, Shogo wrote his findings in his Christmas card to Shelly, which he learned Americans send on their biggest holiday. Shelly, in turn, sent Shogo a New Year's card, which he taught is a national custom for Japanese to celebrate their biggest holiday. In the card, Shelly wrote her sincere gratitude to Shogo for his long and undaunted effort to assist her Japanese learning.

Principles

Principle 1. E-mail tandem helps learners develop linguistic skills by using language as both the medium and the topic of communication. The first and foremost objective of e-mail tandem is to improve participants' L2 communicative ability. According to Brammerts (2003), tandem learners develop their linguistic skills not only by using both languages as the *medium* of their communication (i.e., practicing L2 they have learned, and receiving L2 models provided by their NS partner), but also as the *topic* of their communication (i.e., correcting, explaining, and discussing linguistic features). The preceding section illustrate how learners on both sides learned acceptable L2 forms from their partners (e.g., English prepositions, Japanese -*ga* and -*wa* distinctions). In each case, they produced and received L2 for communication (i.e., *medium*), and learned from L2 models in the form of corrections, and occasionally of explanations and discussions about what is appropriate or not, and why (i.e., *topic*). This is a unique aspect of e-mail tandem, where, unlike other NS-NNS *monolingual* communication, both learners play the role of L2 experts and support each other's L2 development.

Principle 2. Encourage learners to learn from each other's cultural background. Although developing L2 communicative skills is the main goal of e-mail tandem, learning from each other's cultural background is another important objective of this activity. Tandem learners at secondary school level would talk about their school lives and holidays and get to know the cultural differences between two countries (e.g., research on national holidays in Shogo and Shelly's vignette). University student dyads might share their future plans and help each other generate solutions to achieve their dreams. Tandem communication between two learners who have the same occupation or academic discipline might become a special application in this respect. For example, two postgraduate students specializing in law from different countries will be able to not only improve their L2 skills but also increase knowledge in their field in a unique way which otherwise may not be achieved.

Principle 3. Through e-mail tandem, learners engage in authentic communication. One of the major benefits of e-mail tandem is that it allows learners to engage in authentic communication (Brammerts, 2003). In such situations, learners are required to shift their focus from prescriptive linguistic rules to practical communicative skills, which are, in many cases, missing from FL classroom instruction. For example, Shogo learned the significance of providing compliments when giving negative feedback, and adjusting the level of formality (i.e., register) according to the context. Such pragmatic aspects are seldom taught in EFL classes in Japan, but can be learned through authentic communication, where interlocutors create meaning depending not only on structural L2 knowledge (i.e., linguistic competence), but also in the context of the utterance, such as audience and purpose, which in turn develops learners' sociolinguistic competence. Due to its reciprocal nature of communication, e-mail tandem will benefit learners on both sides in this respect.

Principle 4. E-mail tandem increases learner autonomy. It has been recognized that e-mail tandem increases learner autonomy. According to Little (2003), "tandem learners are autonomous in the sense that they are responsible for managing their own learning" (p. 37). In the previous section, Shelly discussed with Shogo several times to convince him why his sentence was inappropriate (i.e., "I belong to the football club"). Shogo, facing Shelly's linguistic problem in distinguishing Japanese particles *-wa* and *-ga*, spent a lot of time trying to find a grammatical rule and finally had an answer, which cleared up her uncertain feeling. In both cases, NSs of their partners' L2 played a substantial role as an expert and assisted their partners' (i.e., novices') L2 learning to the best of their ability. These efforts were not imposed by someone authoritative such as teachers and caretakers, but initiated and directed by learners themselves. This is considered as an autonomous attitude in learning, and it will characterize successful learning even outside formal educational contexts (Little, 2003).

Principle 5. E-mail tandem raises metalinguistic awareness. Finally, e-mail tandem renders language learners opportunities to be aware of their L1, which raises their *metalinguistic awareness* (MLA). In the feedback phase, each interlocutor is supposed not only to correct his or her partner's errors but also give linguistic reasoning that explains why it is not acceptable. It is, however, often very difficult for NSs to articulate the L1 linguistic rules although they use them intuitively. In fact, Shogo had considerable difficulty finding sound L1 rules to explain to Shelly, but this cognitive effort, that is, analyzing a partner's linguistic errors and generating explicit L1 rules, is believed to raise tandem learners' MLA (Appel, 1999).

Interestingly, in Shogo's case, when he found the distinction of Japanese particles *-ga* and *-wa*, he then contrasted his L1 and L2, and recognized that both English and Japanese have the same function to denote first and subsequent mention, but use different linguistic systems (i.e., *a* and *the* in English, and *-ga* and *-wa* in Japanese). Some researchers suggested that this kind of metalinguistic analysis, that is, contrasts between L1 and L2, occurs when learners possess highly developed MLA, which enhances the development of L2 proficiency. For example, Jessner (1999) mentioned that MLA helps learners perceive similarities and differences between L1 and L2, which can activate their prior linguistic knowledge, reduce the cognitive load related to L2 learning, and eventually guide them in the development of an L2 system. Sasaki & Takeuchi (2011) reported that, in their e-mail tandem study, Japanese learners with a higher level of MLA tended to be more successful in English learning. Given these arguments, e-mail tandem has a great potential to improve participants' L2 ability not only by allowing them to practice and receive L2 but also by raising their MLA through its feedback component.

Applications

E-mail tandem is beneficial to any learner of any language, but there are two basic requirements: a tandem partner and computer. With regard to the former, their partners should be both a NS of their L2 and a learner of their L1. Learners in an institutional context, such as the one conducted by the author and Mayumi, where e-mail tandem is pedagogically designed between two schools, will be assigned to an appropriate partner by the instructor. Individual L2 learners can also find partners through websites that connect language learners from different parts of the world. The resources section presents websites designed for teachers and individual learners who seek e-mail tandem partners.

With respect to the latter, e-mail tandem requires computers with Internet access. Learners also need to have their own e-mail accounts (e.g., Gmail, Hotmail, Yahoo! Mail), which are free of charge and can be accessed from any PC (e.g., home/school PCs, mobile PCs) with a Web browser (e.g., Internet Explorer, Chrome, Safari).

Tandem learners should also have computer literacy such as word processing skills and familiarity with the Internet and e-mail. In the case of the author, where participants had little experience of computer use, he held a workshop prior to the activity, in which students practiced typing text, sending and receiving e-mails, and attaching additional files.

Payoffs and Pitfalls

As already mentioned, there are a lot of benefits from e-mail tandem. The author, however, has seen some challenges that his students encountered during the activities. Most of these difficulties were related to technical problems—for example, American Japanese language students' texts sometimes appeared garbled and totally unreadable (Figure 12.2). This happened either when the character encoding did not function in a written document, or when the document was moved to

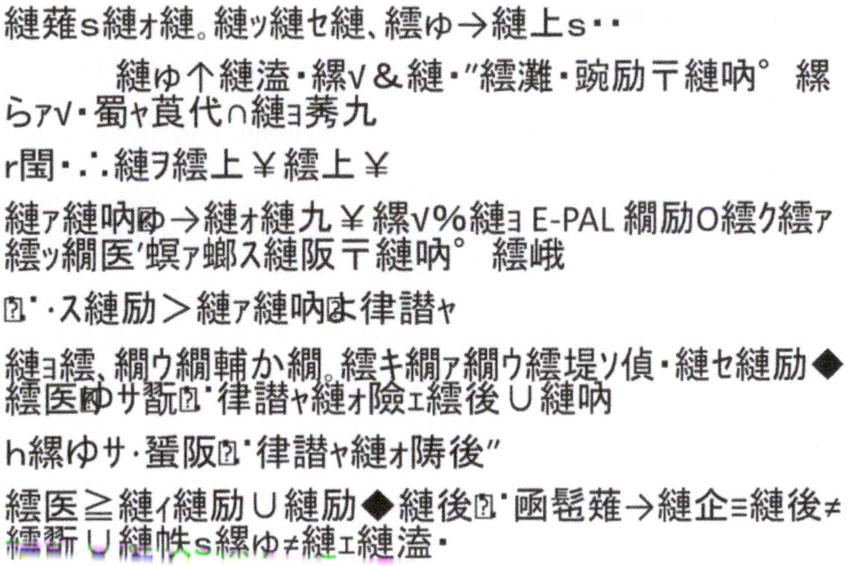

縺薙ｓ縺ｵ縺。縺ｯ縺ｾ縺、繧ゆ→縺上ｓ・・

縺ゆ个縺溢・繝ｖ＆縺・"繧灘・豌励〒縺吶°　繧
らｱﾎ・蜀ｬ莨代∩縺ヨ莠九

ｒ閨・∴縺ヲ繧上￥繧上￥

縺ｱ縺吶Ｚ→縺ｵ縺九￥繝ｖ％縺ヨ E-PAL 繝励Ｏ繧ｸ繧ｱ
繧ｯ繝医'蟇ｱ蠑ｽ縺阪〒縺吶°　繧峨

Ｚｼ・ｽ縺励＞縺ｱ縺吶ｈ律譛ｱ

縺ヨ繧、繝ｳ繝輔か繝。繧ｷ繝ｱ繝ｳ繧堤ｿ偵・縺ｾ縺励◆
繧医Ｚ繧ｩ繧ｫ蠇Ｚ・律譛ｱ縺ｵ險ｪ繧後ｴ繧縺吶Ｕ縺吶

ｈ繝ｶゆ繧ｵ・蟲阪Ｚ・律譛ｱ縺ｵ隍後"

繧医≧縺ｨ縺ｾ縺亥Ｕ縺亥◆縺後Ｚ・函髦薙→縺ゆ≡縺後≠
繧ｽﾎｼ U 縺帷ｳ繝ｖ≠縺ｴ縺溢・

FIGURE 12.2 Garbled e-mail text.

a different encoding system. As a solution, the author instructed students to write and save their messages in Microsoft Word and attach the files to their e-mail. This solved the garbled character problem, but this time some of the attached Word documents were infected by viruses. In response to this problem, students were told to save the documents in the hard disk drive so that they can re-send the file when the partner finds it infected.

Students also had language-related problems. Some students on both sides constantly received e-mail messages with a lot of grammatical errors, and found it exhausting to correct all of them. This happened when their partners' L2 proficiency was relatively low. In this case, the author suggested that students deal only with serious errors which hindered NS comprehension while omitting minor errors. As a result, learners were able to focus more on particular L1 features, which eventually facilitated the development of their MLA.

Past studies indicated that some tandem learners have difficulty in making implicit L1 knowledge explicit, and thus cannot formulate grammatical rules (Edasawa & Kabata, 2007; Sasaki & Takeuchi, 2011). This often occurs when learners are adolescent students, who are cognitively and linguistically immature. It is, therefore, suggested that young learners' tandem learning be at times monitored by tutors such as teachers or adult language users. A linguistic journal is a recommended medium between learners and tutors. In the journal, learners write about their L1 analysis on the partners' language use, as well as what they have thought or learned from tandem communication. Journal entries once a week would help tutors detect each student's problems and support his or her sound e-mail tandem activity.

Discussion Questions

1. If you were an L2 learner, what advantages would you expect from e-mail tandem?
2. What kinds of speech acts do you think learners might learn from e-mail tandem?
3. Have you analyzed your L1 to generalize its rules? Can you give an example?
4. Have you used metalinguistic awareness (i.e., inference and/or analysis of the language) in your L2 learning? If yes, when and how?
5. As an L2 instructor, would you recommend students in your teaching context to join e-mail tandem as an out-of-class language-learning activity? Why? Why not?

Resources

Websites for teachers

- *Tandem-Server Bochum*—http://tandem.uni-trier.de/Tandem/index.html. A comprehensive website on e-mail tandem describing principles and practical tips, presenting useful references, and offering tandem partner search.
- *ePals Global Community*—www.epals.com

Websites for individual students

- *Palabea*—http://www.palabea.com/
- *Tandem Partners Org*—http://www.tandempartners.org/
- *My Language Exchange*—http://www.mylanguageexchange.com/

References

Appel, C. (1999). *Tandem language learning by e-mail: Some basic principles and a case study* (CLCS Occasional Paper No. 54). Dublin: Trinity College, Centre for Language and Communication Studies. Retrieved from http://www.eric.ed.gov/PDFS/ED430396.pdf

Beatty, K. (2003). *Teaching and researching computer-assisted language learning*. London: Longman.

Braga, J. (2007). E-tandem learning for language and culture. *Essential Teacher, 4*, 33–35. Retrieved from http://www.tesol.org/s_tesol/secet.asp?CID=1466&DID=7944

Brammerts, H. (2003). Autonomous language learning in tandem: The development of a concept. In T. Lewis & L. Walker (Eds.), *Autonomous language learning in tandem* (pp. 27–36). Sheffield, UK: Academy Electronic Publications.

Edasawa, Y., & Kabata, K. (2007). An ethnographic study of a key-pal project: Learning a foreign language through bilingual communication. *Computer Assisted Language Learning, 20*, 189–207. doi:10.1080/09588220701489473

Jessner, U. (1999). Metalinguistic awareness in multilinguals: Cognitive aspects of third language learning. *Language Awareness, 8*, 201–209. doi:10.1080/09658419908667129

Little, D. (2003). Tandem language learning and learner autonomy. In L. Walker & T. Lewis (Eds.), *Autonomous language learning in tandem* (pp. 37–44). Sheffield: Academy Electronic Publications.

Nariyama, S. (2002). The WA/GA distinction and switch-reference for ellipted subject identification in Japanese complex sentences. *Studies in Language, 26*, 369–431. Retrieved from http://dx.doi.org/10.1075/sl.26.2.07nar

Sasaki, A., & Takeuchi, O. (2011). EFL students' metalinguistic awareness in e-mail tandem. In M. Levy, F. Blin, C. Siskin, & O. Takeuchi (Eds.), *WorldCALL: International perspectives on computer-assisted language learning* (pp. 55–69). New York: Routledge.

Ushioda, E. (2000). Tandem language learning via e-mail: From motivation to autonomy. *ReCALL, 12*, 121–128. Retrieved from http://journals.cambridge.org/action/displayIssue?decade=2000&jid=REC&volumeId=12&issueId=02&iid=73288

van Lier, L. (1996). *Interaction in the language curriculum: Awareness, autonomy and authenticity.* London: Longman.

Woodin, J. (2001). Tandem learning as an intercultural activity. In M. Byram, A. Nichols, & D. Stevens (Eds.), *Developing intercultural competence in practice* (pp. 189–202). Clevedon: Multilingual Matters.

Note

I wish to dedicate this chapter to the memory of Dr. Leo van Lier. He significantly contributed to my knowledge and skills in the TESOL and CALL field, and the ideas in this chapter stem from his classes at the Monterey Institute of International Studies in California. I would also thank Ms. Louisa Green & Mr. Nicholas Mullins at Kwansei Gakuin Junior High School for their careful proofreading.

PART III
Learning Through Television

13

LEARNING ENGLISH THROUGH THE LANGUAGE OF THE POKÉMON

"Just Watchin' TV, Ma"

Andy Curtis

Introduction and Overview

This particular out-of-class learning opportunity can be described simply as 'watching cartoons on the TV' (television). However, that would be similar to stating that 'in-class language learning is a teacher, a student and a textbook in a classroom.' As all language teachers and learners know, there is far more to it than that. In the same way, although 'watching cartoons on the TV' may seem like a relatively passive-receptive activity and a low level form of 'edutainment'—*education* plus *entertainment*—it can also be much more than that, culturally, linguistically, and on many other levels as well.

As some readers may be unfamiliar with the Pokémon phenomenon, which was at its height in the mid-to-late 1990s and the early years of the new millennium, the first part of this chapter summarizes the phenomenon. That is followed by a vignette, which describes my son and I watching episodes of the Pokémon cartoon series, at our new home in Canada, and what we learned through doing that, in relation to learning English, learning the language of the Pokémon, and learning other important lessons. The title of the chapter comes from the formulaic answer given by our son, Jack, when his mother asked him what he was doing.

The Pokémon Phenomenon

In September 1998, Nintendo of Canada released the Japanese video game Pokémon, which had been released in Japan two years earlier, in 1996. The following month, Kevin Restivo reported that Pokémon was "set to sweep Canada." The word Pokémon comes from the portmanteau of 'Pocket' and 'Monster,' which in turn comes from the original Japanese name 'Poketto Monsuta.' According to Owen Grieve's Pokémon entry in the *Encyclopedia of Play in Today's Society*

(Carlisle, 2009), Pokémon refers to: "a diverse range of animal species with incredible abilities and near-human intelligence" (p. 564).

Pokémon was not only an enormously popular craze for many years, it also became a "multibillion-dollar global franchise … one of the most widely-recognized brand names to have ever emerged from video games" (Grieve, 2009, p. 564). The video game series has sold hundreds of millions of units worldwide, with more than 800 episodes in the cartoon series, and 16 full-length feature films. An example of the popularity of Pokémon in North America was their appearance on the cover of *Time* magazine in November 1999.

Pokémon generated sufficient interest even in the academic world that in November 2000, the University of Hawaii, Center for Japanese Studies Endowment sponsored a two-day conference titled 'Pikachu's Global Adventure,' which resulted in Joseph Tobin's book *Pikachu's Global Adventure: The Rise and Fall of Pokémon* (2004). In addition, a number of scholarly papers in academic journals were also published in the United Kingdom, including the frequently cited article by David Buckingham & Julian Sefton-Green (2003). Their paper, on "structure, agency and pedagogy in children's media culture" in the journal *Media, Culture and Society*, makes use of the English catchphrase for the Pokémon franchise, "Gotta catch 'em all." In terms of definition, Buckingham & Sefton-Green pointed out that "Yet despite the seemingly endless outpouring of adult concern and bewilderment [about the Pokémon craze] it is actually difficult to find a single term to describe it" (p. 389).

Buckingham & Sefton-Green go on to describe what Pokémon is not as well as what it might be:

> It is clearly not just a 'text', or even a collection of texts – a TV serial, a card game, toys, magazines or a computer game. It is not merely a set of objects that can be isolated for critical analysis, in the characteristic mode of academic Media Studies. It might more appropriately be described, in anthropological terms, as a 'cultural practice'. Pokémon is something you *do*, not just something you read or watch or 'consume.' (p. 389)

These aspects are illustrated in the narrative account below.

Vignette

Jack Meets Pikachu in the Frozen North

It is December 18, 1998, in Edmonton, Alberta, Canada. It's still only early afternoon, but it is already getting dark, and it's −28 degrees Centigrade (−18 degrees Fahrenheit) outside. Our ten-year-old son, Jack, who has just been uprooted from his life in China, where he was born and where he lived until now, is watching the first episode of the new Pokémon cartoons on the television. The episode is called

I Choose You! and the opening scene takes place in the laboratory of a Professor Samuel Oak, who has devoted his life to the study of the Pokémon.

At that time, Jack knows little English, so he has gone from being from at the top of his crowded class in China, to not even understanding what people are saying around him in Canada. But he seems happy watching episodes of Pokémon, featuring the lead character, called 'Pikachu.' Instead of attending to the overwhelming number of things that need doing when you relocate as a 'reconstituted' multilingual, multicultural family, from one side of the planet to the other, I sit and watch Jack watching the cartoons, while I make notes.

After some time, I realize that Pikachu's communicative system might, in fact, constitute some kind of 'language,' as Jack appears to understand what Pikachu is 'saying.' Jack manages to explain to me that when Pikachu is happy, it says its own name as "Pika-chooooo" with a long, rising intonation. Likewise, when he is sad, he says his name with a long falling intonation. Pikachu is also able to communicate a surprisingly wide range of emotions through facial expressions and other forms of nonverbal body language.

On closer viewing of more episodes, it seems that Pikachu stores electricity in his chubby cheeks, which he can apparently fire at will to defend or attack or just to heat up a tasty snack. But his aim is sometimes off, so his lightning bolts can accidentally destroy telephone poles and various items of electrical equipment. I note, with an accompanying 'diagram,' that the rodent-like creature appears to have a small mouth and short forearms, with five-fingered paws and three-toed feet.

The more I watch Jack watching the episodes, the more I am struck by this one-word language that each Pokémon character has, based on saying their name in all kinds of different ways. "Imagine that," I wrote in my notes, "a whole language based on a single word?!" I also realized that Jack was able to do much better than I was expecting, when he explained to me the different features of the different creatures, especially Pikachu. Not only did Jack make use of adjectives to describe the number, color, shape and size of the Pokémon, he also tried to describe their facial expressions, their moods, and other features, such as their trademark moves.

Later on, I would ask Jack to tell me about what had happened in the Pokémon episodes that I did not get a chance to see (while attending to the apparently more important matters of life and work), and again I was surprised by how much of the narrative he was able to communicate to me in English. At that time, money was very tight, so Jack did not get into the gaming cards, as we could not afford to buy them for him. But eventually, we did buy some VHS tapes of Pokémon episodes, which Jack and I would watch together sometimes. Using those tapes, we were able to re-watch episodes, pause in the middle of episodes, watch and re-watch short clips of a few minutes from some of Jack's favorite episodes, after which I could ask him more specific questions about particular aspects of what we we'd seen.

Many years later, Jack and I talked about those early experiences of watching Pokémon episodes together. In those talks, we realized that watching those episodes together may have been more important than we realized at the time for he and I to get to know each other, through learning a third language, beyond English and Chinese, that neither of us knew; the language of the Pokémon.

Principles

Principle 1. Use television / video cartoons and games to engage young learners. It is common to think of cartoons and comics as media most suitable for "younger learners," which is a term that, as David Nunan (2011) points out, "covers a large age span: from around 3 years of age to around 15" (p. 2). However, a recent newspaper article was titled "Pokémon gaming draws kids ages 5 to 64," for the 2013 Pokémon World Championships, which shows that learners of all ages can enjoy this kind of 'edutainment.' However, it is possible that children and younger adults may be able to identify with and relate to the Pokémon world more easily than adults, as shown by Jack having to repeatedly explain to me aspects of that world that were clear to him. This relates to Tobin's point that: "The complexity of the Pokémon universe makes for very rich conversations, full of opportunities to achieve social goals by sharing information with others and showing off one's knowledge" (2004, p. 193).

Principle 2. Use songs and rhymes to encourage intensive repetition in an engaging, contextualized way. In terms of what is being learned and how it is being acquired, Nunan also highlights the importance of songs and rhymes, which he states are: "excellent for giving students intensive repetition of language items" and "excellent for teaching core vocabulary" (Nunan 2011, p. 61). In terms of how this kind of repetition can result in the acquisition of cultural and linguistic understanding, Tobin highlights the contextual nature of knowledge and how repetition of songs and rhymes are used in the Pokémon episodes: "Knowledge in this context refers to the ability to give the right name to a monster. This process is performed at the end of each episode in the TV series, in the "Poké-rap'" (p. 193). In my notes from 1998, there are many references to the songs and rhymes being repeated, which Tobin believes is "a prime example of how the manipulation of symbolic referents functions as a core social activity" (p. 193).

Principle 3. Create safe environments for effective learning. Readings books such as Tobin's (2004) and Nunan's (2011), and articles such as Buckingham & Sefton-Green's (2003), many years after those all-important early days with Jack, I realized that there was so much more to those creatures and the cartoons than we noticed at that time. But that form of 'subconscious learning' does appear to be one of the strengths of this kind of out-of-class language learning, perhaps in part because the home-setting may feel much safer and more secure for a child in a new country than a classroom full of strangers.

Principle 4. Exploit the power of narrative to build knowledge. In addition, the narrative structures built into the storylines were also enabling Jack to understand those aspects of language, as they are expressed in English. The importance of this kind of language learning through storytelling is highlighted by Nunan (2011): "Listening to and re-telling stories are fundamental to early learning. In fact, it is argued that stories and story-telling are essential to the human experience" (p. 58). Although Jack and I were not engaged in formal language-learning lessons at that time, the principle of maximizing learner involvement clearly did apply in our case, during those viewings and the talks between us that followed.

"What Pokémon Can Teach Us About Learning and Literacy" is the title of an article by Vivian Vasquez (2003). In the same way that Jack had developed his English through teaching me about the visual features of the creatures, Vasquez's nephew, Curtis, taught her about the written text on the gaming cards: "[H]e was teaching me how to participate in a Poké discourse, the Pokémon way of talking about gaming and using the cards. He was teaching me to break the code so that I could participate with and make meaning of Pokémon text" (p. 119).

Another account of using Pokémon in teaching and learning, which also focused on writing, was by Alleen & Don Nilsen (2000) in a paper titled "Language Play in Y2K: Morphology Brought to You by Pokémon," which is another example of language learning in the home with family, in their case, with their grandchildren. In addition to the importance of home-based language learning with young learners who are family members, another one of the recurring themes of these articles is the focus on first-language learning and development, with relatively few articles found on using this kind of material to teach and learn second and foreign languages.

Also, although a great deal of work has been published on using film in the language classroom (see, for example, Chapple & Curtis, 2000; Curtis, 2007; Curtis, 2012) relatively little has been written on using television for language teaching and learning. This perhaps constitutes the missing of a great opportunity to tap into the pedagogical potential of television series like Pokémon with young second- and foreign-language learners.

Applications

As stated above, regarding what types of learners this kind of medium works best with, the general assumption is children. However, older learners may also be able to access certain aspects of the target language and culture through the same medium. In terms of language input, as discussed below, although the one-word language of the Pokémon creatures is limited, the fact that the language of each character is just one word can make it ideal for younger learners, especially if they have limited target language listening competence.

Also, cartoons on the television, especially if seen at home, with family and friends, are likely to result in far less anxiety than a teacher at the front of the class. Therefore, this kind of out-of-class learning experience could also work well with learners who have limited confidence in using the target language. Also, as the Pokémon show that a single word can be enough to communicate a great deal, such programs can be especially useful for building vocabulary, as well as narrative-structure grammars.

In terms of contexts, one of the recurring themes in the literature is that this particular out-of-class learning experience can be particularly effective when it occurs at home, with family. However, as Tobin observed: "A great strength of Pokémon is that is an activity primarily not of individuals but of social groups and, moreover, one that reinforces the coherence of children as a peer group by allowing them to define themselves vis-à-vis their parents, teachers and other adults" (p. 194). Therefore, this kind of learning experience can be enhanced if groups of younger learners watch together. This is something I saw and took notes on in 1998, when I was watching Jack watching Pokémon episodes together with children of his age.

Another set of contextual and learner-related factors relates to repetition, which is sometimes frowned upon for its lack of creativity. However, for learners who are comfortable with repetition, as part of their preferred learning styles, the repetitive nature of watching the same episodes and/or short excerpts repeatedly can be not only very helpful, but also comforting. That was the case for Jack, coming to Canada as he had done with a traditional Chinese educational upbringing, in which repetition is considered to be highly beneficial and extremely important.

Many learners—again, young and old, but perhaps especially younger learners—need variety for their engagement to be sustained, and with more than 800 episodes of the Pokémon cartoon available, a tremendous amount of variety is possible. Related to variety is the large number of Pokémon characters, more than 150 in total, which means that young learners have no problem finding one or more that are a good fit with their view of themselves, and/or the people around them, thus enabling the young learners to identify with the Pokémon, thereby strengthening the learning.

Payoffs and Pitfalls

In terms of language input, the most obvious limitation of the Pokémon cartoons is the fact that, as Tobin (2004) put it, the "various monsters each have a language of their own that consists entirely of their own name" (p. 193). Tobin's description in 2004 confirmed what I had written in my observation notes in 1998, which is part of the appeal for the young viewers, but which does limit the language input to a single word from each creature. However, Tobin also explained that the name of each creature "essentially reflected their essence and, when said with various inflections, reflected their thoughts and feelings" and which "convey a core characteristic of each creature" (p. 193).

In terms of additional language, there are many human characters in every episode who provide a great deal of oral input through their dialogs. Furthermore, although the language input of the Pokémon is limited to names, single words are where language begins, as Lois Bloom (1976) pointed out in her early work, *One Word at a Time:* "The use of single-word utterances is usually described as the first of the "developmental milestones" in language acquisition" (p. 65). She also stated that "the learning of early aspects of grammar derives from the conceptual notions underlying single-word utterances" (p. 113). Therefore, even though the single-word languages of Pikachu and his Pokémon family provided relatively limited linguistic input, the output generated by Jack far exceeded the one-word inputs of the Pokémon characters, which I described in my notes in 1998 as "Visual Input for Verbal Output, or *VIVO.*"

Another concern expressed at the time was the popularity of the series growing to levels that were considered 'unhealthy' for children. For example, in April 1999, Canadian schools in the Greater Vancouver area banned Pokémon trading cards, each of which had the history, strengths, and weaknesses of a particular character. According to the Canadian Press, "Principals are ordering them [the cards] out of classrooms and in some cases even banishing them from school grounds to put a stop to the fever-pitched trading that too often leads to arguments and tears."

That decision by some Canadian schools was doubtless made in what they perceived to be the best interests of the children. However, it is also possible that such decisions resulted in a common reaction to any kind of ban, which is to make the banned substance all the more attractive and desirable by limiting its supply, which may well then lead to increased demand. For example, Tobin (2004) and his co-researchers found in interviews they conducted with children that "children were very clear about the fact that their parents' and teachers' hostile reactions to Pokémon were key elements in contributing to the definition of Pokémon as a children's universe, a universe that enables them to develop values that differ from those of adults" (p. 191).

Another strength of media like the Pokémon series is that the creators appear to be highly sensitive to the linguistic features of the creatures. For example, one of the first countries in Europe where the Pokémon craze became established was France, where the linguistic creativity with Japanese words would not have worked as well in France as they did in Japan. Consequently, "Nintendo, aware of the importance of naming, translated the creatures' names into terms that artfully reflect the language and culture of French children" (Grieve, 2009, p. 193). This may seem like a relatively small adaptation or accommodation, but according to Grieve, "This is an essential aspect of cultural and linguistic socialization that is necessary if children are to relate intimately to a product" (p. 193).

Another example of this sensitivity to language appeared in the *Pokémon 3* movie, which was released in 2001. In his review of the movie, Earl Calloway (2001) explained that the character Professor Spencer Hale "becomes acquainted with the mysterious Pokémon who is the Unown. There are 26 individual entities in the shape of letters of the [English] alphabet who have the ability to read human dreams, thoughts and emotions and transform them into reality" (p. 20). Such transformations, which are highly sophisticated and worthy of some advanced levels of science fiction writing and film-making, show the creators' awareness of the importance of language and languages in the Pokémon universe.

Discussion Questions

1. If you work with young learners, what kind of teaching and learning materials do you use with them and why?
2. Have you ever tried to teach or to learn a language by watching television programs? If so, how successful (or unsuccessful) were you?
3. What would you say are some of the strengths and weaknesses of using cartoons to teach and learn language?
4. In the British Council website below, they give the following advice: "Choose your cartoons and comic strips with care." What criteria do you use, or would you use, in selecting such material for your younger learners?
5. Principle 2, above, states: "Use songs and rhymes to encourage intensive repetition in an engaging, contextualized way." However, it was also noted that, in some contexts, repetition is "sometimes frowned upon for its lack of creativity." How do you use repetition positively and purposefully in your teaching?
6. Lois Bloom (1976) claimed that: "Single-word utterances are not sentences" (p. 32). Do you agree or disagree with this statement? Why or why not?

Resources

Useful websites

Official Pokémon website—http://www.pokemon.com
Official Pokémon website on YouTube with videos, episodes, etc.—http://www.youtube.com/user/pokemon
British Council, "using cartoons and comic strips"—http://www.teachingenglish.org.uk/language-assistant/teaching-tips/using-cartoons-comic-strips

References

Bloom, L. (1976). *One word at a time: The use of single word utterances before syntax*. Berlin: Mouton De Gruyter.
Buckingham, D., & Sefton-Green, J. (2003). Gotta catch 'em all: Structure, agency and pedagogy in children's media culture. *Media, Culture and Society*, 25, 379–399.

Canadian Press NewsWire. (1999, April 7). Schools ban Pokemon trading cards. Retrieved from http://search.proquest.com.proxy.queensu.ca/docview/359513261?accountid=6180

Calloway, E. (2001, April 11). *Pokemon 3, the movie* is filled with mystery. *Chicago Defender*, 20.

Carlisle, R. P. (Ed.), *Encyclopedia of play in today's Society* (pp. 564–565). Thousand Oaks, CA: Sage.

Chapple, L., & Curtis, A. 2000. Content-based instruction in Hong Kong: Student responses to film. *System*, 28(3), 419–433.

Crawford, T. (2013, August 11). Pokémon gaming draws kids ages 5 to 64. *Vancouver Sun*. Retrieved from http://www.vancouversun.com/entertainment/Pokémon+gaming+draws+kids+ages/8776152/story.html

Curtis, A. (2007). Film in the ESL classroom: hearing the students' voice. In H. McGarrell (Ed.), *Language teacher research in the Americas* (pp. 41–53). Alexandria, VA: TESOL Association.

Curtis, A. (2012). Doing more with less: Using film in the English language classroom in China, *Research on English Education*, 1(1), 30–47.

Grieve, O. (2009). Pokémon. In R. P. Carlisle (Ed.), *Encyclopedia of play in today's society* (pp. 564–565). Thousand Oaks, CA: Sage.

Nilsen, A., & Nilsen, D. (2000). Language play in Y2K: Morphology brought to you by Pokémon. *Voices from the Middle*, 7(4), 32–37.

Nunan, D. (2011). *Teaching English to young learners*. Anaheim, CA: Anaheim University Press.

Restivo, K. (1998, October 19). Pokemon set to sweep Canada. *Computer Dealer News*, 45.

Tobin, J. J. (2004). *Pikachu's global adventure: The rise and fall of Pokémon*. Durham, NC: Duke University Press.

Vasquez, V. (2003). What Pokémon can teach us about learning and literacy. *Language Arts*, 81(2), 118–124.

14

RESOURCING AUTHENTIC LANGUAGE IN TELEVISION SERIES

Anthony Hanf

Introduction and Overview

Many English learners worldwide claim that watching television has benefited their English language proficiency. Indeed, the linguistic benefits of watching foreign language television have been recognized in areas such as listening comprehension, cultural proficiency, and vocabulary acquisition (Danan, 2004; Vanderplank, 2010). This is not to do away with language textbooks, but rather serves as a supplement to enhance the language learning experience beyond the classroom.

In this chapter the author suggests multi-episodic television series as the content of language study. This is because the running time of multi-episodic television series (approximately 20 hours), as opposed to movies (approximately 2 hours), offers far more exposure to the foreign language. This provides language learners with prolonged character development, an unfolding storyline, and thematic episodes all in the context of a familiarized setting.

More than ever before, English language learners have widespread access to technology, which can open a window to rich sources of authentic foreign language usage. With the emergence of high-quality television series in various genres, it would be prudent to take advantage of this language learning opportunity.

Historically, one of the main problems facing language teachers and learners has been the difficulty of accessing 'authentic materials' and making them understandable, whether they be movies, music, newspapers, or famous novels. From the perspective of language learners, authentic television appears daunting. Learners may feel intimidated by its rapid speech, complex constructions, and cultural references. However, learners do not need to fully understand every utterance in order to benefit from foreign language television.

One way of taking advantage of foreign language television series is by using a cognitive strategy called 'resourcing'—taking notes on unknown or desired language (Rubin, 1995). With the aid of textual captions/subtitles, learners have the opportunity of extracting language from native speakers in natural settings, which can be a powerful motivation for some learners. In the foreign language classroom, there is an ever-increasing need to meet students' motivational needs. Watching high-quality and entertaining television series may be one way to meet these needs.

Vignette

Alex is a language teaching professional in his late 20s from Minnesota, USA. He teaches English at a university in Seoul and despite taking occasional Korean classes and having lived in South Korea for nearly four years, his Korean language proficiency remained minimal. In fact, Alex never experienced success with learning languages. His previous attempts at Spanish, French, and Italian ended in relative failure. This was a source of frustration and embarrassment for Alex who teaches language for a living yet could not learn one himself. He recognized that learning Korean would increase his quality of life in South Korea by allowing him to develop closer relationships with Koreans and by gaining a larger degree of autonomy in daily life. Alex thus decided to give Korean another try, but this time in a different way than before.

Alex became fascinated with the phenomenon of how some Koreans spoke nearly flawless English yet had never left the peninsula. "How did you learn English so well?" he asked. Curiously, the most common response included mention of a favorite American television series. Alex developed a hunch that there was something unique about this trend, yet knew it would be naive to conclude that watching foreign language television was the 'key to success.' After some contemplation, he decided it would not hurt to give it a try as his previous attempts of learning a foreign language in the classroom had been unsuccessful. He speculated that perhaps a new method of learning could help him break through the initial barrier of learning Korean.

The next day Alex asked his Korean friends, and searched the Internet, for popular Korean television series. He located several that appeared interesting and was determined to watch them with a purpose by actively paying attention versus passively enjoying for entertainment alone. His study plan targeted two areas of language: communication strategies and politeness strategies. The former was chosen because he often struggled with understanding and being understood in Korean when communication 'broke down.' The latter was chosen because he wanted to learn how to build rapport and maintain relationships in Korean.

He studied these constructs to make sure he fully understood what he was looking for and then began watching from episode one with English subtitles.

He took notes on communication strategies such as "Pardon me?" and politeness strategies such as "That looks good on you!" At first it was tricky and sometimes frustrating because he had to rewind and replay scenes a number of times. However, as time went by not only did his listening skills increase allowing him to "catch" more of each Korean utterance, but he also became adept at spotting useful language. Cognitively speaking, his increased language awareness freed up spare processing capacity for other tasks such as making inferences.

Soon thereafter Alex faced the problem of organizing his notes for efficient review. He then discovered a free flashcard application on his iPad and began creating digital flashcards. He regularly reviewed them and met with language exchange partners for conversation practice. Over a 14-week period, he watched three Korean television series and kept a personal language learning diary.

An analysis of the diary revealed that the most salient theme was Alex's competitive nature as a language learner in the context of living in Korea. This competitiveness spurred Alex to sign up for his first standardized language exam—the Test of Proficiency in Korean. The diary also documented numerous compliments Alex received on his improved Korean ability, particularly his pronunciation. Finally, the diary revealed Alex's improved confidence in using Korean because he felt more prepared to communicate and express himself.

Principles

How does watching foreign language television series enhance language learning? This section introduces key principles and theoretical support for this method.

> *Principle 1. Make use of captions or subtitles.* The use of captions or subtitles is a key requirement which helps learners understand the foreign language. Captions and subtitles are the written form of what is heard. Captions refer to a script in the foreign language that allows learners to visualize what they hear while subtitles refer to a script which has been translated into the learner's native language. In Vanderplank's (1988) study investigating the benefits of watching nine one-hour long sessions of foreign language television, all 15 students reported captions as useful and beneficial to their language development. For getting started, the author suggests learners adhere to the following chart:

Level	Language Script
Beginner	Subtitles (Native-language)
Intermediate	Captions (Foreign-language)
Advanced	Captions (Foreign-language)

> *Principle 2. Develop skills in the cognitive strategy of "resourcing."* One of the best ways learners can take advantage of captions/subtitles is by using a cognitive strategy called "resourcing"—this involves taking notes on unknown or

desired language (Rubin, 1995). With the support of captions/subtitles and the development of technology, learners have the ability to control their learning experience and adjust it according to their needs. In the vignette above, there were occasions when Alex needed to pause and replay scenes a number of times in order to make sense of what he was hearing. As his listening and "resourcing" skills improved, he was able to 'catch' longer streams of Korean utterances with less difficulty.

Principle 3. Find opportunities for comprehensible input and output. With the aid of captions/subtitles, this approach provides learners with large amounts of comprehensible input—a key requirement in Krashen's (1985) second language acquisition theory. Receiving comprehensible input and understanding messages, however, is viewed as insufficient for language acquisition. Learners also need opportunities to produce the language. As learners attempt to communicate, they test their hypothesis about using the language and reflect on its effectiveness (Swain, 1985). These two processes (comprehensible input and output) are recognized as critical for second language development. After watching the Korean television series, taking notes, and reviewing flashcards, Alex met his language exchange partners where he felt safe to "test drive" new language. In that informal setting, he also had opportunities to ask questions. Over time, the combination of receiving large amounts of comprehensible input with opportunities for output supported his Korean language development.

Principle 4. Observe how native speakers use all their linguistic resources to communicate effectively. Foreign language television allows language learners to witness the interactions of native speakers in natural settings (Shrum & Glisan, 2000). This affords learners the opportunity to observe how native speakers behave in a various situations: body language, facial expressions, reactions, and so on. Over time, keen learners develop skills in reading communicative intentions and finding patterns—a theory of how children learn their first language (Tomasello, 2003). Although the processes of learning one's first and second language are different, developing these skills can help learners begin to grasp the pragmatics of a foreign language. In other words, learners have opportunities to make connections between the language and how it's used.

Principle 5. Target specific areas for language improvement. Learners can avoid feeling overwhelmed by breaking down the foreign language into manageable parts. This is achieved by targeting a specific area(s) of language for improvement. This is referred to as a "direct approach" to language learning (Richards, 1990). Richards (1990) suggests looking at the construct of communicative competence and planning a study program around "specific microskills, strategies, and processes that are involved in fluent conversation" (p. 77). Communicative competence is a term used to describe the knowledge and skills of using a language to communicate; it's comprised of sociocultural, linguistic, discourse, formulaic, interactional, and strategic competence (Celce-Murcia, 2007). Alex chose to target communication strategies, a subcomponent of strategic competence, and politeness strategies, a subcomponent of sociocultural competence. One of the benefits of a direct approach to communicative competence is that all components are interrelated. Savignon (2002) asserts that "when an increase occurs in one area, that component interacts with other components to produce a corresponding increase in overall communicative competence" (p. 8).

Applications

This section explains the basic requirements for this study arrangement along with who can benefit from it and how it can be applied to different contexts. It concludes by introducing key management techniques for learner training.

Basic Requirements

A laptop or personal computer is recommended in order to make efficient use of this learning opportunity. Learners need to have basic multi-media skills and know how to pause and replay scenes for taking notes. Alex reported that user-friendly media player software, such as the ones below, greatly enhanced his ability to control his learning experience:

Media Player	Platforms	Cost	Website
VLC Media Player	All	Free	http://www.videolan.org/vlc/
GOM Media Player	All	Free	http://www.gomlab.com/eng/

Learners must also have access to content—a foreign language television series with captions or subtitles. Finally, learners need a convenient way to organize, review, and master new language. One way is to create digital flashcards and organize them by language category. For students with smartphones or tablet PCs, there are a number of free and easy-to-use flashcard applications. Alex recommends Brainscape's Flashcardlet by Holliday (2013) for its sleek design and online support features. The figures below display examples of Alex's three language categories while studying Korean.

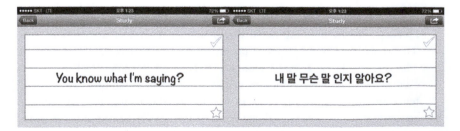

FIGURE 14.1 Communication strategies.
(Holliday, 2013)

FIGURE 14.2 Politeness strategies.
(Holliday, 2013)

FIGURE 14.3 Relationship expressions.
(Holliday, 2013)

Who Can Use Television Series?

Self-directed learners, or those who lack motivation in the classroom context, may find this to be a refreshing approach to language study. This may also be applicable to those who enjoy television series in their native language. Since Alex already enjoyed English-medium television series, he wondered if he could get hooked on any Korean television series. Alex's case revealed that the selection of content was vital to the learner's motivation. He began watching a number of Korean television series and lost interest before locating ones he enjoyed enough to continue.

In the Context of the Classroom

Teachers may utilize this approach by assigning a television series to watch for homework. Language areas of communicative competence may be assigned by the teacher or chosen by students. While exploring components of communicative competence is recommended, teachers and learners may opt for creative categories or desired language, such as Alex's choice of 'relationship expressions' because, as he discovered, romance was an abundant feature in Korean television series.

Other categories learners may 'resource' include the language of slang, humor, or specific registers (modes of speaking) such as how doctors speak in the hospital, how lawyers speak in the courtroom, or how law enforcement officials speak during an investigation. Nevertheless, the teacher may choose not to assign language categories at all by instructing students to merely 'resource' desired or unknown language.

At the outset, the teacher should use some class time to introduce the area of desired language and model the 'resourcing' strategy. Students may not be familiar with concepts of language areas and may need definitions and examples to understand what to look for. When Alex targeted politeness strategies, he first reviewed Brown & Levinson's (1978) taxonomy of the various ways politeness is realized. The teacher may need to locate or create such charts for student reference. With a classroom projector, the teacher should demonstrate how to locate such language by pausing, replaying, and taking notes. Then, the teacher should introduce students to the following metacognitive strategies (management techniques) to help them take more control of the learning process:

1. Planning (what to watch, how to watch a segment, how many replays, etc.)
2. Defining Goals (deciding on what to listen for, etc.)
3. Monitoring (self-assessing comprehension, identifying difficulties, judging strategy effectiveness, etc.)

(Thompson & Rubin, 1996)

During the next class period, students should meet in small groups to discuss the episode they watched and the language they discovered. This is their opportunity to ask questions, particularly of a contextual and/or cultural nature, that only the teacher may have answers to. In large classes, small groups may be assigned different language areas and present their results to the class. Additionally, students might carry out a jigsaw activity in which they participate in reciprocal teaching with students from other groups. The chart below depicts a sampling from Alex's notes on communication strategies which he 'resourced' from Korean television shows. See Celce-Murcia, Dörnyei, & Thurrell (1995) for a taxonomy of communication strategies.

TABLE 14.1 Communication Strategies

Communication strategies	Korean translation	Type of strategy
You know what I mean?	내 말 무슨 말 인지 알아?	Confirmation check
What are you talking about?	무슨 소리야?	Clarification request
The thing is …	그 문제는 …	Gambit
Could you do me a favor?	부탁 하나 할께. 혹시, 이것 좀 해줄 수 있어?	Appeal for help
Can you understand?	이해 할 수 있어?	Confirmation check

Outside the Classroom Context

Learners whose work schedule prohibits them from attending formal classes may also benefit from this approach by arranging their own small groups for language study. In South Korea, adult learners generally work long hours, have limited access to native speakers, and face the rising cost of English education. In this case, Korean learners may choose a television series, 'resource' new language, and meet together for discussion and interaction.

Payoffs and Pitfalls

An obvious payoff of authentic material is that it has the potential of capturing learner engagement, piquing interest, and maintaining motivation. Additional payoffs include a low-cost language learning opportunity and the ability to study at anytime and anywhere. Furthermore, as mentioned in the introduction, research shows that watching foreign language television improves listening comprehension, cultural proficiency, and vocabulary acquisition (Danan, 2004; Vanderplank, 2010). However, this learning arrangement may entail a number of challenges. This section begins by describing payoffs and concludes by addressing pitfalls and their possible solutions.

Potential Payoffs

- *Redundancy*. Both captions and subtitles provide redundant exposure to the foreign language. Koolstra (1999) maintains that learners can profit from this redundancy. The benefit of redundancy, for example, is realized when learners continually hear and begin to notice the use of certain words or phrases.
- *Promotes language awareness*. Both captions and subtitles promote consciousness of language otherwise misunderstood or lost (Borrás & Lafayette, 1994). For instance, subtitled films help learners notice new vocabulary and idioms (Wilson, 2002). Also, captions help learners catch language otherwise lost in the stream of speech (Vanderplank, 1988). Finally, being able to see the written form of speech helps learners notice difficult language such as articles, verb conjugations, and various uncertainties relating to the sound system (deletion, assimilation, etc.).
- *Reduces anxiety*. Both captions and subtitles provide learners with a sense of security by lowering their 'affective filter'—a theory that a psychological barrier may either facilitate or hinder language development. In theory, when learners feel stress and anxiety, their 'filter' goes up and inhibits language development. Conversely, when learners feel safe and comfortable, their 'filter' goes down and they are more likely to 'take risks' speaking the language and thereby creating better conditions for language acquisition.

Vanderplank (1988) reports that captions and subtitles act as a 'safety net' by reducing anxiety in the learner who might otherwise become frustrated and lose motivation to continue.

- *Instant feedback.* Captioned/subtitled foreign language television gives learners the opportunity to receive instant feedback on their hypotheses: comparing what they hear versus what was said. Vanderplank (1988) argues that, from a psychological perspective, the "text provides instant feedback and therefore positive reinforcement for learning" (277). He maintains that this helps learners in the long run by preparing them to watch foreign language films without textual support.

Potential Pitfalls

The potential pitfalls of this approach may include the following: an aversion to a highly self-directed learning experience; the difficulty of acquiring foreign language television series with appropriate captions/subtitles; the extensive time spent viewing; the difficulty of authentic material for lower-level learners. These issues will be discussed along with possible solutions.

- *Acquiring audiovisual material with captions/subtitles.* One of the biggest challenges for Alex was obtaining Korean television series with captions/subtitles. He often located television series he enjoyed yet did not have captions/subtitles and vice versa. One of the most helpful solutions to this problem was asking Korean friends for assistance, especially younger tech-savvy individuals. They helped Alex locate video stores with large selections of Korean television series, some of which contained captions/subtitles. They also recommended paid-subscriptions to Korean websites with large inventories of downloadable and/or streaming Korean television series.
- *Extensive time spent viewing.* While sustained exposure to foreign language television series has benefits, it comes with the cost of time. Alex often felt pressed for time as his teaching schedule left only evenings/weekends for watching Korean television series and meeting language exchange partners. In all, Alex watched three English-subtitled Korean television series totaling 61 hours of exposure, which averaged approximately 37 minutes per day over a 14-week period. Keep in mind that the nature of this method, pausing and replaying, will extend viewing time. Some weeks Alex was able to watch an episode each evening, while others he would only manage time for two or three episodes. He found that the key to success was taking advantage of time when it was available, as his life fluctuated between spells of business. One way to overcome this challenge is to identify a routine that works and stick to it.
- *Difficulty of authentic materials.* One of the major difficulties of using authentic materials in foreign language education is that since they are made for native speakers, their discourse is often far too advanced, especially for

beginners. This can be a huge source of frustration for learners who may lose motivation to continue. At the beginning of each new Korean television series, Alex felt overwhelmed by the new characters and the different ways in which they spoke Korean. In each series, however, Alex progressively became more familiarized with the characters/setting and was surprisingly able to understand more and more as the season unfolded. This may have to do with what Oller (1983) refers to as the benefits that episodic organization provide to learners, which aids comprehension and retention of the story. One solution to the difficult nature of authentic materials is to keep a language learning diary. Learners need to be continually reflecting, self-assessing, and adjusting their own learning experience. This will help them measure their growth and notice when and how to make adjustments. By maintaining realistic expectations for themselves, learners may avoid the pitfall of losing motivation due to the difficult nature of watching authentic foreign language television.

Discussion Questions

1. Would you (or your students) be interested in watching foreign language television series for language study?
2. What kind of language would you be interested in "resourcing" in a foreign language television series?
3. Which English-language television series might be applicable for language learners?
4. What would be some of the biggest challenges for students using foreign language television series in your context?
5. What kinds of activities could you plan for student-generated "resourced" language in your classroom?

Resources

Recommended Media Players

VLC Media Player; runs on all platforms; free. http://www.videolan.org/vlc/
GOM Media Player; runs on all platforms; free. http://www.gomlab.com/eng/

References

Borrás, I., & Lafayette, R. C. (1994). Effects of multimedia courseware subtitling on the speaking performance of college students of French. *Modern Language Journal*, 78(1), 61–75.
Brown, P., & Levinson, S. C. (1978). Universals in language usage: Politeness phenomena. In E. N. Good (Ed.), *Questions and politeness: Strategies in social interaction* (pp. 56–289). Cambridge University Press.

Celce-Murcia, M. (2007). Rethinking the role of communicative competence in language teaching. In E. A. Soler & P. S. Jordá (Eds.), *Intercultural language use and language learning* (pp. 41–58). Dordrecht, the Netherlands: Springer.

Celce-Murcia, M., Dörnyei, Z., & Thurrell, S. (1995). Communicative competence: A pedagogically motivated model with content specifications. *Issues in Applied Linguistics,* 6(2), 5–35.

Danan, M. (2004). Captioning and subtitling: Undervalued language learning strategies. *Meta: Journal des Traducteurs/Meta: Translators' Journal,* 49(1), 67–77.

Holliday, J. (2013). Brainscape: iOS Flashcard Application (Version 3.0.3) [Flashcardlet]. *Available from the iTunes App Store.* Retrieved from https://www.brainscape.com

Koolstra, C. M., & Beentjes, J. W. (1999). Children's vocabulary acquisition in a foreign language through watching subtitled television programs at home. *Educational Technology Research and Development,* 47(1), 51–60.

Krashen, S. D. (1985). *The input hypothesis: Issues and implications* (vol. 1, p. 985). London: Longman.

Oller, J. W. (1983). Story writing principles and ESL teaching. *TESOL Quarterly,* 17(1), 39–53.

Richards, J. C. (1990). *The language teaching matrix.* Cambridge: Cambridge University Press.

Rubin, J. (1995). Learner processes and learner strategies. In V. Galloway & C. Herron (Eds.), *Research within research II.* Valdosta, GA: SCOLT.

Savignon, S. J. (2002). Communicative language teaching: Linguistic theory and classroom practice. *Interpreting communicative language teaching: Contexts and concerns in teacher education,* 1–27.

Shrum, J. L., & Glisan, E. W. (2000). *Teacher's handbook: Contextualized language instruction* (2nd ed.). Boston: Heinle.

Swain, M. (1985). Communicative competence: Some roles of comprehensible input and comprehensible output in its development. *Input in Second Language Acquisition,* 15, 165–179.

Thompson, I., & Rubin, J. (1996). Can strategy instruction improve listening comprehension? *Foreign Language Annals,* 29(3), 331–342.

Tomasello, M. (2003). *Constructing a language: A usage-based theory of language acquisition.* Cambridge, MA: Harvard University Press.

Vanderplank, R. (1988). The value of teletext sub-titles in language learning. *ELT Journal,* 42(4), 272–281.

Vanderplank, R. (2010). Déjà vu? A decade of research on language laboratories, television and video in language learning. *Language Teaching,* 43(01), 1–37.

Wilson, C. C. (2002). Practical aspects of using video in the foreign language classroom. *The TESL Journal,* 5 (11). Retrieved from http://iteslj.org/articles/Canning-video.html

15

INTERNET TELEVISION FOR L2 VOCABULARY LEARNING

Phoebe M. S. Lin & Anna Siyanova-Chanturia

Introduction and Overview

Television, movies and videos have a long history in English Language Teaching (ELT). Since the 1980s, researchers (e.g., Candlin, Charles, & Willis, 1982; Eisenstein, Shuller, & Bodman, 1987) have been exploring the ways in which popular media can be used effectively to enrich the English learning experience. *English as a foreign language* (EFL) learners are particularly encouraged to watch English movies and television outside the classroom since research shows that they can facilitate the learning of English vocabulary, discourse and culture (Meinhof, 1998; Lin, 2014).

To EFL learners who are taught *English for academic purposes* (EAP), television and movies are particularly valuable in that they address learners' lack of experience in casual, everyday English. While these learners can deliver academic essays and professional presentations, many of them find using English outside academic or professional settings challenging. Some of them may, therefore, turn to foreign television programmes, particularly dramas, soaps and comedies, as a source of input of authentic, everyday English. However, access to North American, British, or Australian television programmes has long been a problem. Since satellite television is rather expensive for an ordinary household, learners have had to access it in the school library or self-access language learning centre. Apart from inflexibility in terms of where and when, limited choice of programmes is another issue.

With the advent of Internet television, *ubiquitous foreign language learning* (Chang, Tseng, & Tseng, 2011) can finally become a reality. EFL learners can take Internet television with them wherever they go. In the past, only the very committed EFL learners would take the initiative to visit a self-access language learning centre to watch satellite television. Today, Internet television is accessible with just a few clicks on the Internet-enabled smartphone. This convenience in access means that any EFL learner can receive authentic input, even if they have only ten minutes on the train. The goal of exposure to authentic, everyday English has become much more tangible. There is also a diversity of programmes on the Internet to suit every learner's taste. Most importantly, Internet television is an activity that young people already engage in on a regular basis. According to the Hong Kong Census and Statistics Department (2011, 2012), 94.8% of Internet users in Hong Kong aged 15–24 use the Internet at least once a day, and 88.2% of them use it for online entertainment, including Internet television. So, our task is to advise learners on how they can turn Internet television, which they enjoy, into a unique second language (L2) learning opportunity.

The present chapter is structured as follows. It begins with a story of two Chinese learners of English from Hong Kong—Joyce and Sam—who have been watching Internet television for a number of years. Their examples illustrate the principles behind the use of Internet television, which are the focus of the next section. We then offer some advice on the implementation of Internet television as an extracurricular English learning activity, followed by an examination of the payoffs and pitfalls. The chapter finishes with a list of relevant Internet resources.

Vignette

Joyce loves watching American and British dramas. She watched an episode of *Prison Break* on her local television some years ago and fell in love with the drama series. After watching all four seasons of the drama online, she began to pick up other popular drama series such as *24*, *Bones*, *Sex and the City*, *Doctor Who* and *Holby City*. She often tweets about her favourite scenes on Twitter. Joyce also joined a Facebook group of American and British drama fans. The group of teenagers meets up for an occasional drama weekend where they enjoy drama and food together. Many members in the group, including Joyce, are so familiar with some dramas that they can recite the characters' lines with the exact same tone of voice. They find it amusing to finish the lines before the characters. In high school, Joyce's speech fluency, native-like accent and a vast vocabulary were admired by her classmates.

Sam received a first class honors degree in English language and literature from a Hong Kong university and went on to study for an MA in the United Kingdom. When Sam first arrived in the UK, she was frustrated by her inability to use English in social and interpersonal situations. Despite her excellent performance in all course work, she did not seem to have the vocabulary needed to participate in casual conversations in English. She did not know how to start small talk, tell jokes, fight, or share support and personal feelings. At the time, Sam began watching television programmes on the BBC iPlayer. She could just about follow the language of documentaries and news; the dialogues in dramas and sitcoms seemed too fast for her and there were many unfamiliar expressions. However, she insisted on watching the dramas and sitcoms week after week. Sometimes she watched the same episodes and scenes repeatedly with the English subtitles on. Soon after learning how to download Internet television subtitles from a website, she also began to practise the dialogues of her favourite scenes. A year later, she could make jokes with her local English friends effortlessly and enjoy her favourite British medical drama series without subtitles.

Principles

Joyce's, Sam's and other learners' success in advancing their English proficiency through watching Internet television is the result of a number of factors. Below is a summary of the principles that may help to explain the effectiveness of Internet television for English language learning.

Principle 1. Learners receive extensive exposure to English from watching Internet television. Internet television is an excellent resource for L2 learning. Young people like it and are happy to spend many hours watching it. The dramatic increase in exposure to English outside the classroom is perhaps the main reason for the effectiveness of Internet television. Joyce spent at least ten hours per week watching Internet television, which was almost twice as long as her English lessons in high school. This extensive exposure can improve EFL learners' grasp of English phraseology, which is known to be particularly problematic for L2 English learners (Siyanova & Schmitt, 2007, 2008), and help them to establish an accurate sense of the frequency of use of collocations and other phrasal expressions (Lin, 2014). Nesselhauf (2005), for example, showed that L2 learners often overuse some phrases (e.g., *take into account*) and underuse others (e.g., *take account of*) compared with their native speaker counterparts. In fact, the lack of exposure to English affects not only learners like Joyce, who reside in an EFL region, but also learners like Sam, who have the experience of studying in an English-speaking country. As Ranta & Meckelborg's (2013) survey showed, study-abroad learners do not always receive as much exposure to English as is often assumed.

Principle 2. Learners have the opportunity to observe authentic, everyday speech in English-speaking communities via Internet television. All over the world, the teaching and learning of EAP has been the focus of the English language syllabi in EFL regions (Mauranen, 2006). Since the emphasis is placed on learners' ability to read and write academic and professional texts (Mauranen, 2006), little is done to train learners to engage in informal spoken interactions (or communication for social purposes, such as doing small talk, telling jokes, fighting and sharing support and personal feelings). It is unsurprising then that EFL learners like Sam often notice a knowledge gap when they move to an English-speaking country. Internet television is a useful resource that has helped Sam and Joyce to fill this knowledge gap. It is effective because Internet television gives learners the chance to observe communication in a diversity of informal, communicative contexts. As Lin (2014) shows, the language of Internet television closely captures casual everyday English.

Principle 3. Internet television facilitates contextual vocabulary acquisition. Most vocabulary is learned naturally from context rather than through explicit vocabulary instruction (Sternberg, 1987). Therefore, as useful as the vocabulary learning strategies (e.g., glossing, word lists, bi- or monolingual dictionaries) may be, they cannot compensate for EFL learners' poverty of contextual vocabulary acquisition opportunities in the L2 classroom. In this regard, Internet television may be an ideal channel for contextual vocabulary learning because it offers multimodal, as opposed to bi- or unimodal, contextual cues. Put simply, the multimodal (i.e., orthographical, aural and visual) contextual cues offered by Internet television make it easier for learners not only to work out the meaning of an unknown vocabulary item, but also to learn the new item. Previous research suggests that six to twenty exposures are necessary to learn a word from reading (Schmitt, 2010), which offers unimodal contextual cues. With multimodal contextual cues, fewer exposures may be necessary for vocabulary acquisition to occur. Moreover, the presence of multimodal contextual cues may also reduce the vocabulary demand of Internet television; that is, learners can achieve an adequate comprehension of a programme with a smaller vocabulary size. According to Webb & Rodgers (2009), a vocabulary size of 3,000 word families is sufficient for adequate comprehension of a television programme. A vocabulary size of about 4,000 word families, however, is needed for adequate comprehension of a movie or a novel (Nation, 2006). Finally, recent research (Lin, 2012) has also shown that hearing the intonation and the flow of speech can facilitate the learning of English phraseology.

Applications

Internet television is different from other out-of-class L2 learning activities. It is more likely to appeal to learners from *all* proficiency and motivation levels; even learners with low L2 proficiency and low motivation to learn English will enjoy watching Internet television because it is, after all, entertaining. With all the images, sound effects and subtitles, the content of Internet television may be easier to comprehend than content without images, sounds and/or subtitles (e.g., radio, novels). Television is also commonplace in our everyday life, which is likely to lead to learners' greater acceptance of Internet television.

Joyce & Sam are two of the many young people who are accustomed to watching Internet television, although they have different reasons for doing so. Sam is a highly motivated top scorer in her academic studies. She started watching

Internet television with the clear goal to improve her use of English for interpersonal communication purposes. Joyce, in contrast, was not a particularly motivated student at school, and she did not have any specific L2 learning goals when she first started watching Internet television. She kept watching it simply because she enjoyed the entertainment side of it and also the friendships she made through an interest group. Regardless of their backgrounds, learners have the potential to enhance their L2 proficiency through extensive exposure to Internet television. Their gains will be reflected particularly in their increasingly fluent speech, more native-like accent and a growing repertoire of useful expressions for informal social contexts. To benefit fully from watching Internet television, however, there are some key points to bear in mind.

First, learners need to pay attention to language use while enjoying the entertainment Internet television offers. To promote attention to language, repeated viewing of episodes or scenes is a common strategy. There is no maximum number of times that a learner can watch an episode or a scene. Joyce, for instance, watches some scenes so many times that she has subconsciously internalised the lines and the characters' intonation. That said, there should be a balance between the breadth (i.e., the number of new episodes) and the depth (i.e., the number of repeated viewings).

Second, learners may need training in contextual vocabulary learning skills to help them learn implicitly from Internet television. In an L2 classroom, most learners may be accustomed to receiving explicit instructions and close supervision. These conditions, however, will not be available when learners watch Internet television. To prepare for a transition to this self-directed learning activity, learners may benefit from some guidelines on contextual vocabulary learning skills, such as those proposed by Sternberg (1987). Sternberg's (1987) syllabus familiarises L2 learners with eight contextual cues (temporal, spatial, value, stative, functional descriptive, casual, class and equivalence) and trains them to apply three logical processes—*selective encoding*, *selective combination* and *selective comparison*—to help them guess the meaning of the unknown word X.

To illustrate the operation of Sternberg's (1987) three logical processes, let us consider Extract 1 taken from an episode of the medical drama *Holby City* (series 15, episode 23 "Holby's Got Torment"), accessed via the BBC iPlayer in March 2013:

Extract 1. Medical consultation for a new ward admission
Nurse Chrissie presents a new admission to surgeon Sasha. Sasha meets the patient.

CHRISSIE: Rahim Hussain, multiple abrasions and ED have treated a head wound ...
SASHA: And they sent him on to us because ...?
CHRISSIE: Complaining of amnesia ...
SASHA: Can you book a CT scan, please? Thank you.
SASHA: Right, let's take a look at you. So what happened?

HUSSAIN: I was at a funeral …
SASHA: And?
HUSSAIN: That's it.
SASHA: How do you mean?
HUSSAIN: Went back to the church social club … next thing, I woke up in the ambulance.
CHRISSIE: That's quite a nasty injury.
SASHA: I know.
HUSSAIN: It hurts.
SASHA: So you can't remember anything else?
HUSSAIN: Total blank.
SASHA: Well, if any more details come to mind …

To work out the meaning of the unknown word *amnesia*, the learner needs to apply selective encoding first, which involves separating the relevant from the irrelevant for the purpose of formulating a definition. For example, the patient's loss of memory constitutes relevant information for the definition of *amnesia*, while the patient's attendance at the funeral or social club does not. The second process, selective combination, involves combining relevant contextual cues into a workable definition. In our example, the learner needs to combine at least four relevant cues to figure out the meaning of *amnesia*. That is, (1) the doctor asks the patient specifically about whether he remembers anything about his injury; (2) the patient's reply is "total blank"; (3) the illness is a health complaint serious enough to lead to a hospital admission; and (4) it is linked to a nasty head injury. The third process, selective comparison, is a process by which new information about the unknown word is related to existing information in the learner's memory. In the case of *amnesia*, the learner needs to relate the new information from the dialogue to the existing knowledge that a serious head injury may result in impaired brain function including memory loss.

Third, learners may form groups to share their interest and experience in English Internet television. This will help them to turn an otherwise individual activity into a group endeavour. Joyce, for example, benefitted greatly from joining a Facebook group for drama fans and sharing her views and feelings on Twitter. The friendships she has made through the shared hobby have enhanced her motivation to continue to participate and to pay attention to the language of the characters.

Finally, to enhance the efficiency and effectiveness of the learning process, we believe the following strategies are important to promote attention to language use and to guide learners in their choice of Internet television programmes:

1. *Programme selection.* When EFL learners select Internet television programmes, their individual interests should have priority over other factors. Beyond that, programmes may be chosen based on the extent to which they mirror real language-in-use. A corpus study by Lin (2014) evaluated the extent to which

the vocabularies of 11 genres of Internet television accessible via the BBC iPlayer were similar to those of spontaneous everyday British English. The study found that programmes in the factual, drama and comedy categories were more representative of everyday English than those in the music, learning and religion categories.

2. *Narrow viewing.* Narrow viewing refers to viewing a variety of Internet television programmes on the same topic, or of the same genre or series. By targeting programmes of a similar nature (as opposed to watching single episodes randomly), learners can gradually accumulate background knowledge that will aid comprehension of the content (cf. Schmitt & Carter, 2000). This, in turn, may spare attentional resources needed for the acquisition of new linguistic material. Exposure to recurrent vocabulary items across programs of the same genre or series is also likely to increase the chances of acquiring these items (see Schmitt & Carter, 2000).

3. *Interlingual and intralingual subtitles.* Most Internet television providers give viewers the option to switch subtitles on or off in the same language as the audio stream (also called *intralingual subtitles*). Some may even offer subtitles in a language different from the audio stream (typically subtitles translated into the viewers' first language, also called *interlingual subtitles*). These subtitle options facilitate learners' comprehension of the programme content. Interlingual subtitles offer more comprehension aid than intralingual subtitles. Depending on their level of comprehension and linguistic needs, EFL learners may experiment with interlingual subtitles to begin with, then progress to intralingual subtitles and, finally, to no subtitles in the first viewing. Sometimes, the subtitles can be downloaded and printed directly from the Internet television provider's website or third-party websites run by subtitles fans (see the Resources section).

Payoffs and Pitfalls

There are few alternatives that can compare with Internet television as an EFL learning opportunity in terms of flexibility, accessibility and cost. Inevitably, however, there are also some concerns about its use.

First, some learners may be drawn solely to the entertainment side of Internet television and forget its purpose for language learning. As individuals are generally good at guessing (at least some) meaning by simply attending to visual and audio cues (e.g., characters' gestures, tone of voice, sound effects, the scene), it is possible to enjoy a programme without really paying attention to the spoken input. Although recent psycholinguistic research (e.g., Bisson, van Heuven, Conklin, & Tunney, 2013) shows that incidental vocabulary acquisition takes place even if learners do not make any conscious effort to learn the foreign words, it is important to make use of an array of viewing strategies to maximise the effectiveness of the language-learning process (see previous section).

Second, given that English Internet television is intended for people residing in native English-speaking communities, it does not provide modified input (e.g., foreigner talk) like educational videos do. Therefore, the content may be too challenging for beginner and intermediate EFL learners. Advanced learners may also find the language difficult at the beginning, but comprehension will improve over time with strategies, such as narrow viewing and repeated viewing.

Third, teachers have little control over the content of Internet television programmes. Learners less than 16 years of age may be exposed to inappropriate material, including sex and violence. However, reputable Internet television providers often flag programmes with potentially inappropriate content and request viewers to confirm that they are over 16. Parental locks are also available from the Internet television providers or third-party computer software manufacturers which allow the Internet administrator to block potentially inappropriate content.

Finally, learners' gains from watching Internet television may not be fully reflected in their exam grades because the language of Internet television is not EAP-oriented. In fact, there is a possibility that some learners may confuse the formal register required by the EAP syllabus and the informal register of the Internet television content. Colloquial vocabulary items such as *massive, loads, knackered* and *blown away*, for example, may appear in learners' academic and professional communication if learners are not careful.

In summary, in the modern age, Internet television is part of many young people's daily routine. However, they may not know how to exploit the resource for effective L2 learning. This chapter provided an introduction to Internet television as an out-of-class L2 learning activity. It presented a story of two Hong Kong learners of English, illustrated the principles underpinning the effectiveness of the activity, and discussed its applications, payoffs and pitfalls. All things considered, Internet television can be a useful resource. If used systematically and strategically, it can offer some unique opportunities and unrivalled benefits compared to other, more traditional tools.

Discussion Questions

1. Have your students had experience with Internet television? Do you think that they will welcome the idea of learning English from watching Internet television? Why? Why not?
2. EFL learners in Hong Kong have about five hours of English lessons every week. How many hours of English input do your students get inside *and* outside the L2 classroom?
3. Lin (2014) recommends Internet television of the factual, drama and comedy genres for the acquisition of recurrent expressions in English. Do you know any programs in these genres that you may suggest to your students?

4. Will you consider training students' contextual vocabulary learning skills using Sternberg's (1987) syllabus? How will you adapt it to suit your class?
5. Will you consider setting up clubs for Internet television fans in your school? Why? Why not?

Resources

Some international providers of *Internet television*—www.netflix.com, www.youtube.com, www.hulu.com, www.bbc.co.uk/iplayer

ClipFlair is an all-in-one Web-interface that allows learners to practise transcription and/or dubbing of their favourite video clips. It focuses on listening skills and pronunciation—http://clipflair.net/

Websites run by *subtitles fans*—http://www.subtitlesource.org/, http://www.tvsubtitles.net/, http://subtitles.toh.info/index.html

References

Bisson, M. J., van Heuven, W.J.B., Conklin, K., & Tunney, R. J. (2013). Incidental acquisition of foreign language vocabulary through brief multi-modal exposure. *PLoS ONE*, 8(4), 1–7.

Candlin, J., Charles, D., & Willis, J. (1982). *Video in English language teaching: An inquiry into the potential uses of video recordings in the teaching of English as a foreign language*. Birmingham, UK: University of Aston.

Chang, C. C., Tseng, K.H., & Tseng, J.S. (2011). Is single or dual channel with different English proficiencies better for English listening comprehension, cognitive load and attitude in ubiquitous learning environment? *Computers & Education*, 57, 2313–2321.

Eisenstein, M., Shuller, S., & Bodman, J. (1987). Learning English with an invisible teacher: An experimental video approach. *System*, 15(2), 209–216.

Hong Kong SAR Census and Statistics Department (2011). Results of the 2011 Hong Kong Population Census. Hong Kong: Hong Kong SAR Census and Statistics Department. Retrieved from http://www.census2011.gov.hk.

Hong Kong SAR Census and Statistics Department (2012). Use of new media. *Thematic household survey report number*, 49, 34–62. Hong Kong: Hong Kong SAR Census and Statistics Department.

Lin, P.M.S. (2012). Sound evidence: The missing piece of the jigsaw in formulaic language research. *Applied Linguistics*, 33(3), 342–347.

Lin, P.M.S. (2014). Investigating the validity of Internet television as a resource for acquiring L2 formulaic sequences. *System*, 42(1), 164–176.

Mauranen, A. (2006). Spoken discourse, academics and global English: A corpus perspective. In R. Hughes (Ed.), *Spoken English, TESOL and applied linguistics* (pp. 143–158). Basingstoke, UK: Palgrave Macmillan.

Meinhof, U. H. (1998). *Language learning in the age of satellite television*. Oxford: Oxford University Press.

Nation, P. (2006). How large a vocabulary is needed for reading and listening. *The Canadian Modern Language Review*, 63(1), 59–82.

Nesselhauf, N. (2005). *Collocations in a learner corpus*. Amsterdam: John Benjamins.

Ranta, L., & Meckelborg, A. (2013). How much exposure to English do international graduate students really get? Measuring language use in a naturalistic setting. *Canadian Modern Language Review*, 69(1), 1–33.

Schmitt, N. (2010). *Researching vocabulary: A vocabulary research manual*. Basingstoke. UK: Palgrave Macmillan.

Schmitt, N., & Carter, R. (2000). The lexical advantages of narrow reading for second language learners. *TESOL Journal*, 9(1), 4–9.

Siyanova, A., & Schmitt, N. (2007). Native and nonnative use of multi-word vs. one-word verbs. *International Review of Applied Linguistics*, 45, 119–139.

Siyanova, A., & Schmitt, N. (2008). L2 learner production and processing of collocation: A multi-study perspective. *Canadian Modern Language Review*, 64 (3): 429–458.

Sternberg, R. J. (1987). Most vocabulary is learned from context. In M. G. McKeown & M. E. Curtis (Eds.), *The nature of vocabulary acquisition* (pp. 89–106). Hillsdale, NJ: Lawrence Erlbaum.

Webb, S., & Rodgers, M.P.H. (2009). Vocabulary demands of television programs. *Language Learning*, 59(2), 335–366.

16

EXTENSIVE VIEWING

Language Learning Through Watching Television

Stuart Webb

Introduction and Overview

Television is a source of information and entertainment, and for many people it is an integral part of daily life. A survey of the average household television viewing time in 13 countries revealed that television was watched from 2.43 hours per day in Sweden to 8.18 hours per day in the United States (OECD, 2007). In fact, television might be the greatest source of first language input. Canadians and Americans watch television five times more than they read (Statistics Canada, 1998; United States Department of Labor, 2006).

The greatest value of television for language learning might be its potential to provide large amounts of L2 spoken input, which can contribute to the development of vocabulary knowledge and listening comprehension, as well as other aspects of L2 learning. Perhaps the greatest challenge in L2 learning in the EFL context, where L2 input is typically lacking, is developing a vocabulary size beyond the most frequent 2,000 words. Cobb (2007) found that although extensive reading might be an effective method of developing word knowledge, there are likely to be insufficient encounters with lower frequency words to develop much vocabulary knowledge beyond the high frequency words. Research investigating the lexical profiles of different discourse types indicated that a vocabulary size of 8,000- to 9,000-word families is necessary to understand newspapers and novels (Nation, 2006). Since there is clearly not enough classroom time to teach that many words, L2 learning programs need to find ways to help their learners reach this language-learning target. Watching L2 television extensively as a supplement to extensive reading could help to fill the need for greater L2 input.

Extensive viewing involves regular silent uninterrupted viewing of L2 television inside and outside of the classroom. It was proposed as an approach to improve vocabulary learning through increasing the amount of meaning-focused spoken input that EFL learners receive (Webb, 2009). There is also an argument for including L2 movies within an extensive viewing approach. (See Webb & Rodgers, 2009a and Webb, 2010b.) However, because L2 television offers advantages over movies, such as shorter running times and the development of background knowledge through viewing different episodes of one program, it should represent the core material in an extensive viewing approach. That said, the primary aim of extensive viewing is to encourage regular independent out-of-class L2 television viewing after initial classroom-based viewing. The purpose of a classroom-based viewing program is to raise awareness of the benefits of L2 television for language learning, teach learners strategies that can be used to support their comprehension, and demonstrate that through implementing a principled extensive viewing approach, comprehension may be sufficient for pleasurable viewing.

Although extensive viewing might begin in the classroom, its greatest value lies in out-of-class viewing. The reason for this is that the gains made through classroom-based viewing in one or two courses may be relatively small; 20–40 hours of meaning-focused input, while useful, can account for only so much learning. However, if participation in a classroom-based extensive viewing program motivates learners to do one or two hours of out-of class viewing per week, the gains made through an additional 52–104 hours per year may be considerable. It is the long-term benefits of autonomous extensive viewing that should be carefully considered in any discussion of the value of television rather than the relative language-learning gains of a classroom-based extensive viewing program.

There has been a great deal of research demonstrating the value of extensive reading. However, television has been neglected to a large degree in the language-learning literature. This may be due in part to the perception of television as a source of entertainment rather than education, as well as the greater challenges of researching a discourse type that is not easily manipulated. However, the research findings, while limited to a relatively small number of studies, do consistently indicate that watching L2 television may contribute to incidental vocabulary learning gains in the same way as reading L2 books.

In a corpus-driven study of the vocabulary in television programs, Webb & Rodgers (2009b) found that with a relatively small amount of television viewing of unrelated programs (35 hours), there was a relatively large amount of repetition among lower frequency words. They concluded that with regular viewing over a long period of time, there is the potential for large gains in vocabulary knowledge. Rodgers' (2013) research is the most comprehensive study of language learning with television. He found that university students learning EFL in Japan incidentally learned vocabulary through watching ten 43-minute episodes of an American drama over ten weeks, and that their vocabulary gains were similar in size to those made through reading a graded reader over a similar length of time (Horst, Cobb, & Meara, 1998). The finding that watching television contributes to vocabulary learning is supported by a number of studies that have shown that L2 words are learned through watching short videos (e.g., Rice & Woodsmall, 1988). Rodgers' (2013) research also revealed that the participants' listening comprehension improved from the first episode viewed to the tenth and final episode. Taken together, these studies indicate the potential that television may have as a resource for extensive learning. However, further research is needed to support a learning approach that may initially be controversial.

Vignette

Haruna is a first-year university student in Japan and is beginning her seventh year of formal English language instruction. She has always done well in her English language classes, but despite this feels that her listening comprehension is poor. Although she can understand dialogues from course books, and the speech of her teacher and other students in the classroom, she has struggled to understand English spoken to her when traveling abroad, and conversations between friends who are native English speakers. When she discusses this with her teacher, he suggests that she enrol in the extensive viewing course next semester.

At the end of the course, Haruna's teacher advises students to continue the approach that they have taken in class and watch television using a narrow viewing approach at home. Haruna decides to give this a try and rents several DVDs of English language programs. Once she found one that she liked, she watched it in the same way that she would watch Japanese programs; in sequence from the first episode to the last episode. Sometimes she watches an episode more than once when it is a little more difficult to understand. She is happy to study English in this way; it is fun and she can see that she is making progress with her listening comprehension.

Principles

EFL learners may typically experience language learning through watching L2 television in two ways. First, they might encounter L2 television in the classroom. This will usually involve watching random episodes or short excerpts of television programs and then completing activities designed around teaching points. These short, intensive viewing activities can be an enjoyable change from more common paper-based learning activities. However, they provide little L2 input, and may do relatively little to develop listening comprehension and vocabulary knowledge.

The second way that EFL learners may experience L2 television is on their own outside of the classroom. For some learners, their determination to learn language through watching television may outweigh any comprehension difficulties that they experience and they may persevere and continue to watch L2 television to some extent. However, the majority of EFL learners may be overwhelmed by the speed of the discourse in L2 television, as well as the amount of connected speech, unfamiliarity with the spoken forms of many known words, and the many unknown words that are encountered. Eventually, in these cases, learners may simply assume that they are not at the appropriate level for pleasurable viewing or that L2 television is simply too difficult.

If relatively few learners watch much L2 television, the question is then how can we make better use of television as a resource for language learning? In an extensive viewing approach, L2 television viewing begins in the classroom. Classroom-based programs can be designed to provide support for listening comprehension, educate students about the value of watching L2 television regularly, and teach learners about strategies they can use to better understand programs. Through using a principled approach to watching L2 television, students may develop sufficient listening comprehension to motivate autonomous out-of-class extensive viewing.

Extensive viewing programs should be designed around principles that guide students towards comprehensible and pleasurable out-of-class viewing. The following six principles are of greatest importance to starting up an extensive viewing program.

> *Principle 1. The language-learning benefits of extensive viewing must be clear to everyone involved.* Television is most commonly seen as a form of entertainment rather than a platform for learning. Because of this, students, teachers, program directors, and parents may be sceptical of the value of extensive viewing. Educating everyone involved about the language-learning benefits of extensive viewing is essential before beginning a classroom-based program that aims to move students toward autonomous out-of-class viewing. The benefits include improved listening comprehension and vocabulary learning (Rodgers, 2013). Vocabulary learning may occur through the learning of new words, as well as consolidating knowledge of partially known words, and improving recognition of the spoken forms of words. It should also be clearly stated that the greatest learning gains from extensive viewing may not occur in the classroom, but outside of the classroom. If students watch L2 television regularly over a long period of time, learning gains should be a function of television viewing time; with greater viewing time, comprehension and vocabulary learning should improve to a larger degree.

> *Principle 2. Learners should be at the appropriate level.* Language learners might be motivated to learn through watching television. However, their motivation is likely to be impacted by the extent to which they can understand programs. If learners begin too early, their comprehension may be too low for pleasurable viewing and a lack of enjoyment is likely to discourage further viewing. Because the primary aim of extensive viewing is to increase L2 input, it is important that classroom-based viewing should encourage out-of-class viewing. Webb and Rodgers (2009b) suggested that if learners knew the most frequent 3,000-word families, they may be able to adequately understand television. However, Rodgers (2013) found that learners who knew the most

frequent 2,000-word families but had not yet mastered the 3,000-word level had sufficient comprehension of a television program for extensive viewing. These participants also reported that they enjoyed extensive learning with television and found it useful for language learning. This suggests that once students have mastered the 2,000 high frequency words, it might be appropriate for them to begin a classroom-based extensive viewing program.

Principle 3. Listening comprehension should be supported. An effort should be made to support listening comprehension in the classroom because improved comprehension may lead to more pleasurable viewing. There are several ways that comprehension of L2 television programs can be supported. First, extensive viewing should incorporate a narrow viewing approach (Rodgers & Webb, 2011). Narrow viewing involves watching different episodes of the same program in chronological order. Through narrow viewing students should develop background knowledge of the characters and their relationships, the setting, and the storyline that aids comprehension of subsequent episodes. Another reason for narrow viewing is that the lexical load of different episodes of the same program is lighter than unrelated episodes of different programs (Rodgers & Webb, 2011). This is because each program tends to contain topic-related vocabulary that often reoccurs. This results in a smaller number of different words used in multiple episodes of one program than in random episodes of different programs. Frequent encounters with topic-related words also have a positive effect on vocabulary learning because repetition with the same words increases the potential for vocabulary learning (Webb, 2007). Teachers should raise awareness of the value of a narrow viewing approach with their students to support out-of-class viewing.

Comprehension can also be supported through the creation of glossaries that list key words (Webb, 2010c) and materials designed to increase background knowledge of the characters and storyline. As extensive viewing programs are developed, libraries of materials to support comprehension of different programs can be created and made available to students for their own use. This would be particularly useful in self-access centres where students might be able to choose a program and review supporting materials before viewing. In the classroom, it may also be useful to pre-teach a small number of words that are very frequent in an episode or items that are critical to comprehension. Pre-learning as few as ten frequently occurring words in an episode can have a relatively large effect on the percentage of known words (Webb, 2010a), and this in turn may have a positive effect on comprehension.

Another useful way to support comprehension is to have students watch an episode of a program more than once. Research has shown that multiple readings of the same text can improve comprehension (Dowhower, 1987) and vocabulary learning (Webb & Chang, 2012). In initial episodes of extensive viewing or in episodes that are more difficult to understand, repeated viewing might provide a way to help learners to better understand a program.

There is also some evidence that L2 captions may provide support for comprehension. For example, Winke, Gass, & Sydorenko (2010) found that foreign language learners who watched videos with captions had superior comprehension scores to those who watched without captions. In contrast, Rodgers (2013) found no statistically significant difference between learners who watched ten episodes of television with captions and those who did not. However, the participants in that study did report that they found extensive viewing with captions to be useful. Rodgers recommended that when captions are available they might support learning, particularly for the more difficult episodes of a television program.

Principle 4. Precise comprehension should be a goal rather than a requirement. The degree of listening comprehension when viewing L2 television may move along a continuum from incomprehensible through to degrees of partial comprehension and then finally to precise comprehension. In L1 television viewing, we expect to have precise comprehension. However, in the initial stages of L2 television viewing, comprehension might be less than adequate and the support of teachers may be required. This is why a classroom-based approach is initially necessary. Teachers can support their students' comprehension, make them aware that comprehension should gradually increase over time, and help get them to the point where they can watch L2 television for enjoyment without support.

Principle 5. Classroom-based extensive viewing guides out-of-class viewing. It was suggested earlier that when many language learners try to watch L2 television on their own they may be discouraged from subsequent viewing because of a lack of comprehension. One goal of classroom-based extensive viewing is to make students aware that when they have reached the appropriate vocabulary size, they should be able to understand and enjoy watching L2 television. The teacher's job is to show students that this is possible, as well as to teach them strategies to support their comprehension when they are watching television outside of the classroom.

Principle 6. Learners should watch L2 television as much as possible. Encouraging learners to watch as much L2 television as possible draws on Day & Bamford's (2002) ten principles for extensive reading (see also Chapter 1 in this book). There may be relatively little gained through viewing L2 television if it is rarely or occasionally watched. However, if L2 television is watched often over a long period of time, then there may be substantial development in vocabulary knowledge, listening comprehension, and other aspects of L2 learning.

Extensive viewing can be contrasted with intensive viewing in the classroom, where students watch short clips in order to learn some aspect of language. Although there is also value to this more typical approach to using television in the classroom, the long-term benefits of extensive viewing will likely far outweigh what can be gained through occasional and sporadic viewing. Extensive viewing also differs from how learners may watch television on their own, where comprehension of a program may be challenging and learners may be quickly discouraged. It is the supportive environment of the classroom-based learning program that may help to move learners beyond the point where they are discouraged by imprecise comprehension.

Applications

One of the positive features of an extensive viewing program is that L2 television programs are a widely available resource for language learning. They can often be viewed on television in foreign language contexts, watched online, rented from DVD shops, or purchased. It is best for students to watch in a context where they have control of the material. A format such as DVD or online streaming is ideal, because it is possible to have repeated viewings of an episode.

Selection of programs for out-of-class viewing should be according to interests. What is interesting and entertaining for one learner may be dull and displeasing for another. Making students aware of the approaches to support comprehension in out-of-class extensive viewing is more important than the choice of programs. Students should be taught about the value of using a narrow viewing approach that begins with episode 1 of season 1, as well as watching the same episode more than once when comprehension is particularly challenging. Similarly, students should be encouraged to continue watching television if they are enjoying the content, but do not have precise comprehension.

Teachers should use two criteria to select a television program for classroom-based extensive viewing. First, the selected program should be one that students are likely to be interested in and excited to watch. In a narrow viewing approach where different episodes of a single program are watched, this is particularly important because, if students enjoy the selected program, they are more likely to be motivated to watch subsequent episodes, attend to the language during viewing, and notice their learning gains. The second criterion for selection is the lexical profile of the television program. Freely available lexical profiling software such as RANGE (Nation & Heatley, 2002) and VocabProfile on Tom Cobb's Compleat Lexical Tutor site allow teachers to analyze the scripts of episodes that are available online to determine the proportion of words at different frequency levels that occur in the scripts. Programs that are easier to understand tend to contain a higher proportion of high frequency words than those that contain a higher proportion of lower frequency words. Teachers can quickly use lexical profiling software to get an indication of the lexical difficulty of different programs.

Payoffs and Pitfalls

There are several challenges to implementing an extensive viewing program. Perhaps the greatest challenge is getting everyone involved to buy into the educational value of language learning through extensive viewing. Because of the fact that television is typically viewed as a form of entertainment rather than a source of learning, many people are likely to be sceptical about the benefits of regular L2 television viewing in the classroom. Educating all stake holders about the value of having students watch L2 television regularly is a necessary prerequisite for classroom-based extensive viewing. Teachers may be hesitant to include extensive viewing in a language-learning program if their colleagues and program directors are not aware of the related language-learning benefits. Students may also struggle to understand why something designed to entertain is taking up a portion of classroom time. Moreover, the parents of younger students are unlikely to be enthusiastic about a television-based learning course without being informed of the reasons why extensive viewing is useful.

A second challenge is having teachers accept a supporting role in an extensive viewing program rather than a central teacher-fronted role. In other words, teachers may have a difficult time simply letting their students have continued silent uninterrupted viewing of L2 television. However, it is important that classroom-based extensive viewing does not get broken down into watching short segments with the learners focused on completing intensive learning activities. This will move the nature of viewing away from comprehension of meaning-focused input and toward a more language-focused orientation. Instead pre-learning activities that aim to support comprehension and meaning-focused post-viewing activities that have the objective of consolidating knowledge may be most useful.

A third challenge to extensive viewing is setting up a classroom-based program that involves regular viewing over time. If the greatest language-learning gains made through extensive viewing come from outside of the classroom, it is fair to question the value of implementing a classroom-based extensive viewing program. Furthermore, there might be a belief among teachers that students can simply watch a target L2 television program on their own at home, and that valuable teaching time should be spent on language-focused instruction. However, it is critical that extensive viewing first takes place in the classroom. There are several reasons for this. First, it shows students the value that is being placed on meaning-focused language learning with television. If extensive viewing is dismissed as belonging solely outside of the classroom, then many students may not take the task of viewing seriously or quickly give up. Students are more likely to focus their efforts on the aspects of language learning that are emphasized inside the classroom. Second, initial classroom-based viewing ensures that students watch L2 television in an environment where their comprehension can be supported. Third, regular classroom-based viewing over time with support may help students to reach the point where they are motivated to start the same process outside of the classroom. Furthermore, as more and more language learners begin to watch L2 television, there may be a snowball effect where the value of television as an L2 learning resource becomes better known and more and more learners are encouraged to develop knowledge through extensive viewing. Similarly, because of the popularity of L1 television within society, extensive viewing programs may motivate less proficient learners to reach the point where they can begin a classroom-based extensive viewing program.

Discussion Questions

1. To what extent do you currently use television as a resource for language learning?
2. What are the advantages and disadvantages of using television as material for language learning?
3. Who could benefit from participating in an extensive viewing program?
4. What are the challenges to implementing a classroom-based extensive viewing program in your context?
5. What are the challenges for students moving from a classroom-based extensive viewing program to out-of-class extensive viewing?

Resources

Television shows are widely available. Purchasing DVDs of full seasons of programs is perhaps the most useful way to acquire the materials for classroom-based extensive viewing. This would allow the development of libraries of different programs. Glossaries, background information, and perceived difficulty levels could be created for each new program over time to support comprehension. Television programs can also be purchased in the same way for out-of-class extensive viewing. However, they may often be streamed online at the sites of the networks that air the programs, or purchased for download. Moreover, rental shops may also stock L2 television programs. Thus, if the technological resources are available to students, it should be relatively easy to find material available for extensive viewing.

References

Cobb, T. (2007). Computing the vocabulary demands of L2 reading. *Language Learning and Technology*, 11(3), 38–63.

Day, R., & Bamford, J. (2002). Top ten principles for teaching extensive reading. *Reading in a Foreign Language*, 14(2), 136–141.

Dowhower, S. L. (1987). Effects of repeated reading on second-grade transitional readers' fluency and comprehension. *Reading Research Quarterly*, 22, 389–406.

Horst, M., Cobb, T., & Meara, P. (1998). Beyond *A Clockwork Orange*: Acquiring second language vocabulary through reading. *Reading in a Foreign Language*, 11, 207–223.

Nation, I.S.P., & Heatley, A. (2002). Range: A program for the analysis of vocabulary in texts [software].

Nation, I.S.P. (2006). How large a vocabulary is needed for reading and listening? *The Canadian Modern Language Review*, 63, 59–82.

OECD (2007). *Communications Outlook 2007*. Paris: OECD. Retrieved from http://213.253.134.43/oecd/pdfs/browseit/9307021E.PDF

Rice, M. L., & Woodsmall, L. (1988). Lessons from television: Children's word learning when viewing. *Child Development*, 59(2), 420–429.

Rodgers, M.P.H. (2013). English language learning through viewing television: An investigation of comprehension, incidental vocabulary acquisition, lexical coverage, attitudes, and captions (Unpublished PhD thesis). Victoria University of Wellington, Wellington, New Zealand.

Rodgers, M.P.H., & Webb, S. (2011). Narrow viewing: The vocabulary in related television programs. *TESOL Quarterly*, 45(4), 689–717.

Statistics Canada (1998). *Average time spent on activities, by sex*. Ottawa, Ontario. Retrieved from http://www40.statcan.ca/l01/cst01/famil36a.htm

United States Department of Labor (2006). *American time use survey summary*. Washington, D.C. Retrieved from http://www.bls.gov/news.release/atus.nr0.htm

Webb, S. (2007). The effects of repetition on vocabulary knowledge. *Applied Linguistics*, 28, 46–65.

Webb, S. (2009). The potential for vocabulary learning through watching television and movies (Distinguished lecturer series). Temple University Japan, Osaka, Japan.

Webb, S. (2010a). Pre-learning low frequency vocabulary in second language television programs. *Language Teaching Research*, 14(4), 501–515.

Webb, S. (2010b). A corpus driven study of the potential for vocabulary learning through watching movies. *International Journal of Corpus Linguistics*, 15(4), 497–519.

Webb, S. (2010c). Using glossaries to increase the lexical coverage of television programs. *Reading in a Foreign Language*, 22(1), 201–221.

Webb, S. A., & Chang, A, C-S, (2012). Vocabulary learning through assisted and unassisted repeated reading. *Canadian Modern Language Review*, 68(3), 267–290.

Webb, S., & Rodgers, M.P.H. (2009a). The lexical coverage of movies. *Applied Linguistics*, 30(3), 407–427.

Webb, S., & Rodgers, M.P.H. (2009b). The vocabulary demands of television programs. *Language Learning*, 59(2), 335–366.

Winke, P., Gass, S., & Sydorenko, T. (2010). The effects of captioning videos used for foreign language listening activities. *Language Learning & Technology*, 14(1), 65–86.

PART IV

Out-of-Class Projects

17

AUTHENTIC MATERIALS AND PROJECT-BASED LEARNING

In Pursuit of Accuracy

Jennifer Grode & Adrienne Stacy

Introduction and Overview

It is a common expectation that advanced ESL speakers can express their thoughts both fluently *and* accurately. However, addressing spoken accuracy can be a daunting challenge for language teachers and students alike, as so much of what is done in the era of communicative language teaching is rooted in building confidence and fluency, sometimes at the expense of accuracy. Students thus often struggle to produce accurate grammatical, pronunciation, and discourse-style features (here, features encompassing register, style, and dialect distinctions). They also may feel frustrated without explicit feedback on how to fix these types of errors. So while fluency and confidence are undeniably important—and often the goal of self-directed study—accuracy is still critical to student success, especially as students advance into more academic or professional realms.

How can accuracy be fostered, though, outside of a traditional ESL course? In this chapter, one means of doing so is discussed. By using authentic materials and focusing on self-guided, project-based learning, students notice target structures and then practice them until they develop automaticity. The project explored is, therefore, primarily an exercise in shadowing, a common practice in pronunciation classrooms in which students imitate short segments of native (or native-like) speech. In practice, however, this multistage project becomes much more.

The first phase involves pairing students strategically based on L1 backgrounds, problem areas, and/or goals. (A student working outside the realm of the classroom may seek out a friend with whom to undertake the project, or do it alone.) Students choose a short, 2–3 minute movie or television scene clip that tells a contained story and has approximately equal speaking parts. After selecting a scene, students work together to transcribe it, then annotate its salient pronunciation features. The goal at this point is then to orally reproduce the scene, so that the performance of it sounds as close as possible to the original. If a student is working independently, he or she can focus his or her attention on just one character, allowing the clip itself to act as a "partner." After extensive practice, the scene can either be performed live and recorded or overdubbed into the original scene. Students completing this project as part of a class then receive teacher and peer feedback. Alternatively, students undertaking self-directed study can simply watch their performance and compare it to the original in order to self-assess (Burston, 2005).

In the second phase, students write either a sequel or a prequel to their scene. This means that they must not only match the characters' style of interaction, but also think specifically about language features used in the original to create an accurate extension. After getting feedback on their script from a teacher or English speaking friend, and once again practicing extensively, they can perform the original scene once more, as well as the sequel or prequel. As in the first phase, teacher, peer, and/or self-assessments can provide students with feedback.

In the final phase, students again create their own script, but this time by revisiting the original scene and shifting its discourse style. For example, if their original scene was conversational and used slang, they might adjust the style into a more formal manner of speaking. They may also examine the relationships between the characters. For example, if the original scene is a conversation between friends, the students might choose to change the relationship in order to examine the language of power distance. This phase thus allows students to investigate different registers and dialects and to have fun changing the vocabulary, grammar, and pronunciation features of their scene. Again, students perform the original scene first, followed by the discourse style-shifted scene, and then receive feedback and reflect upon that feedback and their progress in general.

Vignette

A Japanese woman in her late 20s, Keiko had been studying English on and off for years—in both Japanese and American universities—when she joined our program. Her outgoing personality and the value she placed on authentic communication allowed her to achieve a high level of fluency, though as her goal in speaking was often simply to get her point across, her accuracy suffered. Intent on fixing this deficit in order to apply for translation and interpretation MA programs, she enrolled in our Accuracy in Spoken English class.

Keiko's limitations in language use spanned across the previously mentioned categories: pronunciation, grammar, and discourse style. She frequently made errors with subject/verb agreement and verb tense and aspect. She also had pronunciation issues that are fairly common among native Japanese speakers, such as difficulty differentiating between /l/ and /r/ and difficulty producing certain vowel sounds. Furthermore, as a result of only using English up to that point for communication with peers, her vocabulary was informal and she used inaccurate word forms.

Keiko worked on this project with another Japanese student who had similar challenges and was consequently able to delve deeply into fixing her ingrained issues. For the project, Keiko and her partner selected a scene from the American TV show *Sex and the City*. This scene was of high interest, as Keiko already enjoyed the show. However, this scene was also selected strategically, as it provided the opportunity to practice specific features previously identified as problem areas.

The pair worked through each of the three phases of the project. During the first phase, they listened to their scene repeatedly in order to transcribe it and then annotated features such as reductions and intonation in the transcript. Next they practiced with the transcript, in an effort to focus on the specific features they had marked. Finally, they shadowed the original scene by listening to a few seconds of the original at a time, pausing it, and then attempting to imitate it perfectly, giving one another feedback as they went along. Keiko recorded several of these shadowing exercises so she could listen to the original and the imitation back-to-back. This provided her with recorded evidence of the mistakes she was making, raising awareness of her own deficits so that she could continue to improve. These recordings ultimately acted as a record of her considerable progress over time.

As the pair moved into the sequel/prequel phase, they were able to extend their primary focus from accuracy in pronunciation to accuracy in all three areas previously mentioned. Indeed, by co-creating her own script, Keiko was required to produce her own accurate grammar structures and match the discourse style of the original scene. This was the most challenging phase for her, due to the fact that she was forced to pay attention to tense/aspect as well as accurate word choice and vocabulary. However, through extensive revisions and peer feedback during the writing process, she and her partner were able to produce a mostly accurate scene. Additionally, through the chance to perform the original scene again, Keiko showed steady improvement from her initial performance.

The project's final phase again built on the skills from the previous two phases, with the addition of a shift in discourse style. Due to Keiko's previously mentioned interpersonal skills, she already had some knowledge of American slang and dialects. For the project, though, Keiko decided to focus on a specific discourse style commonly associated with her new home in California—that of surfers. This dialect has been immortalized and, to a certain extent, exaggerated in such films as *Fast Times at Ridgemont High* and *Bill and Ted's Excellent Adventure*. In order to determine not only the vocabulary and grammar necessary for the rewrite of the *Sex and the City* scene, but also the intonation patterns used, Keiko did extensive research. She and her partner watched scenes from the aforementioned movies, but decided they were too exaggerated and searched for more modern and authentic examples. Fortunately, she lived in an area where she could walk a few blocks down to the beach to listen and talk to native speakers of this style. She also found other films and interviews highlighting similar speech. While she understood that there was variation within the dialect, she collected enough data to successfully "translate" her scene to this discourse style.

As Keiko moved from imitating a native speaker verbatim to producing language in a new discourse style, she learned more about her own patterns of errors—including those she previously never realized she was making. This resulted in Keiko ultimately improving her day-to-day speech by using a wider variety of accurate grammatical structures, self-correcting more frequently, and developing strategies for overcoming communication breakdowns resulting from errors. Through evaluations from Keiko and other students, we learned that the project, while challenging and time-consuming, was effective and enjoyable.

Principles

So why does this project work and what are the underlying principles that foster its effectiveness? At its core, the project embodies the following principles, which we believe are critical to growth in spoken accuracy:

> *Principle 1. Base input on authentic materials.* In today's language classrooms, teachers are expanding the range of materials used beyond the traditional textbook and empowering students to become a part of the materials selection process. With the spread of communicative language teaching, many language teachers have shifted away from a textbook-centered curriculum (Kumaravadivelu, 2003). These teachers assert that *authentic materials*, or those materials "that occur naturally in the target language environment and that have not been created or edited expressly for language learners" (Larimer & Schleicher, 1999, p. v), are largely superior to *instructional materials*, or those that, in contrast, are created for pedagogic purposes. Authentic materials are purported to increase students' interest in learning, capitalize on students' pre-existing literacies, and maximize the "naturalness" of received linguistic input (Larimer & Schleicher, 1999). Therefore, allowing students to interact with actual English-language films and TV shows is a core part of this project.
>
> Many researchers and instructors also criticize instructional materials for not adequately conveying cultural content (Cortazzi & Jin, 1999), while praising authentic materials as "giv[ing] students direct access to the culture and help[ing] them use the new language authentically themselves, to communicate meaning in meaningful situations" (Melvin & Stout, 1987, p. 44). Thus the cultural component of this project is certainly a strength; indeed, for Keiko, who also had the goal of finding and using a strong female voice in English, the cultural aspects of her chosen scene, in which she engaged in an argument, were particularly powerful.
>
> While there is still much debate as to what actually constitutes *authenticity* in the language classroom (Gilmore, 2007; Roberts & Cooke, 2009; van Lier, 1996), the debate is primarily important in terms of how learners themselves perceive and value it. Chavez's 1998 study determined that of twelve identified *authenticity factors, native speaker inception* was most critical in students' judging a

material to be authentic. This factor was also related to learners' viewing texts or activities as positive contributions to their learning, as well as to their reporting enjoyment in using those texts or activities (Chavez, 1998). Given the nature of this project, then, it is important for students to choose a scene that they perceive as authentic. Of course students may choose to imitate speakers with different accents or dialects, but it is important for them to be invested in the accent or dialect they choose as one that is aligned with their goals.

Principle 2. Strive for automaticity. In terms of spoken accuracy, one of the biggest challenges seems to be automaticity in use. Keiko, for example, could frequently identify and correct her own errors if stopped during a turn, but would continue to make the same errors shortly after. One of the ways we have found to naturally build automaticity is in using a more cyclical "syllabus," in which concepts or objectives are continually reviewed and retaught. But even in the context of a single lesson or practice period, this strategy can be maximized through exposure to rich linguistic input, in addition to multiple opportunities to practice target concepts and structures in context, as Keiko did with her /l/ and /ɹ/ contrast at each phase of the project.

In other words, the facilitation of extensive practice is also an underlying principle of improving spoken accuracy, for the basic notion of repetition in teaching is a solid one that can lead to automaticity of use (DeKeyser, 1996; Gatbonton & Segalowitz, 1988). Indeed, while many teachers associate the word "drill" with thoughts of rote grammar practice and correspondingly bored students (Gatbonton & Segalowitz, 1988), most students actually "judge drills to be useful" (Peters, Weinberg, & Sarma, 2009, p. 893) and revel in some sense of routine that allows them to become increasingly confident in their own abilities. Of course, the "drills" used must be meaningful and extended in order to be effective (Ellis, 2006). Therefore, practicing with an authentic movie scene in a cyclical, repetitive way can be a powerful tool, in that "being able to execute a basic repertoire of ... phrases with little effort enables a learner to perform other aspects of speaking more easily and fluently" (Gatbonton & Segalowitz, 1988, p. 476).

Principle 3. Raise awareness. Just as Keiko did, most students who complete this project note a distinct increase in awareness of their speech, as well as a greater awareness of English in general. This awareness is perhaps at the heart of strategically improving spoken accuracy. Svalberg (2007) writes more generally about a language awareness approach to teaching and summarizes its five primary features—the first four of which are discussed below as underlying principles of the spoken accuracy project.

The first feature of this approach is the "ongoing investigation" of language (Svalberg, 2007, p. 290), a process which is very learner-centered, as students have the opportunity to explore and engage in a language itself.

When Keiko conducted research at each stage of the project, she was, in some sense, participating in this type of investigation. Additional supports in class extended the investigation, as inductive mini-lessons were conducted on topics from relative clauses to politeness in speech acts.

The second feature of the approach involves "talking analytically" (p. 291) about language, which students do as they analyze and check their transcripts and begin shadowing and comparing their production to the original. In this sense, the process is similar to the concept of *languaging* (Swain, 2006), whereby students' interactions "mediat[e] [their] language learning by drawing attention to languagerelated problems they [have]" (pp. 105–106). While in our experience this process is more generally used in the writing classroom, it can certainly be extended to the oral communication classroom with positive effects.

The third feature of a language awareness approach involves interaction, which promotes awareness through feedback, reflection, and negotiation. Keiko engaged in focused interaction with the scene daily, and with her partner and teachers three or four times a week. This combination of approaches was particularly effective in maximizing achievement.

The fourth feature includes "learning skills," which foster independence (Svalberg, 2007, p. 291). We believe this aspect came into play through in-class scaffolding, as well as through additional support activities, such as self-recording and transcription, with subsequent coding and tracking of error types. The project thus seems at every stage to emphasize the importance of language awareness, especially as described in this particular approach.

Principle 4. Foster autonomy. Discussing autonomy in entirely self-directed learning is almost redundant, but within a blended or strictly classroom environment, giving students options and opportunities for self-directed learning can "enhance intrinsic motivation because they allow people a greater feeling of autonomy" (Ryan & Deci, 2000, p. 70). Ryan & Deci go on to identify autonomy as key to promoting self-motivation, which is essential to the development of spoken accuracy in a second language. Without it, students will almost inevitably fall into old patterns of errors, much like Keiko before her enrollment in our class.

In other words, allowing students choice as much as possible helps invest them in the learning process and empowers them to extend their sense of ownership and autonomy beyond a project into other realms of language learning (Kumaravadivelu, 2003). Keiko, for example, indicated both in oral and written reflections on the project that she felt this sense of empowerment as she chose her own scene and made decisions about how to extend it and adapt it. Her continued growth and development after leaving our classroom suggest empowerment leads to improvement.

Applications

While this project was originally conceptualized as part of an advanced-level elective course, in which students were encouraged to tailor their work to fit their own needs, not all programs offer such courses and many teachers lack the freedom to stray from a curriculum. Teachers who are interested in implementing this project could do so as part of an oral communication class with student learning outcomes that include presentations. For while the student is not necessarily disseminating information about a topic in this project, many of the other skills are the same—especially in the first and second stages. Of course, a learner of any language could undertake all or part of this project as independent practice. With the availability of clips online, it is easy to find something to practice with—even if a student is simply interested in improving pronunciation through shadowing.

With that said, we do suggest some guidelines. Students undertaking some or all of the components of the project should be at a proficiency level that allows them to understand structures, even if they do not necessarily use them. In other words, while lower-level students can complete (and have completed) variations of this project in a classroom environment with teacher support, advanced learners may benefit more from the exercises we have mentioned due to their ability to identify and correct their own mistakes, even if they must transcribe them first. This is especially true when talking about self-directed study. Additionally, as the project is somewhat hierarchical with each phase building more skills, it is important that students begin with the first foundational phase. The remaining phases are optional or could be rearranged, depending on time and goals.

Payoffs and Pitfalls

This project can be very effective for a learner who is willing to invest time and effort to imitate authentic language. Students develop a greater understanding of the components that go into spoken accuracy, while practicing those components simultaneously. They gain not only a new awareness of their own specific problems, but also a measure of their own personal growth as English speakers. Since this project is primarily learner-centered, it allows students autonomy, which leads to a level of buy-in that not all projects have. It is also fun—students enjoy working on this project and practicing structures that they might otherwise find dull. Even for students who may be shy or reserved, the first phase has enough structure to ease them into the more creative and demanding second and third phases. Additionally, since one of the few requirements is that they choose a scene from a movie or television show in the target culture, their level of cultural awareness, particularly pragmatics, is subsequently raised.

Of course, there are pitfalls to any project. Since we stressed selecting a scene strategically, many students spent too much time finding the perfect scene; occasionally this was due to being unfamiliar with American popular culture.

Therefore, it is important for teachers to have some backup scenes to suggest to struggling students. Another challenge to overcome, particularly in the case of a student working on this project independently, is the danger of feeling over-whelmed. Most students have many problems they wish to work on and have trouble prioritizing them. Addressing every issue is not the goal here; students attempting this project on their own are encouraged to focus on a few of their problems at a time—focusing first, for example, on clarity of speech before rate of speech. A student working independently should ensure that they pay particular attention to their own recordings of shadowing practice. Constantly comparing their own recordings to the original and seeking feedback from more advanced speakers should be good "checks" on progress.

This project and its accompanying supports allow students—whether in a classroom or studying on their own—to work strategically and efficiently on improving their spoken accuracy through extensive and intensive listening, shad-owing, and ultimately original speech production. In each phase of the project, marked progress in pronunciation, grammar, and appropriate discourse style—especially related to overcoming ingrained errors—can be made and celebrated.

Discussion Questions

1. For students working on the project described in this chapter in pairs, the authors suggest working with someone who shares a first language, or at least similar accuracy deficits. Do you think this is the best approach? Could you make a case for pairing students with entirely different weaknesses?
2. The authors mention that this project could be scaled down to take a shorter amount of time both in and outside of class. How could that be done with-out losing the benefits mentioned in the chapter?
3. The authors emphasize accuracy in *discourse style*, which is not as frequently mentioned in the literature as, say, grammar. Do you think this is an impor-tant area to cover in an oral communication class? What are other ways for students to investigate or practice appropriate discourse style outside of class?
4. Some students are wary of using technology. How could the ideas in this chapter be adapted for technophobes? How about for students and teachers that don't have access to technology?
5. What other ways can you think of for a student to independently practice spoken accuracy? What other creative ways can teachers incorporate accu-racy-related tasks into existing courses?

Resources

Short movie scenes, searchable by title, genre, etc. —movieclips.com
Practice activities centered on movie clips, searchable by grammar point—moviesegmentstoaddressgrammargoals.blogspot.com.br
Pronunciation tutorials and shadowing exercises for scaffolding and practice—*rachelsenglish.com*

References

Burston, J. (2005). Video dubbing projects in the foreign language curriculum. *CALICO Journal*, 23(1), 79–92.

Chavez, M. M. (1998). Learners' perspectives on authenticity. *IRAL*, 26(4), 277–306.

Cortazzi, M., & Jin, L. (1999). Cultural mirrors: Materials and methods in the EFL classroom. In E. Hinkel (Ed.), *Culture in second language teaching and learning* (pp. 196–220). Cambridge, UK: Cambridge University Press.

DeKeyser, R.M. (1996). Exploring automatization processes. *TESOL Quarterly*, 30, 349–357.

Duarte, S.A., & Escobar, L.A. (2008). Using adapted material and its impact on university students' motivation. *Profile*, 9, 63–87.

Ellis, R. (2006). Current issues in the teaching of grammar: An SLA perspective. *TESOL Quarterly*, 40(1), 83–107.

Gatbonton, E., & Segalowitz, N. (1988). Creative automatization: Principles for promoting fluency within a communicative framework. *TESOL Quarterly*, 22(3), 473–492.

Gilmore, A. (2007). Authentic materials and authenticity in foreign language learning. *Language Teaching*, 40, 97–118.

Kumaravadivelu, B. (2003). *Beyond methods: Macrostrategies for language teaching*. New Haven, CT: Yale University Press.

Larimer, R. E., & Schleicher, L. (Eds.). (1999). *New ways in using authentic materials in the classroom*. Alexandria, VA: Teachers of English to Speakers of Other Languages.

Melvin, B. S., & Stout, D. S. (1987). Motivating language learners through authentic materials. In W. Rivers (Ed.), *Interactive language teaching* (pp. 44–56). New York: Cambridge University Press.

Peters, M., Weinberg, A., & Sarma, N. (2009). To like or not to like! Student perceptions of technological activities for learning French as a second language at five Canadian universities. *Canadian Modern Language Review*, 65(5), 869–896.

Roberts, C., & Cooke, M. (2009). Authenticity in the adult ESOL classroom and beyond. *TESOL Quarterly*, 43(4), 620–642.

Ryan, R. M., & Deci, E. (2000). Self-determination theory and the facilitation of intrinsic motivation, social development, and well-being. *American Psychologist*, 55(1), 68–78.

Svalberg, G.M.L. (2007). Language awareness and language learning. *Language Teaching*, 40, 287–308.

Swain, M. (2006). Languaging, agency, and collaboration in advanced second language proficiency. In H. Byrnes (Ed.), *Advanced language learning: The contribution of Halliday and Vygotsky* (pp. 95–108). New York: Continuum.

van Lier, L. (1996). *Interaction in the language curriculum: Awareness, autonomy, and authenticity*. London: Longman.

18

LEARNING-TO-LEARN WITH OURSELVES AND WITH OUR PEERS THROUGH TECHNOLOGY

Catarina Pontes & Marilisa Shimazumi

Introduction and Overview

In this study we report on a *learning-to-learn* program carried out with higher-level learners at Cultura Inglesa São Paulo. This study focused on fostering not only peer mediation and co-operative learning experiences but it also aimed at improving students' oral communicative potential.

The technological learning tool used in the out-of-class experience with the aforementioned learners—Common European Framework (CEF) Level C1—was the *VoiceThread*© online program. This cloud application does not need any specific software installation, but it does have some requirements which can be found at https://voicethread.com/about/features/. With this collaborative tool, users can create, comment on and share documents, presentations, images, audio, and video files.

This *VoiceThread*© experiment involved about 30 higher-level learners officially enrolled in a CEF C1 English course at a private language institute in the state of São Paulo, Brazil.

These learners were in the second term of a three-semester course leading towards the Cambridge Proficiency Exam (CPE). They were from two different groups studying in different cities and, in their needs analysis, it was diagnosed that they presented average writing skills, but needed to gain more confidence in their speaking skills.

The idea of working with VoiceThread© was proposed to them after having carried out a diagnostic speaking task in class in which they had to compare and contrast different lifestyles in cities they had been to. The follow-up to this task was for them to find more information on the chosen place at home, produce a short recording (the average oral samples were of approximately two minutes each) and upload it to their restricted area on VoiceThread©. Once all the recordings had been uploaded, teachers and learners would listen to them and record their comments, impressions and general feedback. Learners would then listen to the comments made on their production, and record different versions each time they incorporated aspects they considered relevant from their peers' or teacher's feedback.

This tool played a fundamental role in encouraging self-awareness of students' linguistic performance over the period of a term. Learners reported to having certainly profited from this experience especially because of the interactive nature of the project and the level of awareness raised concerning their speaking skills.

Vignette

Luciana, a 37-year-old translator at the time, who already held the CPE but wanted to keep in contact with the language, was rather sceptical about learning with this sort of technological tool. Nevertheless, throughout the process, she ended up being one of the most active participants in this project. She constantly contributed with both written and oral samples, read and listened to her peers' comments, and gave them feedback in a consistent manner.

Cristiano, a 31-year-old teacher of English in the public sector, was very open to the initiative. However, he had tremendous language issues and needed a lot of support from peers and teachers. Together with Luciana, Cristiano was also extremely involved and contributed immensely to the implementation of the project by posting written and oral comments, as well as responding positively to his peers' work.

Both Luciana & Cristiano saw in VoiceThread© an opportunity to improve their discourse competence (both at aural and written levels) and to have a different audience other than their teacher. The audience consisted of peers who were genuine listeners and readers, who would not hesitate to pose questions for clarification or make suggestions for change. At first, they did not believe very much in the project due to the technological challenges the tool presented at the time (e.g., it was not common for our learners to have microphones to be used with their computers at home). Thus, adaptations had to be made in order to cater to this need (a microphone was installed in the computer used in the classroom, which meant a few minutes of their regular lesson had to be dedicated to the project). While some of the learners were either doing or checking language practice exercises in class, others would do the recording and make their comments.

The main challenge faced by these learners in the beginning was the vulnerability factor because they were exposing themselves and being corrected by their peers. This also led to a face validity issue, as they were uncomfortable in receiving feedback (not always praising them) from somebody who was not their teacher.

As time went by, Luciana & Cristiano not only saw the advantage of giving and receiving peer feedback, but also started to notice the benefits the project offered them and how much they were developing. This progress went beyond their linguistic gain, and was also noticed in the way they developed trust amongst themselves, built group cohesiveness and worked collaboratively in the editing of the posts. This collaborative process contributed to the development of most of the skills which are desired in the twenty-first century, such as critical thinking, problem solving, communication, and collaboration as well as information, media, and technology skills recommend by 21st Century Skills (see www.21stcenturyskills.org).

A collaborative cycle of work, such as the one implemented in this project, consisted of (1) the teacher setting the task and having learners perform it; (2) learners would then analyse, select, and evaluate the information gathered and proceed to organising the texts for their posts; (3) the material would then be made available on their VoiceThread$^{©}$ restricted area for peers and teachers to comment on and respond to; (4) learners then had the chance to revisit their work and incorporate (or not) the feedback they received by producing a new post; which led to (5) a new opportunity to receive further feedback. This last move would conclude the cycle and the teacher could (6) proceed to a new project, resuming a new collaborative cycle of work.

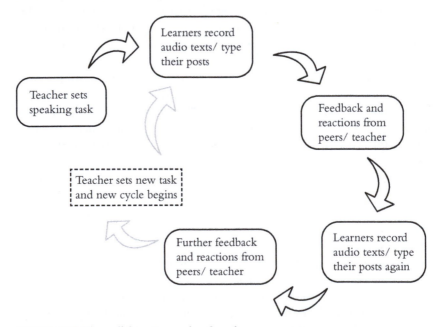

FIGURE 18.1 The collaborative cycle of work.

Everything was documented and made available to all learners in both groups. A visual representation of the collaborative cycle of work is described in Figure 18.1.

Principles

The design and implementation of this project has as main theoretical pillars Knowles et al.'s (2005) six principles of andragogy (i.e., the teaching of adults) and Kolb's (1983) experiential learning cycle which comprises four stages. Moreover, the role of 21st Century Skills (with a special focus on language learning) in this process was of vital importance, especially because of the relevance of life and career skills in learners' lives, as well as covering and developing the four Cs—critical thinking, communication, collaboration, and creativity. This process was also permeated by another important sphere of 21st Century Skills—information, media, and technology skills—all of which were inherent in the program proposed to learners involved in this project.

The andragogical principles referred to above (Knowles et al., 2005) aim at better understanding how adult learners gain knowledge more effectively and in which ways teachers can contribute to these students' successful learning experience. The experiential cycle (Kolb, 1983) illustrates the process which learners (especially adults) can go through while developing their language skills. As for the twenty-first-century skills previously mentioned, they functioned as a gateway to putting into practice the theoretical pillars of andragogy and experiential learning.

The six principles underpinning our project adapted from the work of Knowles and Kolb are as follows:

Principle 1. Ensure that learners know why they have to learn a particular thing. Knowing why they have to learn something beforehand helps adults to invest the right amount of energy and dedication in the process.

Principle 2. Respect learners' self-concept and sense of self-direction. Adults are self-directed and might resent it when others tell them what to do.

Principle 3. Make learners' experiences central to the learning process. Taking into account what learners already know can maximize and contribute to the learning experience.

Principle 4. Match instruction to learners' needs. Adults are motivated to learn when instructional content matches what they need to learn.

Principle 5. Ensure links between the teaching/learning context and the real world. When faced with real-life situations, adult learners tend to be more focused and willing to learn.

Principle 6. Focus on intrinsic motivation. External factors may trigger motivation, but what really drive adults to learn are internal factors (such as quality of life and self-esteem).

In this project, we tried to cater to adult learners' needs by taking into account the principles above. They knew why they had to publish their posts (e.g., to share knowledge, develop language skills, give and receive peer feedback); their background experience was taken into account, as they had the opportunity to choose the content of and the language to be used in their posts; and with the feedback peers gave to each other learners were able to perceive progress and kept on task throughout the process. Kolb's experiential learning cycle came into practice when students posted their production based on their own experience (CE—concrete experience), reflected upon the feedback received (RO—reflective observation), revisited their work in the light of the comments peers made (AC—abstract conceptualisation), and uploaded their revised and improved contributions (AE—active experimentation).

Our visual adaptation and application of Kolb's experiential learning cycle is illustrated in Figure 18.2.

In Figure 18.2, the components of *search for knowledge and experience*, *decision making*, and *further critical reflection* functioned as a bridge to the aforementioned 21st Century Skills, especially if we take into account critical thinking, communication, collaboration, and creativity, with the help of media and technology skills.

For a learning experience to be memorable and effective then, it is not enough to simply go through it. Learners should reflect upon the experience, learn from it and be able to apply the knowledge and experience gained in other contexts and

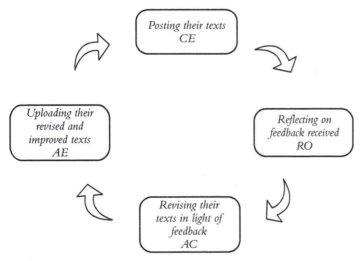

FIGURE 18.2 Students' cycle of learning.
(Adapted from Rogers, 2002, p. 110)

situations, especially with the support and collaboration of their peers and teacher, who will facilitate the process of making assumptions and formulating concepts. These will then be reapplied to similar contexts, when this knowledge will be tried out. It is the learners' role to make the connection between the learning in the classroom and out-of-classroom situations.

Applications

Learners, in general, can certainly benefit from this distance-learning experience for a number of positive reasons, such as flexibility and convenience (learners can manage both their study time and the place from where they will publish their posts, without the pressure of having a fixed time and place to do it); choice and autonomy (learners can choose how many times they want to record and change their versions before posting them); its collaborative nature involving intense peer mediation and intervention (learners can give and get feedback from their peers while preparing their presentations), and above all the opportunity it offers learners to improve their oral communicative potential.

The VoiceThread[©] project can favour more independent learners who are familiar with technology and also cater to those more introvert ones who might feel overexposed and vulnerable to speak in front of a group. Learners who feel disadvantaged in their oral performance would certainly benefit from this project.

This out-of-class learning experience is versatile enough and can be applicable to different groups of learners and levels of proficiency who would be willing to work on a more autonomous and collaborative mode.

Moreover, although the tool used in the project lent itself to helping learners develop primarily their language skills, it was vital for them to improve their interaction with peers from their class and from the other group as well. We can also say that the applicability of the project was immediate, as learners were most times able to incorporate the suggestions made on their posts when revisiting them.

An example of an interaction that took place amongst learners in this study can be seen on the top of the next page. In this example, they gave their opinions and exchanged different points of view on what they believed *carpe diem* meant to them. Similar tasks which involved opinion giving, agreeing and disagreeing on different topics were carried out throughout the project and provided learners with real-life like situations, thus contributing to their development of twenty-first-century skills.

Payoffs and Pitfalls

In our analysis of learners' feedback at the end of the project, we noticed that more positive than negative aspects were mentioned by learners. Overall, it was quite positive for learners to bond outside the classroom and to build this level of trust that allowed them to give peers genuine feedback without compromising their relationship in the classroom. Below we list what learners pointed out as both advantages and disadvantages from their points of view:

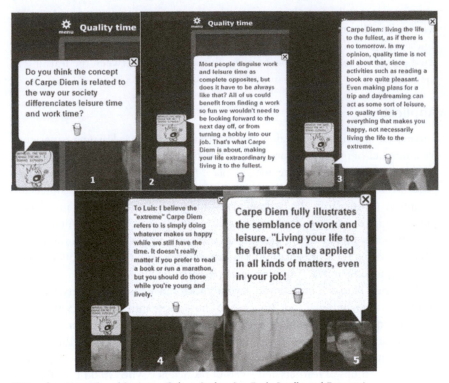

(Taken from VoiceThread Project – Cultura Inglesa São Paulo Intellectual Property)

Advantages

- The first point raised by learners was authenticity—they reported to having felt great improvement in their level of English because of the fact that different people other than their teacher were truly listening to them and giving them feedback on their performance. They felt this was the closest they could get to performing a real-life situation and to being able to gauge how much or how well people would understand the messages they wanted to convey.
- Being able to give and receive peer help and feedback was also pointed out by learners as a positive aspect, once they felt a genuine need to do so because of the nature of the tasks proposed to them. With regard to the first activity they carried out at the beginning of the project (talking about a city they had been to), this reaction was quite natural because of the topic itself.
- Learners also pointed out that the sense of ownership they felt throughout the process kept them engaged in the project and motivated to stay in the course. Seeing their production as materials to be used in the classroom and out of it as well contributed to learners being co-authors of the course and of their learning experience.

- The amount of feedback received (as well as the frequency at which this happened) contributed to learners having a greater sense of accomplishment, especially because most times they were able to incorporate the feedback almost immediately and they had the chance to re-upload an improved version of their posts in the light of the feedback that was given to them.

- Feedback also played a key role in enhancing learners' level of language awareness. After having recorded and posted their contributions, depending on how their peers reacted to their posts, they would revisit their work either in terms of grammar (accuracy), vocabulary (lexical appropriacy), or pronunciation (prosodic features), leading to their linguistic development. This peer mediation also contributed positively towards the development of learners' collaborative skills.

- As stated previously, convenience and flexibility played major roles in the project. Being able to do the recording and publishing the posts at their own time, and from the place they found most convenient, were certainly seen as very positive points by learners, who also mentioned that being able to do things at their own pace contributed to the production of better samples of oral and written texts.

- Last but certainly not least, learners said they had become more self-disciplined; by being responsible for the development of the project and because of the commitment learners had with each other, they felt they developed a greater sense of responsibility and discipline as a result of this need to collaborate.

Disadvantages

- At the time the project was carried out, not all learners had at home (or at work) the equipment needed to record their posts; therefore, it took them longer to publish their contributions because they had to have some spare time to stay in class to do it.

- Still on the subject of equipment, depending on the quality of the device learners had available, the recording produced was not quite clear and therefore made it harder for students to listen to. The suggested procedure was then for learners to spend some extra minutes in class and use the equipment available there, which was of better quality.

- Because some of the learners were not exactly familiar with technology (some were actually technophobes), there was some resistance from their part in getting involved in the project. Only after these digital immigrants started witnessing the first positive results were they more motivated to get involved and share their posts with their peers.

- Although some learners found it easier to manage their own time, others found it extremely hard to discipline themselves to finding the time to contribute to the out-of-class project. The approach taken in class to this issue was to invite learners who had been successfully able to manage their time to share how they had done so and advise their peers on how they could also organise themselves to get involved in the project.

• A last point of attention that was considered a drawback was the fact that some of the learners felt somewhat exposed when they had to post their oral recordings to be commented on by their peers (and to only by their teacher). The work done in class was one to help build an environment of trust and respect together with group cohesiveness, and help learners feel they could work in an out-of-class environment in which there was respect and where they were also building their learner autonomy.

All in all, after having gone through this VoiceThread© project and, as mentioned above, we can certainly state that the benefits outnumber the drawbacks involved in implementing a project of this nature. In the end, we found that the disadvantages of this project were only present in the early stages of implementation and were worked out as the group got more familiar with the experiment, gained more confidence and realised it was worth the investment of their time and, in some cases, even money for the resources (some of the learners invested in equipment to be able to take part in the project from home). Those learners who were quite sceptical at first ended up being persuaded by their peers to join in the project, went the extra mile and even bought a quota so that they could not only upload both their written and oral texts, but they also could upload video snippets alongside their oral production.

Discussion Questions

1. Do you see this as a possible project to be carried out with your learners as an out-of-class experiment? If so, what types of adaptations would you have to implement?
2. Do you think your learners would be open to receiving feedback from their peers? Would it be necessary to have an awareness-raising process with them prior to the implementation of this project?
3. Are your school and your program flexible enough to offer projects of this nature? If not, how could you adapt it?
4. Do your learners have the minimum equipment needed for the experiment? If not, does your school have it/would be willing to have it?
5. How do you think your learners could benefit from this experiment? Do you think this project could help them become more independent and autonomous learners?
6. What would the limitations and constraints be to implement this project in your context? How would you deal with them?

Resources

http://www.p21.org/our-work/p21-framework

References

Knowles, M., Holton III, E., & Swanson, R. (2005). *The adult learner*. Burlington, UK: Butterworth-Heinemann.

Kolb, D. (1983). *Experiential learning: Experience as the source of learning and development*. Englewood Cliffs, NJ: Prentice Hall.

McGrath, I. (2002). *Materials evaluation and design for language teaching*. Edinburgh: Edinburgh Textbooks in Applied Linguistics.

Mishan, F. (2005). *Designing authenticity into language learning materials*. Bristol, UK: Intellect Books.

Rogers, A. (2002). *Teaching adults*, 3rd ed. Glasgow: Open University Press.

19

INTEGRATING CLASSROOM LEARNING AND AUTONOMOUS LEARNING

Leonardo A. Mercado

Introduction and Overview

This chapter will define classroom and autonomous learning integration (CALI) as a concept and discuss the main features of programs that exemplify its application at an institutional level. We will highlight two initiatives that have been applied to thousands of students at the Instituto Cultural Peruano Norteamericano (ICPNA) binational center in Lima, Peru: the Autonomous Learning Project (ALP) and the ICPNA Online Graded Reading Program. The insights that have been learned from these initiatives will be described and suggestions offered for those who might be interested in implementing similar approaches in their own contexts.

Vignette

In 2005, the academic study program at ICPNA had just been reviewed by an external auditor. The results were less than encouraging since, as a whole, students seemed to be lacking an ability to communicate effectively, particularly when compared to proficiency benchmarks as defined by international standards. Consequently, the Academic Department decided to institute a new and innovative autonomous learning program for students that could serve to complement efforts to boost student performance and achievement levels in the classroom. The first component of the program was introduced as the Autonomous Learning Project, or ALP. For the first time in the binational center's history, project work would become a crucial element of the assessment system. The second component was introduced in 2009 as the ICPNA Online Graded Reading Program after the Academic Department reviewed the literature and concluded that the reading content and practice offered by the curriculum fell far short of what was actually needed. Today, both initiatives represent the pillars of autonomous learning at the ICPNA.

Principles

Principle 1. Foster autonomy through out-of-class learning opportunities. Classroom and autonomous learning integration—CALI—can greatly facilitate success in language learning when it is supported by curricula and assessment systems that place a high value on motivating students to learn independently from classroom instruction. Research has shown that ESL/EFL students who maintain contact with the language outside of class and continue practicing on their own are more likely to attain higher levels of achievement as opposed to those whose language learning is limited to opportunities provided within the confines of their regular face-to-face class sessions (Dornier & Cozier, 2000; Islam, 2011). Moreover, by developing ever-increasing autonomy over the course of a study program, or throughout their "lives as ESL/EFL students," so to speak, they stand a better chance of overcoming many of the limitations and barriers that can characterize more traditional second language learning processes, especially those inherent in EFL settings, where exposure to and opportunities for language practice outside of the classroom can be much more difficult to achieve.

Principle 2. Ensure learner "buy-in" to autonomous learning practices. For CALI, teachers should engage students in autonomous language-learning practices that will contribute to the development of their language skills and help them meet their learning goals. However, unless students see value in what is being asked of them, especially if it will take up some of their valuable personal time, positive affect and motivation may be lacking and thus the endeavor may not succeed (McCombs & Whisler, 1989; Dickenson, 1995). CALI seeks to achieve "buy-in" among students by committing them to a graded inquiry, resolution of a problem, task, or extended project that is not only meaningful and engaging but also a unique opportunity to establish and consolidate friendships among classmates, something which is a particularly attractive feature for younger learners.

Principle 3. Integrate in-class and out-of-class learning. Through CALI, students engage in learning pursuits that complement what they have acquired through formal instruction. Most importantly, CALI also provides them with the means through which they can develop strategies for effective inquiry for research, problem-solving, organization of tasks, self-direction towards the fulfillment of one's responsibilities, self-reflection on aims and outcomes, and even skills in teaching others. These are often recognized to be among the most salient characteristics of successful autonomous learners (Chan, 2001; Nunan, 2003). The assignments they carry out can be done either individually or in groups, but the outcome must be presented in class and represent a unique product that clearly exemplifies the language skills and knowledge that students were able to develop on their own.

Applications

An autonomous learning project extends the learning envelope beyond the traditional paradigm of the classroom setting and offers students increased exposure to comprehensible input in the language since they will search for, read, and use what they can most grasp and consider suitable for the task at hand. For teachers, developing ALP alternatives that are suitable for students can be challenging since there are so many factors to consider (see Figure 19.1). First, teachers must make certain that the project bears some relevance to the course's learning goals and outcomes. Students must also find the alternative interesting and meaningful in order for them to have the motivation to make the effort, collaborate with others, and ultimately produce or perform successfully. In addition, teachers should offer students two or more alternatives, or even the possibility to create their own project (e.g., in accordance with a template and specifications), so that they are given a sense of choice, accountability and overall self-determination with regard to their own learning. Affording students the possibility of choosing among meaningful alternatives is likely to have a positive impact on their motivation to carry out a project, persist in the face of difficulty, and use a variety of strategies in order to attain a successful outcome (Paris & Paris, 2001).

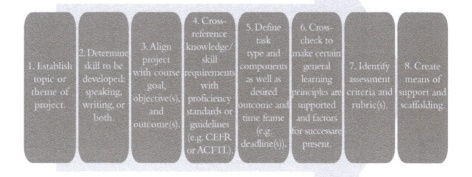

FIGURE 19.1 Steps in creating an ALP that is appropriate for students.

At ICPNA, criteria for evaluation and information about ALP alternatives are provided in print form and online to students throughout the course. Students can also approach their teacher at any time to ask for advice and feedback. Many ALPs require some form of classroom performance on the part of an entire team, so students are reminded several times throughout the month as to how they will be evaluated and how important it is to ensure equal participation on the part of all the team's members. The teacher will assess each member of the team in accordance with predetermined criteria and overall performance. Figure 19.2 shows an example of a scoring rubric for assessing student performance during the presentation of an ALP.

ALP SCORING RUBRIC: Presentations				
Performance Category	0	1	2	Score
Effort	Presentation lacked organization and did not fulfill project requirements.	Presentation followed a logical sequence but only partially fulfilled task requirements.	Presentation was well organized and completely fulfilled project requirements.	
Content	The information was insufficient, irrelevant, or off-task.	There was information that addressed the problem or task, but it seemed incomplete at times.	There was detailed information that addressed the problem or task.	
Language	No attempts to use target language forms.	Some target language forms were present.	Thorough use of target language forms.	
Support	Insufficient visual aids, audio, or video support for presentation.	Some use of visual aids, audio and/or video to support presentation.	Thorough use of visual aids, audio, and/or video to support presentation.	
			Average:	

FIGURE 19.2 Example of an ALP scoring rubric.

In terms of determining whether the ALP endeavor has actually resulted in additional learning, the teacher must assess the end result. What students should make evident is that they have engaged in investigative inquiry through the Internet or other resources, constructing new understandings of the themes, topics, and communicative discourse reflected in the goals of the course. As they work, it would be best if there were support available as needed, such as guidelines and referential rubrics for assessment. But these should not prescribe courses of action or hinder student creativity in terms of expected outcomes. In addition, ALPs should aim to help students develop not only their speaking and writing but also their ability to organize their work, collaborate with others, make decisions, and share accountability. Table 19.1 lists and describes some examples of ALP alternatives.

In practice, the ALP concept has been applied successfully at ICPNA ever since it was first introduced in 2006. Not only has it served to make students more autonomous in their learning, it has also allowed them to learn through the socialization that takes place. Many of them fall in the 14–19 age group, so being able to make friends and work together outside of class through the ALP is important

TABLE 19.1 Examples of Actual ALP Alternatives Used with Students at ICPNA

Name	ICPNA Course Level	Skill	CEFR / ACTFL Level	Summary	Application
Fashion Today!	Basic 4	Speaking & Writing	A1–A2	Make a fashion magazine with pictures of models. Describe each of the models and the clothes they are wearing.	Students will bring their fashion magazine and talk about the contents with their classmates.
Let's Sell!	Basic 12	Speaking	B1	You are representatives of a large technology company at a convention. Convince the audience that your technological products are worth buying. Describe them (2–3) and talk about their features.	Students will talk about their company, product line, features, prices, and comparisons with the competition. Audience will ask questions.
Global Warming & Peru	Intermediate 12	Speaking	B2/C1	As members of the Peruvian Environmental Commission on Global Warming, research the topic and create a project that addresses the issue.	Students should summarize the problem, examples, measures that need to be taken, and what it would cost. The audience asks "challenge" questions.

to them. Consequently, this can increase the chance that they will continue enrolling in the study program, improving retention rates and thus maintaining a steady flow of revenues, a factor of interest to general management. The statistics shown in Figure 19.3 attest to the importance of the ALP.

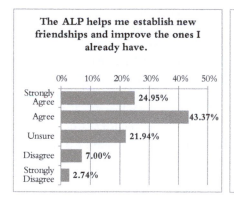

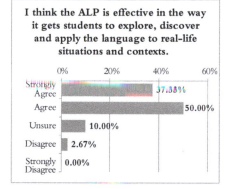

FIGURE 19.3 Selected responses from student (A & B; *n* = 10,024) and teacher (C; *n* = 150) survey results on the ALP/ICPNA Online Graded Reading Program.

Reading has long been advocated as an important source of input to language learning (Krashen, 2004; Schmitt, Jiang, & Grabe, 2011). An effective reading program should provide students with the means to learn through both intensive and extensive reading as well as the support needed to make their success likely. However, how can we make it worthwhile for students to read on their own outside of class, providing opportunities for further language learning and practice? How can we make certain that readings will be both interesting and appropriate for the grade level? And can we maximize student participation without incurring excessive costs that would make such a program unviable? ICPNA has instituted program-level graded reading that addresses these and other issues.

The ICPNA Online Graded Reading Program seeks to significantly increase the students' exposure to English, enhance the development of reading skills and strategies, and promote extensive reading. Also, in order to maximize student access both in terms of availability and cost, it relies on a variety of free, Internet-based readings for each course level. These readings are graded so that they suit course and general proficiency requirements. The overall strategy or goal is to make the intensive reading component of the learning experience as fulfilling as possible so that students feel motivated enough to continue reading beyond what the course actually requires. In other words, under certain conditions, successful intensive reading can and should lead to habitual extensive reading.

Research has established that language learners must have acquired a core of essential vocabulary before they can start to learn independently from context (Nation & Waring, 1997), and that an intermediate level of proficiency may be the minimal threshold level (Rott, 1999). The ICPNA Online Graded Reading Program gradually prepares students to reach this level through a greatly increased focus on reading starting at a basic level of instruction. Each course has an inventory of ten online readings that have been graded, of which five are selected by the teacher or students as alternatives (see Figure 19.4). They complement the readings in the official course book materials. The teacher provides instructions on how to access the readings, make a selection, and prepare for the in-class activity, which may take the form of a speaking or writing task. What is most crucial from the very beginning of the process is that students be provided with the opportunity to choose the reading for the month rather than be told what to read by the teacher. Learner choice in reading materials is one variable that can lead to a greater sense of motivation and improved levels of achievement on the part of second language learners (Grabe, 2009).

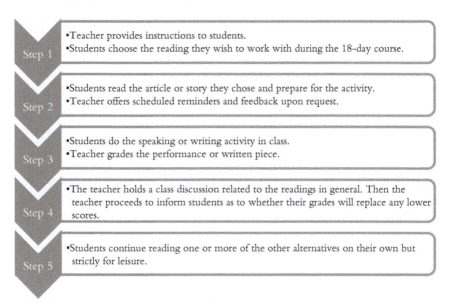

Step 1
•Teacher provides instructions to students.
•Students choose the reading they wish to work with during the 18-day course.

Step 2
•Students read the article or story they chose and prepare for the activity.
•Teacher offers scheduled reminders and feedback upon request.

Step 3
•Students do the speaking or writing activity in class.
•Teacher grades the performance or written piece.

Step 4
•The teacher holds a class discussion related to the readings in general. Then the teacher proceeds to inform students as to whether their grades will replace any lower scores.

Step 5
•Students continue reading one or more of the other alternatives on their own but strictly for leisure.

FIGURE 19.4 Sequence of events in a typical course.

Making certain that the readings are at the right course and general proficiency level is essential if students are to make the most out of the experience. According to Bett (as cited by Anderson, 2008), students should understand at least 90% of a text if they are to be able to read it independently, without assistance from a teacher. There is an abundant collection of printed graded readers currently available, and publishers are now making digitized versions of reading materials as well. However, costs can be prohibitive for students and thus a limitation in terms of making them accessible when the goal is actually to maximize their use—an important factor, particularly in large institutions. Therefore, the other alternative would be to make use of the large variety of reading texts that can be found on the Internet, which is something ICPNA has done. As a result, tens of thousands of students have access to online graded readings at no cost. But how can we grade such readings? Here is a simple breakdown of the process:

1. *Selection.* Course planners choose reading genre types, themes and topics, and word length for each course. This can be aided by input from students in terms of their preferences.
2. *Grading.* Readings are chosen depending on whether they are deemed appropriate for the course level in terms of difficulty and degree of comprehensibility. This can be gauged by doing the following:
   a. Reading text is copied and pasted into a Microsoft Word document.
   b. Spelling & Grammar Checker is used to determine readability statistics in terms of: number of words per sentence, percent of passive sentences, Flesch-Kinkaid Reading Ease, and Flesch-Kinkaid Grade Level. These figures are compared to course specifications and evaluated.
   c. You can use websites like LexTutor and Oxford 3000 to cross-check difficulty level and appropriateness.
   d. Comprehensibility can also be verified in a more conventional way by working with printed samples in class and finding an average comprehensibility level for the entire group.

Once the teacher has found a text that is appropriate, the next step is to provide an incentive for them to do the reading. In the ICPNA Online Graded Reading Program, students are informed in advance that there will be a graded speaking or writing activity based on the reading of their choice and that their performance could result in a grade that replaces a lower score they was obtained on another occasion. In the process, it is hoped that students will find the actual reading fun and engaging enough to feel satisfied with the experience and want to do additional reading. In order to allow for choice when selecting readings and still make in-class group work for the readings possible, activities should be generic in nature as Figure 19.5 illustrates.

The most difficult aspect of the work is ascertaining whether students are really benefitting from the process and if they actually do go on to engage in extensive reading once they have fulfilled the course's requirements. A research study is still pending on whether engaging in the ICPNA Online Graded Reading Program actually leads to tangible language development in specific areas, but what we

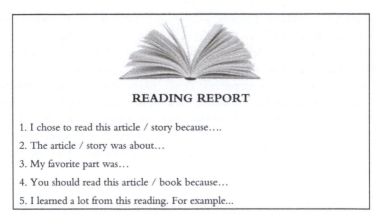

READING REPORT

1. I chose to read this article / story because....

2. The article / story was about...

3. My favorite part was...

4. You should read this article / book because...

5. I learned a lot from this reading. For example...

FIGURE 19.5 Prompt for speaking activity based on online graded reading.

have been able to establish so far is a high level of student and teacher satisfaction with the program, high overall performance on the reading sections of international proficiency examinations (e.g., basic and intermediate levels), and, most importantly, the fact that most students seem to be engaging in extensive reading. Figure 19.6 lists some statistics.

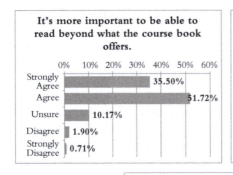

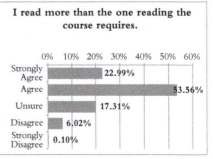

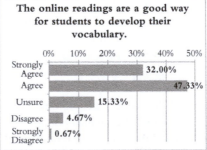

FIGURE 19.6 Selected responses from student (A & B; n = 2,945) and teacher (C; n = 150) survey results on the ICPNA Online Graded Reading Program.

Payoffs and Pitfalls

When classroom and autonomous learning integration (CALI) is implemented systematically over the course of a study program, many of the challenges teachers often face in their work with students can be overcome more easily. For example, teachers often complain about the restricted amount of time they have to carry out the curriculum. CALI makes students more prepared for what they will be asked of them in class, with a greater degree of confidence and a wider range of skills and knowledge. Because the content for classroom lessons may be more familiar to them as a result of independent inquiry and practice, lessons may go more smoothly since time may be saved on presentations, explanations and examples. Motivation is likely to be enhanced if students succeed in class more often and associate their achievements with their efforts to learn and practice on their own. Students will also develop autonomous learning strategies that will help them maintain their level in the language long after they have completed the study program; this addresses the common problem of L2 language reversion or attrition over time as a result of lack of continuous exposure to and use of the language (Bardovi-Harlig & Stringer, 2010).

Another important feature associated with CALI is that it is highly amenable to the needs and expectations of today's generation of millennials, most of whom could also be considered "digital natives" (Prensky, 2001). "Millennials" generally look forward to working in teams, want empowerment and freedom of choice, depict and understand the world in their own terms, are the "chief technological officers" in their own homes, and seek opportunities for learning and entertainment that are authentic reflections of their own lives (Gross, 2012; Friedman, as cited by Sanburn, 2013). The autonomous learning project caters to millennials offering them the opportunity to mold a project alternative according to their own interpretations of "real-life" situations. It fosters teamwork through social networking so that tasks are not just seen as assignments to be done but rather opportunities for further bonding and shared success with friends. As for technology, ALPs are highly dependent on it as a means for students to engage in inquiry, exploration, discovery and consolidation of knowledge in English; who better than millennials and digital natives to take advantage of something to which they are so accustomed? Likewise, the success of the ICPNA Online Graded Reading Program is highly contingent upon students having a sense of choice and making use of technology to access content and materials that would be unavailable otherwise.

In terms of potential drawbacks, one possibility is that students will not be able to work together effectively or get the most out of the experience. A well-known issue is "groupthink," which is when a group tends to follow the direction of one or two of the more dominant members in order to avoid disagreements and conflict; this in turn is commonly believed to lead to poor decision making (Esser, 1998). This can be very difficult to monitor and control, but a well-designed ALP alternative will demand a significant contribution from each of the learning team's members, allowing individuals to apply their creativity and decision-making power to the fullest within their scope of responsibility. As for in-class, reading-based activities, carefully selected discussion questions will serve to elicit an equal amount of language from each of the participants. Another issue with groups or teams is that the amount of work may be unequal when one compares what each member of the group did. This can be offset by using an anonymous survey, which will ask each student to rate their teammates' contributions. The teacher can then make adjustments to a grade if someone stands out as not having done their share of the work.

Another challenge is making certain that the students' language production is in accordance with the activity or project's specifications and overall course level. With tasks that require autonomous learning and practice, the final outcome may fall short when it comes to the amount of content, level of complexity, and frequency of use in terms of selected language features. Yet teachers can help students remain on target by offering them exemplars of the language that is expected, either in the instructions or ongoing feedback prior to delivery. When available, sample writings or video recordings of previous performances can be shown. Students will then have a clearer idea as to what is expected and prepare accordingly.

Discussion Questions

1. What are some ways to ascertain that learning has taken place through classroom and autonomous learning integration (CALI)?
2. What is the role of technology in CALI? Is CALI possible without it?
3. What are some independent study habits and learning strategies students might develop as a result of CALI? How could you follow up in the classroom so that students can consolidate their ability to learn on their own?
4. What are other ways to carry out CALI in addition to the examples related to project work and reading provided in this chapter?

Resources

Recommended websites

TeacherWeb® *Webquests*—http://teacherweb.com/tweb/webquests.aspx
Life in Space Webquest—http://teacherweb.com/PE/ICPNA/LifeinSpace/index.html
Compleat Lexical Tutor—http://www.lextutor.ca/
The Extensive Reading Foundation—http://erfoundation.org/wordpress/
References

References

Bardovi-Harlig, K., & Stringer, D. (2010). Variables in second language attrition: Advancing the state of the art. *Studies in Second Language Acquisition*, 32, 1–45.

Chan, V. (2001). Readiness for learner autonomy: What do our learners tell us? *Teaching in Higher Education*, 6(4), 505–518.

Dörnyei, Z., & Csizér, K. (1998). Ten commandments for motivating language learners: Results of an empirical study. *Language Teaching Research*, 2(3), 203–229.

Dickenson, L. (1995). Autonomy and motivation: A literature review. *System*, 23(2), 165–174.

Esser, J.K. (1998). Alive and well after 25 years: A review of groupthink research. *Organizational Behavior and Human Decision Processes*, 73(2–3), 116–141.

Grabe, W. (2009). *Reading in a second language: Moving from theory to practice*. Cambridge: Cambridge University Press.

Gross, T.S. (2012, July 5). The new millennial values. *Forbes*. Retrieved from http://www.forbes.com/sites/prospernow/2012/07/05/the-new-millennial-values/

Islam, M. N. (2011). Independent English learning through the Internet. *Journal of Language Teaching and Research*, 2(5), 1080–1085.

Krashen, S.D. (2004). *The power of reading*. London: Heinemann.

McCombs, B. L., & Whisler, J. S. (1989). The role of affective variables in autonomous learning. *Educational Psychologist*, 24(3), 277–306.

Nunan, D. (2003). Nine steps to learner autonomy. Retrieved from http://www.su.se/polopoly_fs/1.84007.1333707257!/menu/standard/file/2003_11_Nunaneng.pdf

Paris, S. G., & Paris, A.H. (2001). Classroom applications of research on self-regulated learning. *Educational Psychologist*, 36(2), 89–101.

Prensky, M. (2001). Digital natives, digital immigrants. *On the Horizon*, 9(5), 1–6.

Richards, J. C., & Rodgers, T.S. (2001). *Approaches and methods in language teaching*, 2nd ed. Cambridge: Cambridge University Press.

Rott, S. (1999). The effect of exposure frequency on intermediate language learners' incidental vocabulary acquisition and retention through reading. *Studies in Second Language Acquisition*, 21(4), 589–619.

Sanburn, J. (2013, May 14). How MTV decided to abandon rebellion. *Time*. Retrieved from http://business.time.com/2013/05/14/how-mtv-decided-to-abandon-rebellion/

Schmitt, N., Jiang, X., & Grabe, W. (2011). The percentage of words known in a text and reading comprehension. *The Modern Language Journal*, 95(1), 26–43.

Waring, R., & Nation, I.S.P. (1997). Vocabulary size, text coverage, and word lists. In N. Schmitt & M. McCarthy (Eds.), *Vocabulary: Description, acquisition and pedagogy* (pp. 6–19). Cambridge: Cambridge University Press.

20

THE ECOLOGY OF ENGLISH

Real-World Experiences in Sustainability and Language Learning

Kelley Calvert

Introduction and Overview

Due to the urgent ecological challenges facing humanity, the idea of integrating sustainable principles in the language classroom is gaining traction in higher education. In such a context, a key question presents itself: "What does it mean to be educated in a biosphere that is suffering ecological degradation at a rate that is unparalleled in human history at a time when demand for ecosystem services is growing rapidly" (Kelly, 2009, p. 9)?

This chapter focuses on one modest attempt to address this question in a graduate-level English for Academic and Professional Purposes (EAPP) course at the Monterey Institute of International Studies (MIIS). The course, entitled, "EAPP 8315: Integrated English Skills: Focus on Sustainability," included students with diverse fields of study, including international business, international policy, and nonproliferation.

Vignette

During the semester, students from Korea, Japan, Togo, China, and Iraq engaged in several out-of-classroom experiences via field trips to (1) the Recology waste management facility in San Francisco, (2) Stanford's Hopkins Marine Lab in Pacific Grove, and (3) Doc Ricketts' Lab in Monterey. After brief introductory remarks regarding each field trip, the vignettes below use the students' own words to describe their experiences.

Trip 1: Recology Recycling Center, San Francisco, California

The city of San Francisco has set the goal of zero waste by 2020, making Recology one of the most innovative "waste management" facilities in the country. Recology provides recycling, composting, and artist-in-residence measures, all aiming to reduce waste. During their visit to Recology, students engaged in a lecture providing an overview of the Recology business model. Then, they toured the facilities, including the artist-in-residence studio, the recycling center, the dump, and the garden decorated with art projects made from waste.

Hyuk (Korean student of nonproliferation): Before taking this class, I had never thought about sustainability in everyday life. To be candid, if someone had asked me to go to a recycling factory like Recology, I never would have visited this kind of place. As time goes by, however, my heart is getting soaked by sustainability. Especially, when I saw the workroom of two artists, coupled with the Brazilian artist addressed in our class, I was reminded me of the term, cradle to cradle [Author's note: *Cradle to cradle* is a design concept focused on renewing, restoring, and contributing to ecosystems through products' lifecycle.] After our visit on Recology, it is quite intriguing that I find myself always thinking about and considering sustainability. For example, when students in my Policy Analysis class had to figure out the effects of New York's Soda Law preventing manufacturers from selling sodas exceeding 16 ounces, I naturally answered that we can reduce the trash due to the size of the bottle.

Kouassigan (Togolese international environmental policy student): I was delighted in the training that the center offers to artists. The works of the artists on the site were very beautiful, and more they appeal to thinking. The works reveal power and ingenuity beyond measure because they are created out of landfills. It is just amazing how beauty can be crafted out of mess and throw-aways. It is quite understandable to use good standing materials to create arts, but using trash and materials that were at a specific time judged useless and "socially dead" and thrown onto the landfills denotes more of the high degree of creativity. These artists rectify the way society uses materials by giving them new life prolonging thus, their usefulness. How much more art could have been created if all the landfills of the world were put into robust recycling processes!

Aoi (Japanese nonproliferation student): Visiting all the facilities of Recology reminded me of my experience when I was five years old. I did visit this kind of factory in my hometown, Japan. I was surprised that Japan has had this kind of industry for a long time, while Recology is one of the most famous recycling companies in the United States. I guess it took a while for the U.S., one of the largest consuming country, to accept the concept of recycle and actualize it. All the functions and concepts of Recology were almost same as the one I visited in Japan. Except one thing: Art. Through visiting Recology, I was really impressed by its idea of creating arts from "trash."

Trip 2: Stanford's Hopkins Marine Station in Pacific Grove

For the second out-of-classroom experience, students visited the Hopkins Marine Station in Pacific Grove. The marine station provides a home to Stanford University researchers and biologists. Stephen Palumbi, the current director of the marine station, co-wrote a book entitled, *The Death and Life of Monterey Bay*. The book describes the ecological collapse of Monterey Bay and its subsequent recovery. Students attended a lecture by Dr. Palumbi before taking a tour of the marine station. The reflection below details one student's mental process, making connections between the reading of *The Death and Life of Monterey Bay* and his experience at Hopkins Marine Station:

> *Ougar:* Prior to attending this class, I had limited knowledge on how sustainability is germane to water resources and marine life. I simply thought that climate change and the increase in temperature reduces water level; I was not fully aware of the influence of human practices, such as overfishing. I better understand the unfavorable impact when I read *The Death and Life of Monterey Bay* by Dr. Stephen R Palumbi. ... After reviewing his book, we asked Palumbi a variety of questions and discussed similar problems in other parts of the world. Later, he took us on a short tour in the area and showed us the refuge. The sea otters and seagulls sitting on a floating rock reminded us of the beauty of life and our common goal of saving the planet.

Trip 3: Ed Ricketts' Lab, Monterey, California

In the third out-of-classroom experience, students went on a tour of Doc Ricketts' lab on Cannery Row in Monterey. Edward "Doc" Ricketts was a self-trained biologist made famous in John Steinbeck's novel *Cannery Row* and one of the first scientists to consider ecology in biology. Interestingly, Stephen Palumbi's *The Death and Life of Monterey Bay* details Ed Ricketts' life and influence on ecology in Monterey Bay, a natural connection between the two trips.

In a collaborative writing exercise, students described their experience at Doc Ricketts' Lab in the following way:

> *Group Reflection:* The lab looks out on the sea, so we could hear the sounds of the waves. In the backyard, there were concrete holding tanks for sea creatures. Seaborn explained that the water tanks were used to

keep specimen and Ed studied them. Then, Seaborn showed us a book, "Between Pacific Tides," which is very important to him. He looked so excited because at the age of 12, he received the book from his mother as his birthday gift. Since then, he has pursued his dream, becoming a biologist. And now, he was talking about the book to us at the same place where Ricketts wrote the book 80 years ago. We were so fortunate that we could share that history with him!

Besides Seaborn, there were also two other great men in the lab who welcomed us with their heart-warming hospitality. These men were Michael Hemp & Frank Wright. Interaction with them was such an amazing experience for all of us; they made us feel as if we were at Doc Ricketts Lab with John Steinbeck & Ed Ricketts in the 1930s. By the end of the workshop, Seaborn taught about life: family, love, friendship, food, and travel. He instructed us to write our thoughts on a piece of paper and collected them. He showed that we could tear one paper up easily, but can't do so for the combined papers. We, as a group, are very strong. Nobody can break it.

Principles

Principle 1. Utilize higher education as an empowering conduit for teaching language in tandem with sustainability principles. The first widely-used definition of sustainability was provided by the Brundtland Commission of the United Nations in 1987: "[S]ustainable development is development that meets the needs of the present without compromising the ability of future generations to meet their own needs" (United Nations, 1987). Today, the word *sustainable* is necessarily attached to several fields: sustainable development, sustainable energy, sustainable agriculture, sustainable transportation, sustainable architecture, and sustainable forest management, to name a few. The principles of sustainability have the ability to touch every student's field of study, making it ideal for content-based language instruction.

Why sustainability? Current challenges to the environment are unique in human history and require a unique response. In designing courses, it behooves us to consider how concepts of sustainability fit into the curriculum, even if sustainability itself is not the content fulcrum of the course. For instance, how can we assist our learners to begin viewing themselves in the stoic tradition of being a citizen of the world? How can we help them in embodying "a series of expanding concentric circles that extend from the individual to the family, community, state, nation, world, and ultimately to the greater cosmos"? (Kelly, 2009, p. 43). We see this concept in action in the vignette provided by Hyuk above. Prior to studying sustainability in our English class, he rarely considered impacts of business or legislation on the environment. However, during his policy analysis class, he noticed a change in his perspective: When looking at New York's Soda Law, which prevented manufacturers from selling sodas exceeding 16 ounces, he "naturally" commented that smaller bottles would mean less waste.

Teaching sustainability means helping students view themselves as part of a larger whole, sharing a commitment to nurturing the foundation of life and guaranteeing a better quality of living for everyone on the planet. Interestingly, the concept of sustainability is fundamental to every field of study, making it an ideal building point for an English language classroom. The concept leaves plenty of opportunity for language instruction while encouraging students to incorporate a "global sustainability outlook into their civic and professional lives regardless of their area of specialization" (Kelly, 2009, p. 2).

Principle 2. Offer experiential education to students through field trips. As a teaching philosophy, experiential education indicates a learning experience in which a teacher integrates direct experience into the classroom (Itin, 1999). Experiential learning also involves a reflection process, whereby learners increase their knowledge, develop skills, and come to understand and co-create their new value system. For genuine knowledge to develop, the learners must meet four requirements (Itin, 1999). First, they must be willing to involve themselves fully in the experience. They also have to genuinely reflect upon the experience. Third, they must have the capability to analyse and conceptualize the experience before finally utilizing and applying their new knowledge.

Why field trips? In their working paper, "Learning Styles and Learning Spaces: Enhancing Experiential Learning in Higher Education," Kolb & Kolb (2004) define experiential learning as a process of constructing knowledge involving a learning cycle where the learner experiences, reflects, thinks, and acts in a recursive process. Learning, according to experiential theory, is "the process whereby knowledge is created through the transformation of experience" (p. 5). This transformation of experience was key in the EAPP vignettes included above. For instance, Ougar mentions his limitations in understanding how principles of sustainability extend into marine biology. However, through the trip to Hopkins Marine Station, he came to understand "a number of factors that directly threaten the welfare of marine life." That knowledge was solidified by the experience of seeing "the sea otters and seagulls sitting on a floating rock," which "reminded us of the beauty of life." *Seeing* allows for a *transformative* experience that solidifies classroom learning.

As Kolb & Kolb (2004) point out, the ELT (Experiential Learning The-ory) model includes four modes of understanding experience: Concrete Experience (CE), Abstract Conceptualization (AC), Reflective Observation (RO), and Active Experimentation (AE) (see Figure 20.1).

FIGURE 20.1 The simplest experiential learning cycle. (Compiled by Andrea Corney www.edbatista.com/2007/10/experiential.html)

In constructing knowledge through experience, the learner has concrete experiences that serve as the basis for observations and reflections that are inte-grated into abstractions that bring new implications. From these implications, the learners are able to actively test their hypotheses and create new experi-ences. By visiting Recology, Hopkins Marine Station, and Doc Ricketts' Lab, students were exposed to concrete experiences. Immediately following these field trips, they were given the opportunity to reflect on their experiences via personal blog accounts or collaborative discussion and writing. Making space for students to integrate their experience into reflection encouraged them to take ownership of their learning. As Keeton, Sheckley, & Grose (2002) point out, reflection has the power to deepen learning from experience.

In their reflections, students often noted how their abstract conceptu-alization (AC) became real through the concrete experience. For instance, many vignettes above noted the cradle to cradle concept, which is a design concept focused on renewing, restoring, and contributing to ecosystems through products' lifecycles. After visiting Recology, numerous students reflected on this concept and how it came to life. After seeing how artists used landfill waste to create amazing pieces of art, Kouassigan wrote, "Using trash and materials that were at a specific time judged useless and 'socially dead' and thrown onto the landfills denotes more of the high degree of cre-ativity." In the vignettes above, we also see this recursive process through the application of old knowledge to new experience when Aoi compares her experience at a landfill in Japan to the trip to Recology. "All the functions and concepts of Recology were almost same as the one I visited in Japan. Except one thing: Art."

Principle 3. Experiential education has the potential to increase student motivation. Motivation, as it relates to language learning, has been variously defined and classified in the literature (e.g., Gardner, 1982; Crooke & Schmidt, 1991; Dornyei, 2001). For the present research into language learning and sustainability, the everyday definition of motivation applies: it is a psychological characteristic that impels individuals to reach a goal. Still, it cannot be denied that learners come to any language class with a variety of motivations. As Dornyei & Kubanyiova (2014) assert, people learn languages for several different reasons; meanwhile, "an equally wide array of reasons keep their motivation alive," and "the vision of who they would like to become as second language users seems to be one of the most reliable predictors of their long-term intended effort" (p. 3). This relationship between motivation and vision is particularly relevant in the present discussion of language learning and sustainability, as it is hoped that students will integrate a vision of themselves as responsible global citizens based upon experiential learning.

Motivation. In "Motivation and Motivating in the Foreign Language Classroom," Dornyei (1994) provides 30 strategies for motivating language learners. The most relevant strategies for the current chapter are the following: promoting student contact with L2 speakers, promoting students' self-efficacy with regard to achieving learning goals, arousing and sustaining curiosity and attention, and encouraging group cohesion.

To give opportunities for student contact with the L2, Dornyei (1994) recommends field trips outside of the classroom, pen pals, or exchange programs. In the current case, contact with L2 speakers was promoted by creating the space for authentic communication to occur. Students had the opportunity to interact and ask questions of native speakers at Recology, Hopkins Marine Station, and Doc Ricketts' lab. To create these opportunities, it should be noted that the author had to tap into local community resources. Meanwhile, to scaffold these opportunities, the author promoted self-efficacy in students by teaching learning and communication strategies (Dornyei, 1994). Prior to each field trip, the class brainstormed questions to ask the speakers and practiced communication strategies. However, perhaps the most important strategies employed were the arousing and sustaining of curiosity and attention as well as the creation of group cohesion. To arouse and sustain curiosity and attention, Dornyei recommends "introducing unexpected, novel, unfamiliar, and even paradoxical events; not allowing lessons to settle into too regular a routine" (p. 281). Frequent out-of-classroom learning experiences motivated students by preventing routine from setting in.

Applications

Though the content of this course was sustainability, this model of out-of-class learning could be applied in multiple contexts. It is ideal for content-based classrooms where field trips can enhance the learning experience of students through authentic communication, community building, and classroom cohesion. This chapter makes five suggestions for adopting this particular out-of-class learning model: (1) utilize local resources, (2) scaffold communication for authentic contexts, (3) provide space for students to reflect on out-of-class learning experiences, (4) discuss ways to apply new knowledge into daily life, and (5) take every opportunity to build classroom cohesion.

To utilize local resources for out-of-class learning, we have to consider the context in which our classroom resides. Monterey Bay provides a particularly rich environment for a sustainability class. In brainstorming potential field trips for the class, I had an array of options due to the presence of resources like Recology, the Monterey Bay Aquarium, Hopkins Marine Station, and so on. Nonetheless, it takes reaching out to partners in the community to effectively utilize these resources. Regardless of the topic, the instructor can brainstorm a list of available local resources and make contact with stakeholders in the community to connect learners with authentic contexts for communication.

Once these local resources are located and a trip is organized, it then falls upon the instructor to scaffold the communication context. For instance, our class read *The Death and Life of Monterey Bay* prior to visiting Hopkins Marine Station and hearing the author's lecture. Through discussion in class, students came to understand the issues and concepts presented in the book as well as its vocabulary prior to our visit. In addition, students composed possible questions for the author before we went to visit the lab.

After an out-of-class learning experience has occurred, it is important to allow students to reflect on the experience. The experiential model of learning highlights the importance of letting students incorporate their experience into their worldview, thus enabling them to form new hypotheses and take action. Inside the classroom after these experiences, students were given time to reflect on their field trips. They wrote individual reflections or composed group narratives about their experiences after each trip.

To further the learning process even more, it is important to encourage students to think of ways to incorporate this knowledge into their daily lives. In the classroom, we frequently did activities focusing on an important question: What can *I* do to help this situation? Students were empowered to change their daily practices through simple acts like using their own water bottles and picking up litter rather than just ignoring it. As Kouassigan states in one of his reflections, "I think the biggest thing I am leaving this semester with is the awareness and consciousness about sustainable practices. The semester made me turn this idea into everyday actions, and this is the stage that brings about positive changes."

Finally, it is important to encourage group cohesion wherever possible. In a learning environment where out-of-class engagement is being encouraged, the need for group cohesion becomes particularly important. Students share more intimate ideas, thoughts, and time together than would otherwise be possible.

Payoffs and Pitfalls

Perhaps the most important payoff of this model is the enhanced student motivation and group cohesion. As one student, Clark, wrote of his experience, "Receiving knowledge and practicing it right in the class is such a joyful learning experience, which is hard to find in China." Yufan echoed this joy and added, "During this semester, I learned a lot through reading those books, chapters, and articles, but especially, I learned the history about Monterey Bay, the place where I am living in and studying." In this reflection, Yufan notes the importance of learning about the local context as well as his excitement about learning.

In addition, students built a strong group cohesion following this model. Because students had a chance to bond outside the classroom, they seemed more comfortable sharing ideas inside the classroom. As Yufan writes, students became more than colleagues, considering one another friends by the time the class was over: "We exchanged our thoughts on peers' papers, and in the meantime, we got some really helpful suggestions from our classmates. I appreciate that I had this wonderful class in my first semester. We had fun, we learned a lot, and we are friends now." In addition, students were able to learn about sustainability issues by nation. As Kentaro states, "One of my favorite topics was other country's own problems. My classmates' presentations made me think about it, and their topics were quite interesting."

In terms of pitfalls, perhaps the greatest is the amount of time required to effectively plan field trips and reflection activities. In addition, it is difficult to measure how much students learned from the field trips without any quantitative data. Similarly, the actual impacts of learning about sustainability on behavior could be negligible, as a change in knowledge does not necessarily equal a change in behavior. Nonetheless, in quantitative responses, it seems the benefits of the class outweighed shortcomings. As Ougar notes, "It was difficult to reflect on all that I learned throughout this course. I became familiar with various definitions of sustainability in different contexts. It was with no doubt an eye-opening class that stimulated me to take an action, even simple, to change as much as I can. I will not be able to build huge green buildings, or become a policy maker in my country, but I still can do my part through implementing and sharing what I have learned from my professor and classmates."

Discussion Questions

1. What is sustainability and how can it function as an instrument of language learning and a tool in higher education?
2. What are the cognitive and affective benefits of incorporating field trips as out-of-class learning experiences for students?
3. What resources do your students bring to the concept of sustainability? What are their fields of study? What are their nationalities? What insights can they bring to the classroom about sustainability in their own countries and fields?
4. How might concrete experiences outside of the classroom facilitate true learning in your classroom?
5. How could outside-the-classroom experiences increase student motivation and communicative competence?
6. Could field trips be used to enhance any of your current courses?
7. How might field trips/out-of-the-classroom experiences build group cohesion in your classroom?
8. What local resources could you utilize to illustrate abstract classroom concepts?
9. How can you provide space for student reflection and knowledge building after out-of-the-classroom experiences?

Resources

Bioneers, a nonprofit promoting environmental solutions and innovative social strategies for restoring the Earth—www.bioneers.org

The International Society for Ecological Economics, an organization facilitating understanding between economists and ecologists—www.ecoeco.org

Second Nature: Education for Sustainability, an organization dedicated to accelerating transformation towards sustainability in higher education—www.secondnature.org

Sustainability Institute, the sustainability institute provides information, analysis, and practical demonstrations to foster transition to sustainable systems—www.sustainer.org

References

Crookes, G. & Schmidt, R. W. (1991). Motivation: Reopening the research agenda. *Language Learning*, 41, 469–512.

Dornyei, Z. (1994). Motivation and motivating in the foreign language classroom. *The Modern Language Journal*, 78(3), 273–283.

Dornyei, Z. (2001). Teaching and researching motivation. Harlow, England: Longman.

Dörnyei, Z., & Kubanyiova, M. (2014). *Motivating learners, motivating teachers: Building vision in the language classroom.* Cambridge: Cambridge University Press.

Edwards, A. (2005). *The sustainability revolution.* Gabriola Island, BC: New Society Publishers.

Engellant, K., & Parks, A. R. *The simplest experiential learning cycle.* Retrieved from http://experlearning.wordpress.com/

Freire, P. (1996). *Pedagogy of the oppressed.* New York: Penguin.

Gardner, R. C. (1985). Social psychology and second language learning: *The role of attitudes and motivation.* London: Edward Arnold Publishers.

Itin, C. M. (1999). Reasserting the philosophy of experiential education as a vehicle for change in the 21st century. *The Journal of Experiential Education,* 22(2), 91–98.

Kelly, T. (2009). *The sustainable learning community.* New Hampshire: University of New Hampshire Press.

Kolb, A., & Kolb, D. (2004). *Learning styles and learning spaces: Enhancing experiential learning in higher education* (Working paper). Case Western Reserve University, Cleveland, OH. Retrieved from http://occasionalplanner.com/wp-content/uploads/2013/07/Learning-Styles-Learning-Spaces.pdf

Orr, D. (2005). Forward. In A. R. Edwards, *The sustainability revolution* (pp. xiii-xv). Gabriola Island, BC: New Society Publishers.

The United Nations. (1987). Report of the world commission on environment and development. The Brundtland Report. Retrieved from http://conspect.nl/pdf/Our_Common_Future-Brundtland_Report_1987.pdf

21

TAKING CONTROL

A Digital Video Project for English for Science Students

Lindsay Miller & Christoph A. Hafner

Introduction and Overview

This chapter describes how second language (L2) university students invest their time beyond the classroom when asked to create a digital video project, which documents a simple scientific investigation. This digital video project is part of a credit-bearing EAP course all science students have to take in order to complete their programme in an English medium university in Hong Kong. The project is structured as an integral part of the course and students work in groups outside of class time to create their own scientific documentary which they then up-load onto YouTube. During the course, the students are introduced to the concept of how scientific texts can be presented using different genres: the scientific documentary vs the lab report. They are also introduced to some simple technology which they can use when making a digital video. Then, the students are given freedom to decide on the type of documentary (observational, expository, participatory); write their own script; prepare a storyboard; record the video footage; and present their scientific findings in as creative a fashion as they like. The results show that when given responsibility for creating a scientific documentary these students invest a large amount of their own time out of class and develop a number of skills: cooperative learning, learner autonomy, and language skills. They invest their time for a number of reasons: They are aware of a potentially large authentic Internet audience who may view their work; they want to present their oral skills well on video; they enjoy the process of being creative and want to showcase their work to the best of their ability.

The English for Science course at our university was restructured and redesigned three years ago, from a pedagogy of 'teaching' to a pedagogy of 'learning' (see Brew, 2006). As part of the new course structure, students had to work in groups to create a scientific digital video project. An introduction to the project and student videos can be viewed at our dedicated website (http://www1.english. cityu.edu.hk/acadlit/). In addition, details of the whole video production process and its outcomes can be found in Hafner & Miller (2011); Miller, Hafner, & Ng (2012). As part of the redesign of the English for Science course, we talked to our students, via focus group interviews, about the potential benefits and problems they encountered when preparing their videos. We also tracked the progress of twelve groups over the seven week period of the project with the help of Student Assistants. This chapter outlines how the project operates and describes the experiences of one group of students.

Vignette

Willie, Gwen, Andrew, & Eddie, four Chinese students, formed a group in class to complete the English for Science project. Three of the students were from Hong Kong and one from Mainland China. Gwen & Andrew were studying applied chemistry, Eddy environmental science, and Willie was a mathematics student. The only course where all students could meet regularly was in their English for Science class. They could all speak Cantonese and their English proficiency was around intermediate level. This was the first time any of the group members had prepared a digital video and so it was a new experience for them all.

The students were given time in class to talk about their digital videos, but most of the work on this project had to be done out of class (see Application below). As such, the group had to arrange to meet, communicate with each other about the progress of the video, conduct interviews as part of their data source, and film and edit the video. In order to do all of this, they used a variety of communication instruments: phone calls, e-mail, WhatsApp, and Drop Box, and there was a lot of out-of-class communication between members of the group. From time to time, the whole group met in the cafeteria or library to talk about the progress of their video. They also met as a team to collect their interview data. This was done outside of the library, at the entrance to the university, and in a park. In the final stages of the project, the team met several times to film footage for their video.

In our focus group meetings, we were keen to know which languages the team used to manage, talk about, and prepare their digital video. As all group members were able to use Cantonese, we were not surprised that they often talked on the phone, or face-to-face, in Cantonese. However, we were surprised at the amount of English that was also used: researching their topic via online sources; making notes from their group discussions; annotating their storyboard; writing the script; editing the video with the software; and sometimes while filming (giving instructions to each other). Some parts of the project would make using English the default language, for example, when writing the script or practicing the narrative for the video, but there were other times when the students used English rather than written Chinese or spoken Cantonese.

What became apparent when talking with the students was that they practised their English, both writing (when preparing the script) and orally (for the narrative), many times before they were satisfied with their performance. For instance, the script was drafted four times, and each group member practiced their on-camera narratives about ten times. The group also made use of other resources outside of the classroom to improve their project, for instance, an American friend of one of the students checked their script once it had been written.

In terms of teamwork, the group seemed very happy to have had the opportunity to work together outside of the class time on the video project. They mentioned that they worked well as a group, that a team spirit was created which transcended the project, and that they even started to help each other in other subjects, such as Willie giving some assistance to the others in mathematics.

Principles

There are two main principles which have guided having our students take part in their digital video project. The first is an emphasis on learner autonomy, that is, allowing our students freedom in deciding on how, what and where to film and what the end product will look like. The second is making use of a technology-enhanced learning environment in order to connect with our students' popular cultural experience and motivate them and bridge the gap between in-class and out-of-class learning.

> *Principle 1. Foster learner autonomy by extending in-class learning to out-of-class project work.* The English for Science course adopts a learner-autonomy-based pedagogy. The concept of a learner-autonomy-based pedagogy is that language learning does not stop once the lesson is over, and that learners have the ability to take control of their own learning (see Holec, 1988). Learner autonomy, though, is sometimes mistaken as learners having control over all aspects of their language learning (Hafner & Miller, 2011). We maintain that there can be a balance between agency and structure when using a learner-autonomy-based pedagogy. That is, in the project described in this chapter, students are supported in class with a variety of learning activities (structure), which they then use for their out-of-class project work (agency). By supporting learners in class with a variety of activities, and then giving them responsibility for their out-of-class project-based work, our learners have the tools they need to complete a digital video. Then, they are encouraged to work collaboratively with their team members and may choose to be more or less independent of each other at different stages while working on their project (see Dickinson, 1987).

> *Principle 2. Support out-of-class learning with a technology enhanced learning environment.* Figure 21.1 shows that the project progressed through three

main stages: planning, filming and editing, and then sharing. At each stage of the process, different types of technology were introduced to the learners who were then encouraged, out of class, to explore the usefulness of this technology for completing their project. This in-class/out-of-class format to the course is an integral feature for the success of the students' digital video projects.

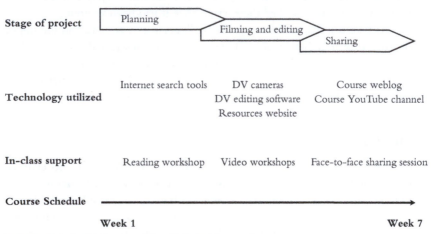

FIGURE 21.1 Architecture of the digital video project.

By using a digital video project, we encourage the students to work with new technologies and new literacies, to experience a range of resources, tools and environments for their out-of-class learning experiences (see Benson, 2001). Black (2007) and Lam (2006) provide useful examples of how technology-rich environments can enhance chances for autonomous language learning. We believe that by combining a learner-autonomy-based pedagogy in class, with an out-of-class digital project we heighten the students' learning experiences as they create and share multimodal texts using images, videos, texts and sounds. In order to create their videos, students must combine a range of skills including: researcher, writer, organizer, and presenter working collaboratively, problem solving, and evaluating their work. By working with others to produce a significant piece of work, learners reflect on what they can and cannot do well, and are encouraged to seek out resources which will assist in their project, and which will possibly have wider implications to their future learning.

Our experience of using a learner-autonomy-based pedagogy within a technological learning environment is that when given such a video project to complete students invest time and effort into their work over and above what they would normally do in a purely structured learning environment, and are happy to collaborate with each other to showcase what they have learned.

Applications

There are many published examples of successful project work at all levels of language learning; for example, Dam (1995) had her young learners work on language projects, while Becker & Slater (2005) write about their experiences of using projects with young adults. Regardless of the learners' language level, for project work to be successful the learners need to be exposed to a variety of learning opportunities and they have to be able to work collaboratively.

In our context, we were working with young adult university students who had intermediate language level abilities. Even so, we had to manage the structured learning environment of the classroom with the type of out-of-class activities in which we encouraged our learners to engage. Table 21.1 shows the structure of the digital video project.

TABLE 21.1 In-Class and Out-of-Class Activities

Time	In-class course structure	Expected out-of-class activities
Week 1	Introduction to the course and making a scientific digital video	None
Week 2	Planning project work; arrange groups and hand out topics	Meet to discuss their project
Week 3	Creating a scientific documentary using multimedia; introduce the software useful for the project	Meet to practice using the software; brainstorm ideas on how to present their project
Week 4	No class, data collection, lab work	Meet to collect data for their project and film the process
Week 5	Preparing storyboard and script	Write, review, edit their storyboards and scripts
Week 6	Video trouble shooting	Film and edit the digital video
Week 7	Video viewing	Post comments about peers' videos to the course blog

Our students engaged in a lot of out-of-class communication and work as evidenced in the vignette. Sometimes they worked independently on one part of the project, but then they shared their knowledge in a collaborative effort to complete their project as a team effort. The choice of which language to use was left up to the students, but a lot of English was used. We contend that having students work in groups on such a project helps to create a language-rich learning environment for them over and above what could normally be achieved with an exclusively classroom-based course.

Given the freedom to work to their own schedule and decide on the amount of effort to expend on doing the project, it was surprising how much out-of-class time the students spent on completing the task, as the following focus group extracts show:

LINDSAY: So how much time did you spend?

GWEN: Yes, hmmm, I guess two hours a day ... every day ... and during the main project period for it was the month [weeks 2–5 of the project].

WILLIE: Yes, I guess we spent more time in Week 5 ... finding the pictures ...

GWEN: ... and thinking how to fix the video ... editing ...

ANDREW: ... a lot of time ... (*laughs*)

The students were also keen to expend their time on "getting it right":

LINDSAY: What happened when you were doing the narration, the story? Did you do that once?

WILLIE: No, recording my voice at least one half day in my room and then they did their own later on.

GWEN: Yes I did my own again at home because I thought my voice was maybe too nervous ... not good enough, so I need to do it again.

LINDSAY: Do you know how many times you recorded it before you were happy?

GWEN: Oh ... more than ten times! (*laughs*)

WILLIE: Yes, more than ten times, it's like only five minutes when we are actually recording ... so totally speaking it's like three to four hours to practice (for all four students).

LINDSAY: What kind of things were you not happy with when you heard your voice?

WILLIE: It's very strange for me to hear my voice (*laughs*) ... and I kind of think "Is that me?" ... and it's not fluent, and sometimes we will speak a wrong words and so we will start over again.

LINDSAY: How about you Andrew?

ANDREW: About ten times also ... because I wasn't very natural the first time ... some pronunciation is wrong, like I don't know (how to say) special words ... like decibel.

Our students also enjoyed the freedom of being autonomous and appreciated the amount of peer support they were able to obtain from each other:

LINDSAY: Did you enjoy working on the project out of class time?

WILLIE: Yes, because it is free and we can set our own time and we can set our own agenda and no pressure when we are doing the project.

LINDSAY: How about you Gwen?

GWEN: I think for me this is a bit precious because this is the first project I do in CityU, so I cannot say there was no pressure, but I quite enjoy the style as we do it all by ourselves, just as Willie have said, we can do the research and have our own schedule on it, and plan the time well so I think it is quite good.

LINDSAY: Did you learn anything from being part of a group?

GWEN: How to communicate with each other ... we are from different disciplines so when we communicate with each other we can get some new ideas, other than just from our own discipline ... because students from difficult disciplines will have some special ways of looking at the same things.

EDDIE: I feel very happy working with them ... my teammate will help me a great deal ... also I'm not too familiar with the computer ... to create a video ... and my teammates just call me and ask me to do something easy and do something I can do ...

Completing the digital video project was not always easy. The students had challenges with preparing their "perfect" script and when using the technology. However, they found ways to overcome any challenges they had:

ANDREW: It's hard to write naturally cause when I first write the script I write some sentence that it is weird so I gave my draft to my friend and he said, "Oh, it is so weird we don't say it." So he helped me to change the sentence a little bit ... so I learned how to write in a natural way ...

LINDSAY: Thinking about the technology again ... you said you were a little bit familiar with the technology.

GWEN: Not this software ... Willie helped me a bit find the soundtracks ... and also Eddy did the filming and soundtracks.

ANDREW: I also learned some technical skills because I was sometimes holding the camera and I didn't hold it at the right angle so they would tell me I didn't do a good job ... if I do it alone I would not notice this.

GWEN: If I had a problem with the editing then I went to the Internet and found out how to do it.

ANDREW: I encountered some technical problem when I downloading the music from some website ... and so I just find another website ...

Payoffs and Pitfalls

One of the biggest benefits we noticed in having students complete their digital video projects was that each group took control of their learning and a strong collaborative group-learning experience emerged. Although the students were introduced to the different stages of the project in class (see above, Application), what happened after class exceeded our expectations, as evidenced by the well-presented and creative scientific videos each group presented.

As the students were working in groups of three of four, each member had to negotiate his or her role within the group. This allowed students with special skills in one area the chance to 'shine,' and contribute to the overall product. For instance, we often found that one student would take charge of writing the script, while another was the "actor" on screen, and yet another would take over the technical aspects of getting the digital video ready to upload to YouTube. This role allocation was nearly always done by the students discussing their strengths and weaknesses and, hence, becoming more aware of their learning skills and strategies. Where no one seemed to have the relevant skills, these were learned in other ways, often by seeking advice from friends, family or surfing the Internet. Therefore, the learning opportunities for the students expanded well beyond the classroom as they progressed through the project.

When talking to our students after viewing their videos, we were often informed that their ten-minute video had taken several hours of practice, filming, and editing. We were particularly impressed to discover that our students were often highly critical of their on-screen performance and narratives and would redo a shot several times until they got their delivery right. This type of practice is something English language teachers would rarely see in class.

Of course, one of the biggest dangers in handing over a project like this to groups of students who share a similar first language (L1) is that most of the work will be conducted in the L1 and, as we can see from the vignette above, our students did use Cantonese. Often this was done in order to speed things up, to negotiate technical terms they were not familiar with in English, or simply to maintain the social cohesion of the group. We also noticed this happening in class time. In one lesson, when we introduced the digital software to the students and had them practice using it on laptops, there was a lot of Cantonese used by the groups. However, as everyone was on task and all they were trying to do was make sure they knew how to operate the software, we decided to allow the L1 to be used in this context. We came to see our students not just as L2 learners but rather as emergent multilinguals for whom it is natural to draw on multiple linguistic codes in a strategic way.

When teaching an in-class English for Science course, the tutor can manage the learners' use of L1 and L2. In the digital video project, we have described here, the teacher has to give up some of this control and rely on the demands of the project, which requires students to create a documentary in English, to engage students in the L2. As illustrated in the vignette, students working on their video project must make use of the L2 in a variety of situations and communicative events As a result of talking with our students about the processes they went through to complete their digital video projects we became more aware that in a multilingual context like Hong Kong students are likely to rely on a range of linguistic codes in their interactions out of class. It therefore seems to us that in future courses it is necessary to discuss such multilingual strategies with our students. For example, when is it appropriate to draw on the L1 and when does such reliance hinder potential progress in learning the L2? What is an appropriate code choice in the context of doing Internet research, conducting the field study, or socializing with teammates? How do such code choices affect language-learning opportunities?

Having taken part in producing their digital video, most of our students appreciated the experience they had gone through and were able to apply what they had learned in more ways than may have been possible with a purely classroom-based course. One aspect of this was their ability to critically analyse each other's videos in the peer feedback session. As all the students had gone through the process of making a video they were able to appreciate what their classmates had done:

LINDSAY: So by going through the process of making a digital video did that make you more aware of the good and bad points of the other group's videos?

WILLIE: Yes ... sure. I remember when I watch some of their videos I immediately see that they don't have good structure ... they don't organize it well ... they don't have a logic to their video.

GWEN: I remember some boys act out something when in Central and it is like a television programme, so that is quite good approach.

ANDREW: I remember one that they included the behind the scenes shots ... how they shot their video ... it is quite interesting.

Discussion Questions

1. Are students you teach familiar with project work? What types of language-based projects have they done before?
2. How much freedom can you give learners to explore their language skills and strategies and at what levels of language proficiency can learners begin to do this?
3. How often do your students use technology? What types of technology are they most familiar with? Do you capitalize on this use of technology for language learning?
4. How do you feel about students in a language class using their L1? Can you think of situations where use of the L1 is more appropriate than the L2?
5. What do you understand by the terms 'pedagogy of teaching' and 'pedagogy of learning'?
6. We talk about "structure" and "agency" as a guiding principle of the course described here: What do you understand by these terms and can you give examples of how they operate in a course you teach?

Resources

We have compiled a list of useful websites for both students and teachers which can be accessed at our website, http://www1.english.cityu.edu.hk/acadlit.

American TESOL provides a variety of free podcasts and videos on how to prepare classes for project work at http://www.livebinders.com/play/play_or_edit?id=107380.

The following blog at *World Teacher*, http://worldteacher-andrea.blogspot. hk/2011/06/project-work-in-efl-classrooms-eltchat.html, is a very good point summary of what, why, and how to do project work with ESL learners.

Edutopia includes a range of resources such as videos of success stories for project-based learning in school contexts at http://www.edutopia.org/ project-based-learning.

References

Beckett, G. H., & Slater, T. (2005). The project framework: A tool for language, content, and skills integration. *ELT Journal*, 59(2), 108–116.

Benson, P. (2001). *Teaching and researching autonomy in language learning.* Harlow, UK: Longman.

Black, R. (2007). Digital design: English language learners and reader reviews in online fiction. In M. Knobel & C. Lankshear (Eds.), *A new literacies sampler* (pp. 115–136). New York: Peter Lang.

Brew, A. (2006). *Researching and teaching: Beyond the divide.* New York: Palgrave Macmillan.

Dam, L. (1995). *Learner autonomy 3: From theory to classroom practice.* Dublin: Authentik.

Dickinson, L. (1987). *Self-instruction in language learning.* Cambridge: Cambridge University Press.

Hafner, C. A., & Miller, L. (2011). Fostering learner autonomy in English for science: A collaborative digital video project in a technological learning environment. *Language Learning & Technology*, 15(3), 201–223.

Holec, H. (1988). *Autonomy and self-directed learning: Present fields of application.* Strasbourg: Council of Europe.

Lam, W.S.E. (2006). Re-envisioning language, literacy, and the immigrant subject in new mediascapes. *Pedagogies: An International Journal*, 1(3), 171–195.

Miller, L., Hafner, C.A., & Ng, C.K.F. (2012). Project-based learning in a technologically-enhanced learning environment for second language learners: Students' perceptions. *E-Learning and Digital Media*, 9(2), 183–195.

PART V

Interacting with Native Speakers

22

LANGUAGE AND CULTURAL ENCOUNTERS

Opportunities for Interaction with Native Speakers

Jane Arnold & Carmen Fonseca-Mora

Introduction and Overview

Language learning has at times been put into two categories: the monastery and the market-place approaches. The monastery approach refers to organized language learning in a classroom with students and a teacher following a formal, rule-based plan while the market-place approach would involve being in a context where the language is spoken, not specifically to learn the language but using it to get something done (McArthur, 1991). What we discuss in this chapter would fall between the two because, on the one hand, it involves the direct intention to learn the language and also differing degrees of assistance available for the learning process but, on the other, it provides opportunities for developing communicative competence outside the classroom.

Language and cultural encounters, defined here as voluntary out-of-class learning experiences based on contact with native speakers[1], can be found in a variety of contexts and language-learning situations. The starting point of these experiences is learners' desire to improve their language skills and increase their knowledge of the culture in situations of authentic communication. Diverse types of opportunities for connections by learners of different languages with native speakers are readily available today. One example would be the formally organized tandem language exchanges where learners of two different languages are paired for conversation practice, with each partner being a native speaker of the language the other wants to learn. Another option would be virtual contacts with target language speakers which are very common now and may be established informally through social networks or e-mailing. Also Massive Open Online Courses (MOOCs), Skype lessons, or other online language courses are readily available; all are delivered by native speakers who add interaction through the chats. However, to improve their language learning, learners often opt for naturalistic language encounters where they learn by communicating in the language, but at the same time have support by expert teachers. Some of the most effective out-of-class language experiences are those where pedagogically structured contacts and naturalistic contacts are combined.

One of the most common options for facilitating encounters with native speakers is study abroad which, while generally designed for language learners, may also include opportunities for professional development of nonnative teachers or pre-service teachers in a target-language context. Another type of encounter would be through intensive immersion in language villages located in the learner's country of origin. In this chapter, we explore these ways of improving language learning through interaction with native speakers in different social settings. This has advantages over other useful outside-the-classroom work with the language in that, among other reasons, learners have more direct channels for receiving feedback. It can also help to develop their sociolinguistic, strategic, and cultural competences, and learners' confidence in being capable of interacting successfully in the target language.

Vignette

1: Study Abroad

Alice, a student from the United States who studies Spanish at her university, was not feeling confident about actually using the language. She had learned it well enough to pass her exams but she didn't know if she could pass the most important exam: being able to understand and be understood in a real communicative situation. As this was one of her main goals, she decided to look for a study-abroad program for the first semester of her last year at the university. She made an exhaustive search and chose Seville for its historical and cultural importance and because of its reputation for a friendly environment where foreigners were very welcome.

Before leaving for the study-abroad semester, she conferred with her professors about how to get the most out of the experience and was given useful advice. The onsite program director in Seville also answered several questions she had, so when she arrived she felt better prepared to "pass the test." She had requested home stay with a Spanish family in order to be able to have as much access as possible to native speakers, and before leaving she prepared many phrases in Spanish that she expected to need to be able to communicate with her host family. She knew she was a little shy about speaking in a language she didn't totally control, but she also knew that this could limit the success of her venture so she prepared herself not only linguistically but also psychologically to be ready to communicate in Spanish and not to be overly worried about making mistakes. She had read that the people in Seville were quite used to foreigners and were helpful and patient with the attempts of foreigners to express themselves. She visualized herself communicating fluently with people in Spanish in many different situations and this gave her more confidence that she would actually be able to do it.

At the University of Seville, Alice had a good selection of interesting courses to take given by native speakers of Spanish but her experiences in these classes were not so different from those in her home university but the rest of her day, outside the classroom, was radically different. She made a real effort to communicate with her host family at mealtimes. She found that at first, perhaps out of politeness, they didn't ask her a lot of questions but were very pleased to answer questions she had, and they gradually began to inquire about her life in the United States and her new life in Seville. She needed to use Spanish at many moments of the day and she tried to avoid spending a lot of time with other English speakers. She was always on the lookout for opportunities to speak Spanish, and at the university she found a program for volunteering with a local NGO, which gave her the chance to meet more native speakers and led to deeper immersion in Spanish society and an increase in her intercultural sensitivity.

For developing her ability to communicate with greater fluency in Spanish, Alice found it very useful to participate in the tandem conversation exchanges offered at the university. While only half the speaking time was in Spanish since her part of the exchange was to help the Spanish student with his English, she found it to be a great opportunity to speak with someone with similar motivation towards learning the language spoken by the conversation partner. To bring in written communication, Alice and her partner also agreed to keep journals and correct/comment on each other's weekly entries. Both in their spoken and written exchanges they were able to get important feedback from their partner which meant not only greater fluency from the exchange but also greater accuracy.

During her study-abroad experience, Alice both improved her language competence and extended her knowledge of Spanish culture. Instead of admiring photos of the Plaza de España in Seville, which she was already familiar with as the setting in several films such as *Star Wars* and *Lawrence of Arabia*, or the cathedral with its famous Giralda tower, she was able to "live" the culture she was learning about. She was very moved when she visited the room in the Alcazar Palace, where over five centuries ago Columbus was received by Queen Izabella after his second voyage to America, and she then went to the nearby town of Huelva where she could go on board the life-size replicas of the original ships in which Columbus and his crew sailed from there to America. Culture left the pages of her textbook and became part of her life experience.

2: Language Villages

Elena, a Spanish business woman from the south of Spain, wanted to become more fluent in her international business negotiations and in general to feel more confident when interacting in English. As she currently had only a week free, she decided to enroll in an intensive course at a language village in the north of Spain. Before being accepted, she had to take an oral exam on the phone to ensure she had a sufficient level of English to benefit from this experience. In the group, there were as many native speakers from different English-speaking countries as Spanish learners of English.

Sessions started at 9.00 AM with breakfast, and then learners were paired each hour with different native speakers for one-to-one activities in English such as practicing telephone conversations, talking about common interests or preparing presentations on a given topic. The afternoon sessions included general group dynamics activities for team building and preparation of the entertainment for the evening sessions. After dinner, there were social activities, including drama, karaoke singing, telling jokes, poetry reading or dancing.

During this immersion experience, Elena improved her communicative skills in English but also her social skills. Participating in authentic communicative situations in a nonthreatening, supportive atmosphere gave her confidence in her ability to express her ideas in English. The activities in the language village were all very success-oriented, and this helped Elena to lose her fear of speaking in English. The varied kinds of activities carried out led her to feel more comfortable when relating to native speakers in different types of situations.

As the native speakers she interacted with were from different English-speaking countries, she became familiar with different accents and cultural backgrounds. She found that knowing about those different cultures could help her when conversing. She understood that to be successful in her professional context where she has to negotiate with people from many places, intercultural competence needs to be developed as well as linguistic competence. She also reflected on how to interact successfully with English speakers from different educational backgrounds and in diverse environments to be able to adapt to each communicative situation. She arranged to keep in contact by e-mail with all the native speakers she had met because she knew that this could help her with her writing skills. Finally, while she was aware of the limitations of an intensive course lasting only six days, she felt she had achieved her main goal: losing her fear of interacting with native speakers and thus gaining confidence that she could use her English successfully in professional and other contexts.

Principles

Most language learners want to do more with the language than translate texts or understand the basic grammar concepts; they want to be able to communicate in the language, to understand the culture, and move comfortably between different registers depending on the communicative situation. The following are some principles that support these purposes:

> *Principle 1. Using language in authentic as well as pedagogically and culturally structured contexts outside the classroom can significantly enhance the language-learning process.*

Here the word *authentic* is very important. In the classroom, students often do activities that involve role playing of situations such as those they would find in the real world and this is good practice—but learners know that it is not the "real thing." When actually living in the country for a study-abroad experience or while immersed in a sociolinguistic experience with native speakers in a language village, using the language in real communicative situations is much more meaningful for learners. Authentic use of the language also includes understanding the social context of speech acts, which refers to "the culture-specific context embedding the norms, values, beliefs, and behavior patterns of a culture" and which implies development of learners' sociopragmatic competence and includes factors such as "the role of the participants in a given interaction, their social status, the information they share, and the function of the interaction" (Alptekin, 2002, p. 58). This, of course, is something much more readily available to learners in a target-language context.

Another advantage of being in a context where their concern is not just to learn the rules of the language but to actually communicate with native speakers is that learners develop useful compensatory strategies to overcome the inevitable conversation breakdowns. This progressive improvement of learners' strategic competence makes them feel more confident, lowering their anxiety.

In the case of Alice, when she came to Spain, she was somewhat worried at first that she might not be understood when speaking with Spaniards. However, she found that the need she felt to make herself understood was stronger than her fear of making mistakes, and so jumping in and using the language, with some difficulties at first, enabled her to make even more progress than she had hoped for. Part of her success was due to her realizing that just being surrounded by the language would not help as much as if she had a plan for getting the most out of the opportunities afforded her to interact with native speakers. She was proactive about finding ways to be in contact with native speakers.

In research on the topic, it has been found that study-abroad learners do not always make greater gains than their peers at home in all aspects of language learning (Segalowitz et al., 2004; Collentine, 2004). The conclusions of these and other studies indicate that results, as regards proficiency in all areas of language learning, are not always optimal in study-abroad programs because learners may take learning too much for granted and because they are not given adequate support in the form of strategy training to take full advantage when abroad of the encounters with the language and culture (Paige et al., 2004). Thus even in a study-abroad context, pedagogical orientation to maximize the benefits of opportunities outside the classroom can be important.

Principle 2. Opportunities for conversations with native speakers about topics of mutual interest can help learners to become skilled communicators. Learning languages by conversing is really nothing new. In the sixteenth century, Montaigne wrote that through conversation "Without methods, without a book, without grammar or rules, without a whip and without tears, I had learned a Latin as proper as that of my schoolmaster" (cited in Savignon 1983, p. 47). In a similar vein, Tarone (2007, p. 842) reminds us of Bakhtin's recommendation that we should learn language from people (not from dictionaries), as "the language varieties we learn from people always retain elements of the personalities and values of those people," and this is exactly what happens through interacting in authentic contexts when participating in language encounters. In conversations, participants both listen and speak. In naturalistic interaction, learners can practice listening comprehension: retaining information and connecting it with what comes next while at the same time they may need to access their schemata knowledge to understand more fully. Speakers naturally tend to adapt to their listener's competence and modify their speech to facilitate understanding.

In the language villages, this adaptation is more evident as the native speakers have been given the mission of helping learners to understand what they say to them, and so their conversational style includes strategies that facilitate language learning. They tend to use verbal or nonverbal means to create discourse contexts where learners can freely express themselves, talking about their thoughts and feelings on a number of topics. For these conversations between learners and native speakers, topics are often selected beforehand; some of them may be on personally relevant matters and others are related to activities the native/nonnative pairs have to present later in front of the rest of the group.

After her course at a language village, Elena, the Spanish business woman, considered that the experience had been very positive and that her spoken English had improved. Research confirms Elena's perception; it has been shown that L2 contact through study-abroad or immersion programs strongly affects learners' fluency (D'Amico, 2012) especially if, as we have seen, learners are given support and orientation for maximizing learning.

Principle 3. *Intensive out-of-class language experiences can connect to broader goals.* Language and cultural encounters are related in many ways to broader social goals. Intensive out-of-class language experiences can facilitate empathy, native speaker–learner rapport and cross-cultural appreciation. Intercultural understanding is often assumed to be an automatic benefit when people from different cultures are in contact, but problems with communication can arise when they hold different cultural references. Cultural issues may be explored with learners to eliminate prejudices and stereotypes.

As Naim Boutanos said, "Man is the enemy of all he ignores: teach a language and you will prevent a war. Spread a culture and you will bring peoples together."[2]

Principle 4. *Learners' attitudes towards the language and culture will have a significant effect on their willingness to communicate and their learning.* Varied learning activities in authentic situations that include cultural exposure will be likely to be appraised positively by learners. During Alice's study-abroad experience, Spanish "culture" (everyday life of the Spanish people) and "Culture" (the historical and artistic heritage of the country) came alive for her, making her relationship with the language more meaningful.

From a neurobiological perspective Schumann (1999, pp. 29–30) explains the importance for the maintenance of motivation of stimulus appraisals in language learning: they include "novelty, and familiarity, pleasantness, goal or need significance, coping potential and self and social image." Appreciation for another culture can relate to several of these and can affect learners' executive motivation, that which occurs while learners are engaged in tasks in language learning.

Language learning has been defined as "a deeply social event that requires the incorporation of a wide range of elements of the L2 culture" (Dörnyei, 2001, p. 159). In a study-abroad experience access to direct contact with these elements is readily available. Many of them are also included in the activities and the contacts established in language villages where great emphasis is placed on providing learners with cultural knowledge and on creating a good intergroup climate. Referring to the latter, Hadfield (1992) says, "A positive group atmosphere can have a beneficial effect on the morale, motivation and self-image of its members, and thus significantly affect their learning, by developing in them a positive attitude to the language being learned, to the learning process, and to themselves as learners" (p. 10). Cultural encounters enjoyed by learners may shape their attitude and help to sustain motivation for language learning that depends on the quality of learners' language-related experiences.

Applications

Study-abroad programs are designed in general for university students to have the opportunity to study languages and get credits for their degree in their home university but in a country where the language is spoken.

While study-abroad programs are generally for undergraduates or masters students, there are also experiences abroad for nonnative language teachers or for pre-service teachers designed to facilitate the improvement of both language and teaching skills as well as providing first-hand knowledge of the target culture, which is something that can greatly enrich their teaching of the language.

Language villages with their short intensive courses are conceived of mainly for busy adult learners who would like to combine language learning and meeting with native speakers. They are generally highly motivated language learners who want to invest their money (or their company's money) in something that can really satisfy their expectations. There are also variations for younger learners such as summer language holidays or summer language camps. They all have

in common that without leaving their home country, learners can have intensive and usefully structured out-of-class language and cultural experiences with
native speakers of the target language.

Payoffs and Pitfalls

The most obvious advantage of learning a language in an immersion situation is
the easy access to native speakers of the language studied. Thus, developing communicative competence is, at least theoretically, much easier.

Some students such as Alice are able to take full advantage of a study-abroad
learning experience but not all study-abroad students behave in the same way.
Some of them prefer to remain in their safety zone and to spend a lot of time
with other students from their home country (Magnan & Back, 2007). In research
on communication skills, it has been confirmed that study-abroad students have
not always benefitted from the L2 interaction opportunities they have had. Stephenson (2002, pp. 90–93) speaks of three different factors that can influence
the results of study abroad: individual characteristics of students, opportunities
for interaction with the host culture and characteristics of the program for study
abroad and the staff involved, but she points out that each factor by itself is not as
important as the relationship between the three.

In the case of the Erasmus study-abroad programs, this initiative has greatly
increased student mobility within different countries and language contexts in
Europe. Large numbers of university students have studied abroad in another
university with an Erasmus grant. However, many of these programs do not have
a focus specifically on language learning. Also, students may not be studying in a
country where the language they are learning is spoken; for example, students of
English from France may have a grant to go to Rumania where they take courses
in English at the university but they do not have the extensive out-of-class contact
with English that greatly facilitates learning the language. Furthermore, Erasmus
students often do not receive the necessary orientation to take full advantage of
the contact with another language and culture.

Language villages offer learners a very important advantage for many adult
learners: they do not have to travel abroad in order to have intensive contact with
the language. In a language village, this can involve much more real contact in a
week than in several months of classes and as much actual use of the language to
communicate as some stays abroad, which are over a longer period of time but
do not provide the direct, structured communicative work with the language
that is found in the language villages. However, while learners are gaining greater
fluency with the language, the intercultural experience in language villages is
much more reduced. They do have access to knowledge of other cultures via
their conversations with the native speakers from different countries but this is
not the same as being in the country where the language is spoken and where

one is surrounded by monuments that are related to the history and culture of the country and where there are possibilities to do the everyday things that people from the country do.

Discussion Questions

1. Learners sometimes experience anxiety when they try to communicate with native-speakers? What do you think are the causes of this kind of anxiety?
2. Why do you think on-line contact with native speakers may be less threatening for learners than face-to-face encounters?
3. In the light of your response to questions 1 and 2, how can teacher prepare learners to try out their communication skills with native-speakers?
4. What features of a home-stay experience do you think are likely to benefit language learners? Are there features of the experience that could also sometimes be problematic in terms of language learning?
5. How do you think tandem conversation-exchange experiences can be structured to facilitate effective language learning?
6. Which aspects of language learning and use do you think are most likely to benefit from an English-village experience? Which are not?
7. What features of authentic language use do you think are facilitated by study abroad and language-village experiences?
8. What aspects of cultural knowledge and awareness are such experiences most likely to facilitate?

Resources

In this chapter, we have stressed the importance of not just studying abroad but studying strategically to get the most out of the experience. The following link to the Center for Advanced Research on Language Acquisition (CARLA) provides research and resources on strategies for studying abroad. http://www.carla.umn.edu/strategies/SBIinfo.html

References

Alptekin, C. (2002). Towards intercultural communicative competence in ELT. *ELT Journal*, 56(1), 57–64. doi: 10.1093/elt/56.1.57

Collentine, J. (2004). The effects of learning contexts on morphosyntactic and lexical development. *Studies in Second Language Acquisition*, 26, 227–248.

D'Amico, M. (2012). L2 fluency and willingness to communicate: The impact of short-term study abroad versus at-home study. *US-China Foreign Language*, 10(10), 1608–1625.

Dörnyei, Z. (2001). *Motivational strategies in the language classroom*. Cambridge: Cambridge University Press.

Hadfield, J. (1992). *Classroom dynamics*. Oxford: Oxford University Press.

Magnan, S. S., & Back, M. (2007). Social interaction and linguistic gain during study abroad. *Foreign Language Annuals*, 40(1), 43–61.

McArthur, T. (1991). *A foundation course for language teachers*. Cambridge: Cambridge University Press

Paige, R. M., Cohen, A.D., & Shively, R. L. (2004). Assessing the impact of a strategies-based curriculum on language and culture learning abroad. *Frontiers: The Interdisciplinary Journal of Study Abroad*, 10, 253–276.

Savignon, S. (1983). *Communicative competence: Theory and classroom practice*. Reading, MA: Addison-Wesley.

Schumann, J. (1999). A neurobiological perspective on affect and methodology in second language learning. In J. Arnold (Ed.), *Affect in language learning* (pp. 28–41). Cambridge: Cambridge University Press.

Segalowitz, N., Freed, B., Collentine, J., Lafford, B., Lazar, N., & Diaz-Campos, M. (2004). A comparison of Spanish second language acquisition in two different learning contexts: Study abroad and the domestic classroom. *Frontiers: The Interdisciplinary Journal of Study Abroad*, 10, 1–18.

Stephenson, S. (2002). Beyond the lapiths and the centaurs: Cross-cultural "deepening" through study abroad. In W. Grünzweig & N. Rinehart (Eds.), *Rockin' in Red Square: Critical approaches to international education in the time of cyberculture* (pp. 85–104). Munster: Lit Verlag.

Tarone, E. (2007). Sociolinguistic approaches to second language acquisition research, 1997–2007. *The Modern Language Journal*, 91, 837–848.

Notes

1. When using the term *native speakers* in this paper we also mean any speakers of the language who have a level of proficiency similar to that of a native speaker.
2. As cited in Regional Ministry of Education, *Plurilingualism Promotion Plan: A language policy for Andalucian society*, http://www.juntadeandalucia.es/averroes/plurilinguismo/planing.pdf.

23

STUDY-ABROAD PROGRAMME DESIGN AND GOAL FULFILMENT

"I'd Like to Talk Like a Kiwi"

John Macalister

Introduction and Overview

Study abroad, or the opportunity to have trans-national educational experiences, is a feature of many language-learning programmes. There is considerable variety in the implementation of study-abroad; programmes vary, for example, from short visits to protracted stays in a foreign country, and from an emphasis on cultural tourism to a firm focus on learning the target language. There can also be variety in the goal of the study-abroad experience; a short course may be aiming at affective change, motivating learners to learn the language more enthusiastically when back in their home country, whereas longer courses may have clearly defined language proficiency development goals.

Trans-national experiences are found not only in language-learning programmes but also in language teacher education programmes. The benefits for participants are believed to be multiple. Sahin (2008), for example, claimed that for 26 Turkish pre-service teachers a two month internship experience in the United States contributed to the professional, personal, and cross-cultural changes that the teacher education programme sought to make. A different example of such a programme is the focus of this chapter. Supported by the Malaysian government, it saw pre-service teachers spending two years abroad at selected universities in New Zealand, Australia, and the United Kingdom. This was a typical 'sandwich' programme; the time abroad was sandwiched between preparatory and final years in Malaysia, with the teaching practicum forming a significant part of the final year.

An examination of the perceptions about the purpose of the programme held by different participants in the programme—the Malaysian pre-service teachers, their Malaysian lecturers, and lecturers in a New Zealand university—found considerable differences (Macalister, 2013). The New Zealand-based teacher educators focused on pedagogical knowledge, while the dominant theme for the Malaysian teacher educators was on the role of the teacher—the characteristics of a teacher generally, and, more specifically the teacher as developer of critical thinking and the teacher as an agent of change. For the pre-service teachers, however, who were training to be English language teachers, the focus was firmly and primarily on content knowledge; they spoke of knowing more about the language, of being better able to use the language, and of developing cross-cultural knowledge. Language proficiency development was neatly encapsulated in one student's response when asked about the anticipated benefits of two years in New Zealand.

STUDENT: Well, first I hope that ah, I hope that my English can improve.
J.M.: Yep, yep.
STUDENT: I'd like to talk like a Kiwi.

It is worth emphasising here that the students were not enrolled in an English language-learning programme; while abroad they were studying academic content courses. The focus of this chapter, then, is on what teacher educators can learn from the ways in which these students did—or did not—engage in language use and language-learning activities in order to pursue their own language-related goals.

Towards the end of their two years in New Zealand, 12 student participants volunteered for a follow-up interview, during which they talked about their time in New Zealand and the ways in which they had, or had not, engaged with opportunities to develop their English language proficiency. There was a mixture of experience, and the following two vignettes tell the stories of, first, a more successful experience and, then, a less successful one. While each is essentially one person's account of their engagement with language learning opportunities, details have been borrowed from other people's stories in order to ensure greater anonymity. In what follows, the words are those of the students; my contributions to the discussion are signalled by the initials 'J.M.'

Vignette

Selma was one of a sizeable minority among the cohort of 60 students who was not ethnically Malay. She also stood apart for coming from a family where English was the primary language of the home. This put her at an advantage over some of her peers, but even so she admitted to being initially self-conscious about the grammatical correctness of her speech when talking with native speakers.

> Um ... probably not thinking too much because when you talk to a Kiwi you tend to be very cautious with your grammar, but after some time I realize it's not about the grammar at the end of the day, it's about the message you're trying to bring across.

Of course, she was only able to come to this realisation because she made conscious decisions to do things apart from the group. She found work—in a Malaysian restaurant admittedly—but her interactions were mainly with the customers, so English was needed. She also tried to take elective courses which her peers were not taking, in order to create opportunities to interact with others.

> Yeah. Although … this might really sound bad, but I try to distance myself from Malaysians from time to time. You know I don't want to go back to that comfort zone because I actually had a class on with two Asians and me being the only Malaysian, and the other one's a Japanese so. … So, well the first class wasn't that fun because that's the first problem: Where do I sit? 'Cos everyone's a stranger. But then I've been trying to look for classes like this, you know. Where you don't have any Malaysians so that you automatically manoeuvre yourself towards them and you sit beside them for the whole three months and don't make friends.

In class, she was also ready to contribute.

> No I mean, I don't know, maybe because, it depends on the person I'd say. So for me I'm kind of extrovert person, so I like to ask. Whether it's in lecture or in an informal conversation I just like to ask people. So that's one of the things that might put me up outside of my comfort zone. You know you are forced to ask because you don't know, if you are not asking then you cannot understand for this kind of assignment for example. Like, you know, when I am having difficulty in doing an assignment I'm going to see [a learning advisor] for example. So I'm actually talking. Speaking to the native speakers so … mmm

Prior to beginning her two years abroad, she had received advice from her 'seniors,' the students who had preceded her to New Zealand, and on the basis of this advice she registered for a university programme that required her to engage broadly with the university and the local community.

> Yeah. I um … despite it taking a lot of my time from my Malaysian friends, um … I thought that's a sacrifice I've got to make for my two years just because that is what my government sent me for, might as well just make the most out of it. I met a lot of people from different majors. I wouldn't have met them if I didn't join the programme. They wouldn't even have sat with me and discussed about international issues. I wouldn't engage with the society. I wouldn't get to know, you know normal people like the nuns in the church and all that if I didn't, you know, volunteer. Yeah.

But what made her most different from her contemporaries was a willingness to be independent. She travelled around the country alone, did seasonal work, lived with non-Malaysians, and through these interactions discovered yet more opportunities, such as going to tramp a famous walking track.

SELMA: And I backpacked around New Zealand last summer. I mean I …
J.M.: Not by yourself I hope?
SELMA: All by myself *(both laugh)*.
J.M.: Selma!
SELMA: Sometimes I join the Krazy Kiwi Experience Tour. Oh I met a lot of Canadians and Londoners and crazy people too. *(JM laughs)* Up to Cape Reinga and down to Stewart Island. I met a lot of old ladies who were tramping alone. Fifty, sixty …
J.M.: Yeah?
SELMA: And they were like "Oh Milford Track? Oh I've done that." They showed me pictures.

Salmah, on the other hand, had not enjoyed the same success. She shared characteristics with the majority of the group—female, ethnically Malay, and Muslim. She began, as almost all the students did, with good intentions. She was going to meet new people, take different electives from those of her friends, and so on. She soon found, however, that it was easier to stick with her friends. As she admitted, "It's not that we don't want to mix with others, it's just that we're comfortable with those groups."

Like Selma, she had found employment—in another, but different, Malaysian restaurant—but for her this proved a hindrance to participating in a range of other activities. When she did have spare time, she tended to join in Malaysian group activities; after all, she had her friends and "it's real hard to be parted from them."

She was also committed to being a successful student. For her, this was also a constraint on using English productively.

J.M.: Yeah, okay. So what about in the university? Have you had much chance to interact with people who aren't Malaysian?
SALMAH: Mmm. Just during tutorial. I'm not the one who really like to talk in the lecture hall.
J.M.: I remember.
SALMAH: Because I think I need to focus in lecture hall. Er … some … because if I have tried in my first year, tried to talk like during lecture but sometime I just lost my focus.
J.M.: Mm. Mm. We all learn in different ways.
SALMAH: Yeah.
J.M.: Yeah, yeah, yeah, okay. Okay. No that's good, that's good.
SALMAH: Specially during [so-and-so's] lecture …
J.M.: Yeah. Yeah.
SALMAH: I need to focus from first the beginning to the end.
J.M.: Yeah.
SALMAH: If I start to talk—oh no!

When asked to what extent she felt she had met her own language proficiency development goals, Salmah rated her performance as average, around 50%.

J.M.: Around 50? OK. OK. And what could have made it more successful?

SALMAH: Because I think it's my own mistake. Not other people. I just don't take the opportunity. You have a lot of facilities here.

Principles

It would be too easy to put Selma and Salmah's different experiences down to learner variables—being a member of the majority group disfavouring local engagement, for instance, or having English as a home language facilitating it. The vignettes are to some extent composites, being true for both Malay and non-Malay, females and males. And from the vignettes certain principles emerge. These are principles for teacher educators and course and programme designers to bear in mind when considering a trans-national programme for students enrolled in content—as opposed to language-learning—courses; they create an environment that encourages engagement.

> *Principle 1. Promote autonomy through real-world communication.* One of the five principles that Cotterall (2000) proposed for promoting learner autonomy in the language classroom was that "Course tasks either replicate real-world communicative tasks or provide rehearsal for such tasks" (p. 111). In the same vein, transnational education programmes need to create situations in which students must engage in real-world communicative tasks with target language speakers. This engagement needs to be autonomous, and based on real-world needs. Among the 60 Malaysian students, those with a defined role and associated responsibilities reported engaging in more English language use than those who did not; the latter tended to allow the others to speak for them. These roles did not need to be formal and within the programme—Selma, for example, seemed to manage interactions for her flatmates, as the interview extract below illustrates.

J.M.: Yeah. OK. Yeah ... yeah ... yeah. And what about outside? Have you had any opportunities to develop your English outside of the university?

SELMA: Mmm. Yes, when talking to my landlord!

(Both laugh)

J.M.: OK, OK. Well that makes sense. Yeah. Yeah.

SELMA: Yes. Yeah. Because there's one time—he's Indian—and then our house always be like a viewing house for the insurance to come in, so we have to talk to the insurance officer so all sort of thing. When our internet going slow I have to contact my internet agent so I speak English with that.

The lesson for course and programme designers is that they should identify and assign roles and responsibilities to students as a means of facilitating such interactions. Examples are roles relating to the organisation of academic and social activities, and to representing others in, for example, sports teams and halls of residence.

Principle 2. Foster positive affect and integrative motivation. Another principle that is found in language curriculum design and that can apply equally to creating opportunities for out-of-class language learning relates to integrative motivation; in other words, to attitudes. As has been said elsewhere, "If learners have negative attitudes towards the language and its users, or if they feel personally threatened by having to use the language, this will make it difficult for them to progress in learning the language" (Nation & Macalister, 2010, p. 62). Selma's engagement with New Zealanders, and others, both on-campus and elsewhere, suggests that she held positive attitudes, and benefitted accordingly. For Salmah, however, it was more difficult:

> But I find it quite hard really to mingle with Kiwis and locals because we have different cultures and stuff ... so. Like last time we went out with them, they ... we went to a bar and they were drinking and stuff. So that kind of thing is quite hard for me. So some just really understand ... but some don't ...

This suggests that at least some of the local students were either unaware of or insensitive to the Muslim prohibition on drinking alcohol; a café may have been a better choice for out-of-class socialising than a bar. Salmah realised this problem when she said, "It's quite hard to mingle with them because you don't socialize like how they did." When reflecting on her language proficiency development goal at the end of the two years in New Zealand, she concluded, "'Cos I don't really get to mingle that much with Kiwis and stuff. I didn't really improve that much."

Principle 3. Provide repeated opportunities for real-world communication. The importance of repetition is well-known in language learning. In vocabulary learning, for example, repeated encounters with words has been shown to be a pre-requisite for learning to occur (e.g., Webb, 2007; Zahar, Cobb, & Spada, 2001). In the context of out-of-class language learning, repetition is also important as a means of supporting the first two principles, autonomy and integrative motivation. Put simply, thought needs to be given to providing repeated opportunities for students to engage in real-world communicative tasks and to interact socially with native speakers.

Principle 4. Challenge traditional views of learning and foster flexibility of learning styles. The final principle derives from Salmah's observation that she needed to focus on understanding the oral input of lectures, and so did not interact with others during the formal content learning sessions. The likelihood is that Salmah subscribed to a transmission mode of learning, a view quite probably shared to a large extent by the lecturer, for this after all is what she appeared to experience, leavened a little by question and answer exchanges between lecturer and students. To change this, the traditional view of the learner as passive needs to be challenged with both teaching staff and students, and alternative ways of teaching suggested to faculty. While the use of question and answer exchanges may work as a means of monitoring comprehension and gathering input with some students, it may not be suited to all and may be particularly unsuited to students, like Salmah, who are also concerned with their ongoing language proficiency development.

Applications

The applications of these principles relate to the support that should be in place around trans-national education programmes, and the preparation that should be undertaken before the programme begins. They are principles that teacher educators need to apply when designing courses if they want students to develop language and cross-cultural communication skills.

One element of preparation should be with university teaching staff to raise awareness of how their own teaching style may not suit the learning style of their students, particularly non-native-speaker students. Taking a critical needs analysis approach, which works from the assumption "that institutions are hierarchical and that those at the bottom are often entitled to more power than they have" (Benesch, 1996, p. 736), Benesch has demonstrated the power of considering the university lecture from the non-native-speaking learners' perspective. She found that learners "want and, one might say, need small classes, informal discussion, discourse that includes humor and personal anecdotes, and the opportunity to ask new questions" (1996, p. 734). Small changes, such as opportunities to discuss with other students in pairs or small groups during the lecture, or the opportunity to ask questions at designated times, can make a big difference both to learning outcomes generally and to increasing opportunities to engage with the target language.

A second element of preparation relates to cross-cultural training. In practical terms, this is most likely to be made available to the students on the trans-national programme, rather than to local students, as the former are a clearly defined group, the latter are not. Such training could, however, prepare students like Salmah for the experience of being taken to a bar and equip her with strategies, such as suggesting an alternative venue, so that the experience becomes more positive, with the possibility of follow-up social meetings enhanced.

Possibly the greatest initiative that could improve opportunities for out-of-class language learning are programmes such as that Selma enrolled in. The Victoria International Leadership Programme (VILP) is an award-winning programme offered at Victoria University of Wellington, New Zealand, that its promoters describe as "an academically oriented extra-curricular programme of seminars, speaker events, and experiential activities relevant to" a range of themes including international leadership and cross-cultural communication. While the requirement to attend and provide reflective feedback on a fixed number of seminars and other speaker events broadens the university experience, the experiential activities add the cross-cultural (and language development) element; examples of such activities include teaching English to refugees and/or migrants in the local community, being a buddy in the University's Language Learning Centre, working as an intern at an embassy, and engaging in learning another language. As Selma said of her experience on the VILP, "I wouldn't get to know, you know normal people like the nuns in the church and all that if I didn't, you know, volunteer."

Payoffs and Pitfalls

By implementing these principles in trans-national education programmes, the claimed professional, personal, and cross-cultural benefits that such programmes are believed to offer are more likely to be delivered. However, even then, there are no guarantees. It is, for example, worth bearing in mind that only one of the 60 Malaysian pre-service teachers in this cohort actually completed the VILP, although Selma was not the only one to begin it. Perhaps this could be described as the "you can lead a horse to water" syndrome. In this case, there were 60 students with much in common; they had already spent 18 months studying together in Malaysia and arrived in New Zealand with well-established friendship groups. It is reasonable to ask to what extent the expectation that students will put aside their shared history simply because they are in a different country, with different opportunities, is realistic. As Salmah herself said, "It's not that we don't want to mix with others, it's just that we're comfortable with those groups."

It is also the case that involvement in a programme such as the VILP does require a commitment that not all students feel they can make. Salmah, for example, found that her academic studies and her involvement with a Malaysian students' organisation did not allow her to complete the VILP requirements. Therefore, attention to teaching style, to cross-cultural training, and to identifying roles for students to take on so that they can engage in real-life communicative tasks with native speakers are also necessary as they create, at least the possibility for, increased engagement with the target language.

The only real pitfall in taking these steps is likely to arise, ironically, from achieving too great a success. There is always a risk that trans-national education programmes may alienate students from their home culture, the culture to which they must return. This was the experience for Japanese students who spent a year abroad in a Canadian university where individualism and critical thinking were encouraged, and who returned to "mope around their home campus bewildered and bitter that their newly found ability to criticise and question is not considered praiseworthy in Japan" (Greenholtz, 2003, p. 129). They had too successfully embraced the change that their trans-national experience promoted, and now found it difficult "to take their places in society" (p. 123).

One payoff, and this could be the greatest benefit, may be for promotion of inter-cultural learning among a group that is generally overlooked when the benefits of trans-national education programmes are being discussed—the local students. After all, if Malaysian students are interacting with New Zealanders, the New Zealanders will be learning about and from the Malaysian students. The trans-national experience becomes mutually enriching.

Discussion Questions

1. To what extent do international students have repeated opportunities to engage with native speakers in your context?
2. From your experience of university teaching, what changes could be promoted to faculty to give students a more active role in their own learning?
3. What cross-cultural challenges exist for international students in your context? Think of groups of students with different characteristics, and how the challenges may vary. What sort of advice or strategies could minimise any challenges?
4. Selma claimed to be an extrovert, and that this made her more willing than others to engage with native speakers. How important are personality traits such as this in determining a person's engagement with the target language? What role can programme and course design play in counteracting any constraints that might arise from considering yourself an introvert?
5. Based on your reading of other chapters in this book, what additional suggestions could you make for promoting language-learning opportunities on transnational language education programmes such as this?

Resources

For information about the *Victoria International Leadership Programme*, see http://www.victoria.ac.nz/students/get-involved/vilp.

References

Benesch, S. (1996). Needs analysis and curriculum development in EAP: An example of a critical approach. *TESOL Quarterly*, 30(4).

Cotterall, S. (2000). Promoting learner autonomy through the curriculum: Principles for designing language courses. *ELT Journal*, 54(2), 109–117.

Greenholtz, J. (2003). Socratic teachers and Confucian learners: Examining the benefits and pitfalls of a year abroad. *Language and Intercultural Communication*, 3(2), 122–130.

Macalister, J. (2013). Desire and desirability: Perceptions of needs in a trans-national language teacher education program. In S. B. Said & L. J. Zhang (Eds.), *Language teachers and teaching: Global perspectives, local initiatives* (pp. 303–316). New York: Routledge.

Nation, I.S.P., & Macalister, J. (2010). *Language curriculum design*. New York: Routledge.

Sahin, M. (2008). Cross-cultural experience in preservice teacher education. *Teaching and Teacher Education*, 24(7), 1777–1790. doi: 10.1016/j.tate.2008.02.006

Webb, S. (2007). The effects of repetition on vocabulary knowledge. *Applied Linguistics*, 28(1), 46–65. doi: 10.1093/applin/aml048

Zahar, R., Cobb, T., & Spada, N. (2001). Acquiring vocabulary through reading: Effects of frequency and contextual richness. *Canadian Modern Language Review*, 57(4), 541–572.

24
TALKING TO STRANGERS

Learning Spanish by Using It

Phiona Stanley

Introduction and Overview

This chapter considers how I learned Spanish by getting out of my 'comfort zone' and pushing myself into situations in which I had to use it, well before I felt ready to do so. I discuss different stages and the various strategies I used, and I analyse the ways in which this approach can be replicated by other language learners in different contexts. I begin with my own background and two language learning vignettes and, throughout the rest of the chapter, I refer back and unpack these experiences to make sense of how transferable this technique may be.

For several years in high school and as an undergraduate, I took classes in various languages and got nowhere fast. Languages, places, peoples, and cultures fascinated me then, as they do now, and every year or two I would make a start in a new language. In those years, I dabbled in French, Italian, Russian, Spanish, and German. In classes, we mostly focused on accuracy and grammar, and although I learned some trivia about each of these languages and a handful of useful phrases (and many useless ones, too), my oral proficiency was sorely lacking. I worried that I was no good at languages. I took some linguistics courses at university to learn more about the structure of languages generally in the hope that this would be the magic bullet. It wasn't. So it was with some trepidation that I set off, straight out of university, to Peru to teach English. Peru had just come out of civil war and I was living in an area of Lima in which most houses had an armed security guard outside the gate. When I walked past I would say hello to these guards, who were bored guys from the provinces, paid little for endless hours of watching and waiting; it was a quiet area. And little by little, I struck up a friendship with Arón, the guard at the house next door.

Vignette

Lima, Peru, 1994

We're sitting on the kerb in the dusty street under a tree; it is evening. I've brought us sugary *Inca Kola* and the two glass bottles sit next to us, collecting condensation in the humidity. We communicate through my fragments of Spanish but mostly through goodwill, sketches, and shared cognates, which we sometimes write down. It isn't early March but we're talking about International Women's Day; *el día internacional de la mujer*. I know the word *mujer* and the rest is cognate-easy. In Peru, Arón says, Women's Day means that men buy flowers for women, just like Mother's Day. I say that, where I am from, it is a bit different, a bit more feminist. He considers the word "feminist," rolls it around his mouth and then dismisses it: "Feminista." It sounds like an insult the way he says it. Arón is one of 13 children, *trece hijos. ("¿Tres? No, ¡Trece! Uno. Dos. Tres. Cuatro. Cinco. Seis. Siete. Ocho. Nueve. Diez. Once. Doce. ¡Trece!"* He counts on all his fingers and three of mine.) He sends his mother flowers on Women's Day. Women, he says, where he is from—which is Pucallpa, in the Amazon basin—the women there work just as hard as men. Harder. Women's Day celebrates this, he says. With *trece hijos*, I imagine his mother's life *is* really hard. I say this (grammatically all over the place but still making meaning): *vida es duro*, I tap on the surface of the stone kerb to show this idea, *duro*, hard. *"Sí, la vida es dura. La vida de mi mamá es bastante dura,"* Arón confirms, correcting my accuracy without even realising he is reformulating it for me. I listen attentively to how he puts it. Then, laughing, I ask if every other day of the year is *el día de los hombres*, and Arón laughs too, and then stops laughing, and says, simply, *sí*.

Warsaw, Poland, 1996

I am trudging through Łazienki Park in the snow. It's Friday afternoon, getting dark, and our breath condenses on the outsides of our scarves. Lots of other people are around, but the breath frozen on our scarves is different from theirs, because ours is forming *las palabras españolas* and not *polskich słów*: Spanish words, not Polish ones. I'm walking with my Polish friends Kinga and Piotr and we're going to our Spanish class at the Instituto Cervantes, which is attached to the white-marble Spanish embassy. Its teachers are Spanish graduates of *filología* and *lingüística aplicada*; well versed in the mysteries of the *subjunctivo*, the *pluscamperfecto*, and the *imperfecto*. They are amused at my Peruvian "street Spanish"; one tells me I sound like I just stepped out of the Amazon. They laugh, gently, that I don't know such simple words as *abrigo*, *bufanda*, and *guantes*, but I've never needed coats, scarves, and gloves in Spanish before. My teachers despair, a little, at the grammatical carnage I make of their royal language, and they bewilder me with their metalanguage and insistence on accuracy. But they cannot deny me this: When we listen in class to the original recording of Juan Rulfo's *Diles Que No Me Maten*, I, alone in our group, understand.

Principles

In Lima, I learned Spanish as I had learned English, by using all kinds of meaning-making strategies to build my language, as needed, from the ground up. The first day I sat with Arón I used, perhaps, 2% Spanish and 98% everything else: cognates, gestures, drawings, and the avoidance of anything complicated. During and in between our chats under the tree, I kept my eyes and ears open, magpie-like, collecting Spanish: I strained to string sentences together and I gathered new words as I needed them. I would make a coffee last all afternoon in the marketplace, poring over a book called, ambitiously, *Spanish in Three Months*. The book was a prop: it, and the lone *gringa*, attracted passersby, many of whom stopped and transformed themselves, momentarily, into Spanish teachers. Everyone was keen to help out. And then the next time I sat down with Arón I used, maybe, 3% Spanish and 97% everything else. And so it went.

What is going on here? There are two main ideas here, used in tandem: acquiring bits of language (input; Krashen, 1985) and using those bits of language, as well as whatever other resources are needed, to make meaning: output (Swain, 1985, 2005). Neither one, on its own, is enough. And sometimes the division between them is blurry: when I sat in the market with my book, I was learning a few words from the page (input) but I was also speaking to people (output), and sometimes those people were explaining new words (input) or I was trying to make meaning without the right words (output) and they would help me fill the gaps (input). The two processes are blended, which is the principle behind the test-teach-test language lesson format (e.g., Cullen, 2001), and what I was doing was perhaps an organic version of that.

> *Principle 1. Find sources of comprehensible input.* Krashen's (1985) input hypothesis posits that in order to acquire new pieces of language—grammatical structures, but also active vocabulary items—learners need to be exposed to language input that is simplified to a level just slightly above their own current language level. So although I may have a Russian TV channel, for instance, unless I'm exposed to slower, simplified Russian speech, I cannot pick up much Russian just from watching it as the input is not sufficiently comprehensible. Krashen called the requisite level "$i + 1$," by which he means the current state of the learner's interlanguage (i) plus one. This is the level at which comprehensible input can be used by learners as a source of development for their own learner language.
>
> So there I was. I would sit for hours in cafés with a dictionary and *El Comercio*, the local paper. It was good comprehensible input because it had a lot of pictures that gave context. I went out with my colleagues, other English

teachers, both *profesores nativos* and local Peruvians, and I listened, noticed the way they constructed things, and got them to write down their words for me. The same words and phrases kept coming up again and again and I looked them up: *pues, entonces, todavía, por lo menos, por si acaso, no es justo, me dijo. Poco a poco*—bit by bit—I built vocabulary; *paso a paso*—step by step—I understood more. I proudly brought all these new acquisitions back to Arón, under the tree. My Spanish was full of mistakes and the effort to speak was exhausting, but I felt the progress I was making. It was exhilarating, motivating, exciting, and fun.

Principle 2: Maximize opportunities for comprehensible output. This principle, proposed by Merrill Swain (1985, 2005), says that in order to develop his or her interlanguage, learners need to do more than simply *receive* comprehensible input. She or he also needs to *produce* language, and to receive feedback from listeners about what "works" or does not. So, for example, as people spoke to me in Lima I would replay their words in my head, making sense of things and sometimes trying them out for myself. A street seller went off to find small change and told me to stay (*no se vaya*) until he returned. I pondered this new construction, not learning its grammatical label until years later. I had never noticed it before, and had certainly never used it. To learn language by speaking it, one must become a language detective: a sleuth, an interrogator of words. I saw the same construction used in the title of a Jaime Bayly book, *No se lo digas a nadie*, on sale on every street corner that year. Both phrases are commands: *Don't go! Don't tell anyone.* I tried using this structure in all commands, and sometimes it worked and sometimes it caused looks of slight puzzlement. This was the negative feedback I needed to tell me that something wasn't quite right. So I restricted its use to phrases in which I knew it worked: *¡no me lo digas! ¡no te vayas!* Ah, these all start with *no*, maybe it is not *all* commands, only the negative ones? I tried that and it worked better.

I was a detective, solving this puzzle using the clues around me. I started hearing these odd verb forms cropping up in other places: *que tengas buen fin de semana; en cuanto lo sepa (have a good weekend; as soon as I know)*. It wasn't until I finally came to study Spanish in class that I was able to iron out the wrinkles and use this structure properly. But by then I had a feeling for when it 'sounded right', and this made it easy to grasp the underlying principles, enjoy some 'aha' moments, and then move on, using it organically. And, finally, I learned its name (it is the subjunctive). Like a native speaker of any language, I learned first to *use* the language and then I learned *about* it.

After six months in Lima, I took off for a while around South America. By then I could defend myself, as Spanish puts it, I could get by. Traveling, I struck up conversations with all kinds of people. I tried my first oyster—*ostra*—tasting of the sea, with some laughing fishermen; later I found out that *aburrido como una ostra* is to be bored as an oyster, that is, bored stiff. I squirreled away new words and idioms as if they were precious stones.

(A squirrel, *ardilla*, is an animal but not a verb in Spanish—and not to be confused with *orilla, águila,* or *anguila*—similar sounds, but different ideas.) Like the oysters, I tasted these new sounds, chewed them, pushed them around with my tongue (*lengua*, which is also 'language'). I rolled the r's and imitated the Latino lilt. I had fun with the language, and I smiled a lot, and smiling is infectious: I met people and they tolerated my lousy Spanish.

These stages seem to be the way pieces of grammar are acquired if you learn a language by using it: at first, it is used rarely, then randomly or in set phrases, then 'properly' (according to rules learned in a grammar book), and then, finally, organically, incorporated into natural use. Other research backs this up (Ellis, 1997; Lightbown & Spada, 1999, pp. 141–149; Scovel, 2001, pp. 50–56). It may not be the most *efficient* way to learn a piece of grammar but it does seem to be *effective*: I have a good 'sense' about what 'sounds right' in Spanish, much as I do in English, and I acquired this through learning Spanish by using it.

And I read. Books are expensive in Latin America but a vibrant bootleg trade exists on the streets. I read whatever they were selling and sometimes I struck up conversations with strangers because we were reading the same book. Many of the words I learned through extensive reading I've never had much use for since. To this day, I know a lot of obscure vocabulary that I've never needed: *eje* (both axis and axle), *destornillador* (a five-syllable screw-driver), enlutado (from the Guillén poem *¡Ay señora mi vecina!*) and *dábale arroz a la zorra el abad* (i.e., 'the abbot gave rice to the vixen,' which is a some-what contorted Spanish palindrome; I learned this, unsurprisingly, in Panama: *A man, a plan, a canal—Panama*).

I did not *need* these words, but 'need' is a slippery concept (*un concepto res-baloso;* I remember deducing *resbaloso* from the warnings of a stranger, while we were both climbing down river rocks near Baños, in the Ecuadorian Amazon). I 'needed' all these curious words because I needed a background to my new self. Words were a question of identity. I loved (and still love) being someone who speaks good Spanish. If you speak English and Spanish you can talk to half the world. Latin America draws me in like nowhere else: it has *chispa*, a sparkle, and it is a place where *no termino en mi mismo*, as Pablo Neruda puts it. I am more than just myself. My Latina self is more confident: That year I spent Christmas with a family of Bolivian silver miners and crossed Lake Titicaca with a Peruvian priest. Learning Spanish was as much a course in culture and confidence as it was in language.

Applications

For this approach to be successful, it helped that I am outgoing and that I didn't feel embarrassed to make language mistakes (Lightbown & Spada, 1999, pp. 54–57). Under our tree in Lima, Arón understood that I spoke English just as well as he spoke Spanish, and that my inability to say what I wanted to say in Spanish was indicative of nothing more than that; I never felt my identity or intellect were threatened by my limited language. Later, when traveling around and talking to strangers I was aware that I sometimes had to push myself to engage with people and that sometimes all I felt like doing was holing up somewhere with a book in English and avoiding the struggle to make meaning. (Sometimes, too, I retreated into the backpacker 'scene,' in English, spending time with other *gringos*.) I'm an extrovert, and I feel so very driven to learn Spanish, and if ever I felt like escaping sometimes, I can only imagine how confronting learning like this might be for someone more introverted and less motivated than me. This is supported by a famous case study of a Japanese artist who learned English in Hawaii, in a similar way how I learned Spanish. Of his subject, 'Wes,' Schmidt (1983, p. 142) writes, "All observers agree that Wes is an extremely extroverted and socially outgoing person, with high self-esteem and self-confidence, low anxiety and inhibition. He is ... not at all afraid of making mistakes or appearing foolish in his use of English."

This whole process, then, relies on three main factors: being in or seeking out a target-language-using environment, finding (or feigning) the confidence to have a go at using language without necessarily getting it 'right', and being sufficiently motivated to collect new bits of language from whatever source and to engage with users of the target language and become part of their social 'world.' Not everyone meets these conditions, but a bit of feistiness and the willingness to step out of a comfortable bubble are good things to develop more generally and are beneficial in areas well beyond language learning.

What about context? Is 'learning by using' something that requires the luxury of an extended period spent in a target-language context and plenty of free time to spend *pateando latas* (literally 'kicking cans,' but in English this might be 'shooting the breeze') among native users of your chosen language? Certainly, being in a target language place helps. (Although without motivation, it is absolutely possible to be in a language-rich environment and nevertheless eschew that language altogether: Plenty of long-term expats are only minimally proficient in the language of the place in which they live.) And it is better to be around the language, physically, viscerally, emotionally, if only to maintain the momentum of motivation. But it is also possible, as my Warsaw experience showed, to keep a language warm in a cold place. While it is *simpático* to speak Spanish in *Sudamérica*, it is perfectly possible to practice among Poles in a park. And now, thanks to the Internet, it is easy to find someone to practice language with, whether online or among others near you who speak the language (whether they are fellow learners or natives interested in a language exchange). My Spanish practice now, in Sydney, is both online with Latin Americans and locally among Australians who also learn and love Spanish. In the mid-1990s, when I started my Spanish journey, the only way to be fully immersed was to go to the target-language place; now, it is just as easy to do this online (and, for most people it is probably less intimidating to start chatting online than it is to make real-life friends in the street or market, as I did).

Payoffs and Pitfalls

The number one issue here, I think, is motivation, both amount and type. I have loved Latin America wholeheartedly from first reading and obsessing about going there during my undergraduate studies of Colombia to the moment I set foot in traffic-snarled Lima, through some very rough travels and my reading of its often brutal history to feeling a little shiver of excitement when I hear Spanish spoken in the street in Sydney. I have Latino friends and I share the values of those cultures that prioritise moment-to-moment enjoyment and the quotidian embrace of the literary and the magical. I keep an eye on Latin American politics and I have an iPhone app that links me to the Guatemalan national news: right now I'm following, with fascination and horror, the trial of Rios Montt. The literature of Latin America—both classic and contemporary—interests me, and the moment I landed in Texas for a conference this year, I tuned the rental car's radio to a salsa station. Caring about Latin America motivates me to learn the language. This is an integrative motivation and it is very strong—strong enough to make me trudge through Warsaw snow to Spanish classes; strong enough to have me listing obscure nouns like *ardilla, águila* and *anguila*.

Is it also necessary to experience, and play to, an otherness of some sort? Being a *gringa* certainly helped me in Lima, and being a language nerd gave me entry in Warsaw into a like-minded circle. But I don't think the mystique of otherness is a necessary condition of this approach. I know a Chinese student in Australia (where Chinese international students are ubiquitous and where it is perfectly possible to remain firmly ensconced in in a comfort zone throughout a university degree) who is managing to do something similar. Having initially taken a part-time job in a restaurant kitchen—speaking only Chinese—she now travels further and does less convenient shifts in an ice cream shop, where her colleagues are Afghani, Indian, and Brazilian and where English is used all day. Laughing one day, she also told me about a strange 'secret hobby' she enjoys: She calls the free phone 1-800 numbers on consumer goods packaging—toothpaste and shampoo packaging, electronic gadget instructions and guarantees, the Ikea helpline—with invented problems and questions for free English practise and, sometimes, a chat with bored call centre operators. This is not dissimilar to my sitting in the market in Lima with *Spanish in Three Months* all those years ago.

Discussion Questions

1. The writer of this piece describes her motivation as 'integrative' in that she wants to become part of Latin American society and culture. This helps her learn Spanish as she enjoys the identity that comes of using it. How would you describe your own or your students' motivation (type and amount) in a language you/they are learning?

2. How would you feel about starting a conversation in a language in which you are beginner level? To what extent is personality important in this 'method'? How might this learning approach be used by a shy person?

3. What was the role of Spanish–English cognates in this account? How could this process be applied to language learning where the learner's first and target languages do not share such linguistic similarities?

4. Learning a language by using it relies on finding something to talk about. Some of the websites listed, such as verbling.com, provide a list of suggested conversation topics on the side of the video-chat screen. If you are hoping to learn or improve a language by using it, what might you choose to talk about? What does this depend on?

Resources

Social networking, retro–style (i.e., get offline and go and talk to people!)

MeetUp—http://www.meetup.com/—provides a forum where like-minded people in your town or city can organize to meet. On it, there are lots of language-focused "meetups."

CouchSurfing—https://www.couchsurfing.org/—is for travelers and hosts looking for/offering free homestays. However, if you don't want to host visitors, you can also use this site to arrange to have coffee with tourists who come to your locale. You can set the language(s) you are learning and the countries you would like to meet people from.

Language exchange websites

These sites allow you to chat online with people whose language you are learning and who are learning your language:

   italki—http://www.italki.com/
   Verbling—https://www.verbling.com/

Language-learning blogs

And it is also worth reading the blogs of people who write (mainly) about *how* they learn languages. Here are some interesting ones but there are many others:

   The Polyglot Dream—http://www.thepolyglotdream.com/
   Fluent in 3 Months—http://www.fluentin3months.com/
   Every Day Language Learner—http://www.everydaylanguagelearner.com/
   Speaking Fluently—http://speakingfluently.com/
   Omniglot—http://www.omniglot.com/blog/
   http://www.janafadness.com/blog/
   http://www.mezzoguild.com/

References

Cullen, R. (2001). PPP and beyond: Towards a learning-centred approach to teaching grammar. In H. Ferrer Mora (Ed.), *Teaching English in a Spanish setting* (pp. 13–26). Valencia: Universitat de Valencia.

Ellis, R. (1997). *Second language acquisition*. Oxford: Oxford University Press.

Krashen, S. (1985). *The input hypothesis and implications*. New York: Longman.

Lightbown, P. M., & Spada, N. (1999). *How languages are learned*. Oxford: Oxford University Press.

Schmidt, R. (1983). Interaction, acculturation and the acquisition of communicative competence: A case study of an adult. In N. Wolfson & E. Judd (Eds.), *Sociolinguistics and second language acquisition* (pp. 137–174). Rowley, MA: Newbury House.

Scovel, T. (2001). *Learning new languages: A guide to second language acquisition*. Boston: Heinle & Heinle.

Swain, M. (1985). Communicative competence: Some roles of comprehensible input and comprehensible output in its development. In S. Gass & C. Madden (Eds.), *Input in second language acquisition* (pp. 235–256). Rowley, MA: Newbury House.

Swain, M. (2005). The output hypothesis: Theory and research. In E. Hinkel (Ed.), *Handbook of research in second language teaching and learning* (pp. 471–483). Mahwah, NJ: Lawrence Erlbaum Associates, Inc.

25
INCREASING THE LINGUISTIC AND CULTURAL BENEFITS OF STUDY ABROAD

Marc Cadd

Introduction and Overview

During the past several years, an increasingly significant number of college and university students have been making time for a study-abroad experience. Although their reasons for doing so vary greatly, many study abroad because they are either majoring or minoring in a world language, or they hope to use the language professionally. Regardless of motivation, students anticipate new experiences, a broad range of linguistic interactions, challenging and rewarding cultural experiences, and personal and academic growth.

Conventional wisdom assures students, parents, and teachers that they will return home with a significant increase in their linguistic proficiency and cultural understanding. The expectation that one will become fluent in the language is an often-heard inducement for students to undertake the experience. Students and educators alike assume this increased fluency can be achieved through greater access to native speakers of the language. As DeKeyser (2007) noted, "For some students, parents, teachers, administrators, and prospective employers, study abroad is not only the best form of practice, sometimes it is the only form they consider to be useful" (p. 208). However, immersion in another culture cannot guarantee linguistic and cultural gains. Research into this topic reveals quite a complex picture. For example, Rohrlich's study (1993, p. 4) determined that only three percent of survey respondents had as their primary reason for studying abroad to learn the target language. Further research is very mixed about the gains students can attain through study abroad.

Those studying abroad need to interact with native speakers. This interaction can occur through a variety of means (see Arnold & Fonseca-Mora in this book). In this chapter, we examine a one-credit-hour course required of students studying abroad and seeking transcriptable certification of linguistic and cultural competence. The assignments for the course are 12 "tasks" that require the students to interact with native speakers so that they do not spend all of their free time with fellow speakers of English. We will look at course requirements in more detail and the resulting experiences of students. We also examine the experiences of one student and learn how she assesses her linguistic and cultural gains.

Vignette

Monica studied in Spain. She was a motivated student, one determined to avoid the pitfalls of interacting with too many English-speaking students. She was majoring in international relations and hoped to work for the government in a Spanish-speaking country. She was concurrently enrolled in the course referred to above.

Monica did have some initial anxiety about speaking with Spaniards. After working her way through the tasks, though, she commented that, "I was really nervous for the first few weeks. This was not the Spanish I had learned in my classes at home. But once I got to know a few students and spoke with them all the time, it got easier. It got to the point I was even dreaming in Spanish part of the time." For her, more practice through the tasks yielded a lower level of anxiety.

Monica's self-perceived level of fluency increased as well as she completed the tasks: "If I can introduce myself to a person and get the person to see that I can speak Spanish well enough to hold a conversation, they are much less likely to keep switching back into English. They are appreciative that someone can speak their language fairly well and so I get more practice."

Finally, she expressed and demonstrated the belief that her cultural understanding had increased. She had this to say about how September 11 was perceived where she studied:

> In Barcelona, as well as the rest of the region, September 11 has an entirely different meaning than most Americans have known for the past ten years. What has become one of the darkest days in the history of the United States is, in fact, a day of celebration throughout the region known as La Diada.

> The day was officially designated Catalan's National Day in 1980 but previously it marked a loss of liberty to the region's inhabitants. On September 11, 1714, during the War of Spanish Succession, Barcelona fell to forces of the Bourbon Dynasty. After the defeat, Philip V punished the people of Cataluña by outlawing the language and traditional cultural practices of the region.

> Especially after years of oppression under Franco, the people of Cataluña have developed immense pride of their heritage, language, and culture. Now the annual national holiday has become a day of parades, poetry readings, and a showing of Cataluñan pride. ...

The more I thought about it the more I realized how similar the two meanings of September 11 are. Both symbolize loss—in America of our security, in Cataluña of culture. Both have become national rallying points as well as points of discord within the population. And both force its citizens to look toward the future.

Monica overtly compared the two meanings of September 11 for residents of Cataluña. She synthesized elements of history, culture, and current events to conclude that both cultures view that day as a day of loss.

Monica's persistence in using the language resulted in less anxiety, greater fluency, and increased cultural understanding. She realized that her linguistic and cultural gains were dependent upon the effort she put into her study-abroad experience.

Principles

Principle 1. Success with foreign language learning is significantly enhanced with out-of-class learning experiences. This is the primary principle underlying this chapter, and, indeed, the whole book. Students need to practice the language they are learning both in and out of the classroom, and a blend of in-class and out-of-class optimizes the chances of success with foreign language learning. There are many ways to have out-of-class learning experiences. In this chapter, I deal with one experience that has the potential to maximize the acquisition of a foreign language: the study-abroad program. By providing a more structured study-abroad experience, instructors can aid students pursuing an increase in both linguistic proficiency and cultural competence.

Principle 2. The success of a study abroad program hinges on the extent to which the learner interacts with native speakers. As the research demonstrates, students who are left to their own devices to locate and interact with native speakers may or may not exhibit gains in their linguistic skills and cultural competence. Many students studying abroad surround themselves with fellow speakers of their native language and seldom leave their comfort zone. In order to increase the likelihood that the desired positive gains occur, instructors should provide a more targeted approach that ensures students interact with native speakers.

Principle 3. In courses where students receive credit for their study-abroad program, provide structured tasks requiring students to interact with native speakers. One means of ensuring that students interact with native speakers is to require them to complete a series of tasks that require interaction with native speakers. Students at the author's university who were participating in a certificate program completed a series of such tasks as part of a one-credit-hour course. The primary objective for this course is that students complete a variety of functional tasks requiring competence in the language and culture. The 12 tasks and related cues for student blogging are delineated in the application section below.

Principle 4. Create experiences that result in students undergoing decisive interventions. A fourth principle that results in an increase in cultural understanding, as Laubscher (1994) noted, is that the student undergo some sort of "decisive intervention" (having an "insider perspective" provided) usually from a "key informant" (a native speaker). He concludes that simply "having the data available is no assurance that substantive learning will take place" (p. 106). This observation supports having students interview native speakers.

Riedel (1989) concurred when she stated that "[t]here is now a greater emphasis on 'forcing' students to take advantage of relative accessibility to personal contact with experts in their field and national institutions where firsthand information and experience is available" (p. 775). She has students interact with professionals in the target culture who are actively employed in the students' major field(s) of study. Riedel made two recommendations that appear to lead to positive gains in linguistic proficiency and cultural understanding:

> One, what is taught inside the classroom must always be related to what students will experience outside of the classroom. Two, students must be required to actively integrate the knowledge gained from the classroom with their extra-curricular activities. (p. 776)

These activities include internships and interviews with politicians, etc. Archangeli (1999) echoed this position, positing that once the students have arrived in the host country, instructors can best assist them by forcing the students to interact with native speakers in a meaningful fashion. By doing so, she believed the students' fear of speaking would decrease. The tasks described below attempt to integrate these two observations into course assignments.

Applications

The extent to which students benefit from their study-abroad experience is dependent on a large number of variables. These variables may be personal, academic, linguistic, and/or cultural. Such factors as whether students reside in a dormitory or have a homestay experience, the personality of the students, their reaction to the new environment and their ability to adjust to it, the types of courses in which they enroll, the length of their stay, and their previous knowledge of the culture all potentially play a role in determining the degree to which students demonstrate an increase in oral proficiency and cultural understanding. By requiring students to complete a required, structured set of tasks, the likelihood that these positive gains occur can be increased.

In Cadd's study (2012), he described 12 tasks that appear to be beneficial to all students, regardless of where they studied or for how long. The 12 tasks are outlined in Table 25.1.

TABLE 25.1 The 12 Tasks

Task One	Identify a current event that is controversial. Read two newspapers and compare/contrast the information there. Also speak to at least one member of the culture about the event. Ask how important it is, whether it will have a long-term impact, etc. What was the topic about which you read and spoke? When you spoke with someone about the culture, did you notice any differences in the way you speak in your culture and the way s/he did in hers/his? For example, was s/he more or less formal than you? Did you have problems understanding her/him? If so, what did you do about it? Did you use any strategies to make the conversations flow more smoothly?
Task Two	Introduce yourself to at least three members of the culture. What did you say about yourself? Which questions were you asked? Were you asked anything that you didn't expect? Was it easy or difficult to speak with these people? Why? Did you learn anything meaningful about the culture? Did you notice any differences between your style of communication and theirs? If so, what were they? Did you have problems understanding them? If so, what did you do about it?
Task Three	Identify a food dish not readily available in your culture. Go to a restaurant, store, etc. where that food can be found and ask a server, cook, or store employee about it. Which food dish did you investigate? What is its history? Why is it representative of that culture? Could you easily prepare that dish in your culture? Why (not)?
Task Four	Identify a museum, park, means of transportation, etc. that is representative of the culture. Find at least two members of the culture and inquire about why it represents that culture (e.g., what does the Washington Monument tell about the United States). Which museum, park, or means of transportation did you investigate? What did you learn about it? Did you learn anything meaningful about the culture? If so, what? Did you notice any differences between your style of communication and theirs? If so, what were they? Did you have problems understanding them? If so, what did you do about it?
Task Five	Attend a festival, fair, public event, etc. celebrated in the culture. Speak with at least two members of the culture who are present. Choose two who are quite different, e.g., young vs. old, male vs. female, etc. Ask why the event is important. Which festival, fair, public event, etc. did you investigate? What is its history? Did you learn anything meaningful about the culture? If so, what? Did you notice any differences between your style of communication and theirs? If so, what were they? Did you have problems understanding them? If so, what did you do about it?

(Continued)

Task Six	Speak to at least two people about your age or younger who would be familiar with some of the slang currently being used. Ask for their help in identifying at least 15 words or phrases. In your post, list these and tell when they would be used. Give the English equivalent, too.
	Did you encounter any surprises in this undertaking? Did you learn anything meaningful about the culture? If so, what? Did you notice any differences between your style of communication and theirs? If so, what were they? Did you have problems understanding them? If so, what did you do about it?
Task Seven	Call a business you are interested in and ask when it is open and where it is located.
	How do people answer the phone there? Did you find it more difficult to speak on the phone than in person? Why (not)? If it was more difficult speaking on the phone, how did you compensate for that? Did you learn anything meaningful about the culture? If so, what? Did you notice any differences between your style of communication and theirs in talking on the phone? If so, what were they? Did you have problems understanding them? If so, what did you do about it?
Task Eight	Go to a post office and mail something. Compare this experience to a comparable one in the United States or your native culture.
	How much does it cost compared to what you are familiar with? How did the person working there interact with you? Did you learn anything meaningful about the culture? If so, what? Did you notice any differences between your style of communication and theirs? If so, what were they? Did you have problems understanding them? If so, what did you do about it?
Task Nine	Ask three members of the culture for directions to a bank, restaurant, post office, movie theater, etc.
	How did they respond to you? Were they ready and willing to help? Did they ask where you are from or other questions? Did you learn anything meaningful about the culture? If so, what? Did you have problems understanding them? If so, what did you do about it?
Task Ten	Ask two members of the culture for their views on the United States, President Obama, etc. Ask if they view the people of the United States any differently than they view the government.
	What did you learn? Was it the same as you expected? Was it difficult to talk about this topic? If so, why? Did you notice any differences between your style of communication and theirs when talking about politics? If so, what were they? Did you have problems understanding them? If so, what did you do about it?

(Continued)

Task Eleven	Find two people who are members of a minority in the culture you are in. Ask about how they feel they are treated, why they are there, what kind of work they do, etc. Learn as much as you can without becoming too offensive or obtrusive.
	What did you learn from the people with whom you spoke? Did you learn anything meaningful about the culture? If so, what? Did you have problems understanding them? If so, what did you do about it?
Task Twelve	Find two members of the culture and ask about how people give gifts.
	When do people give gifts? What kinds of things are given for the various events? Is one expected to reciprocate? Should one bring a gift when invited to someone's house? Did you learn anything meaningful about the culture? If so, what? Did you have problems understanding them? If so, what did you do about it?

Students blogged periodically about their experiences in completing the tasks. Because the students studied abroad for one semester and it was imperative to encourage them to interact with native speakers throughout that period of time, the instructor advised the students to complete approximately one task per week. The tasks could be completed in any order so as to allow the students to take advantage of any serendipitous opportunities that presented themselves. Instructors regularly read and commented on the blogs as well. The language instructors in the United States who were reading the blogs were very proactive early in each student's study-abroad experience; if students did not blog early and/or did not reflectively assess their experiences, the instructors provided early direction. Cadd (2012) noted that students completed the tasks quite well, but they often required assistance in commenting appropriately and in a timely fashion.

The tasks did not vary by culture. Students did not sign an agreement to complete the tasks, but the supervising professors monitored blog posts closely so as to ensure to every extent possible that the students had, indeed, actually completed the tasks.

The students in the study were enrolled in programs in various countries. The majority of the students (69%) were female. In a sample of 13, two were seniors, eight were juniors, and three were sophomores.

The rationale for having students complete the 12 tasks is clearly expressed in Wilkinson's ethnographic study (1998) of students studying abroad that challenged the assumption that the students will automatically encounter ample opportunities to interact with native speakers. Such students need "encouragement" to interact with native speakers. In Cadd's (2012) survey, administered after the study-abroad experience, Monica noted that her level of anxiety decreased as a result of working her way through the 12 tasks and that being persistent about speaking Spanish led to fewer attempts on the part of the conversation partner to switch to English. This helped her decrease her anxiety and increase her fluency.

Anxiety

Generally, students tended to comment in the survey that their level of anxiety had decreased as a result of completing the 12 tasks (Cadd, 2012). Initial anxiety is to be expected, but increasing familiarity with the language and exposure to varied situations benefit all language learners. Indeed, as one additional participant noted, "[I] went from not wanting to open my mouth to being anxious to speak with my new friends. It meant so much more than what I had been doing in the classroom."

Fluency

Becoming "fluent" in the language is a goal mentioned casually by many students wanting to study abroad. They have been told by teachers and parents that they will be fluent only if they study abroad. Although "fluency" is definitely relative, student comments generally revealed that the more tasks a student had completed, the more fluent he or she felt him- or herself to be. One student, speaking toward the end of his semester abroad, commented that, "I wouldn't say I'm fluent, but I'm much more fluent than I was before I came. I feel I am more fluent because I can talk about things not in a textbook and with a greater variety of people. I can make myself understood."

Cultural Understanding

Students referenced the tasks while commenting on the extent to which their cultural understanding was enhanced. Being "forced" to interact with native speakers seems to increase cultural understanding. For example, one student who lived in Spain during the World Cup wrote:

> I asked a girl I knew if she was a big soccer fan or what was so great about World Cup time. "Soccer is cool, sure. Whatever. It's more fun for me that I get an excuse to ... be proud of Spain." This is not the attitude of everyone. A lot of the students will discuss the technicalities of the game ... I'm American and I have not watched too much soccer in my time ... But I'm much more interested now than I was before I came to Spain. It's an important part of the culture and I want to get to know more about it.

Payoffs and Pitfalls

One positive indicator is that students forced to interact with native speakers appear to gain confidence, fluency, and cultural understanding. Many variables mentioned above cannot be controlled by the teacher, but requiring students to complete tasks of the sort mentioned here provides an equalizing effect. Students find a real-world application for what they acquire in class. They are forced to "think on their feet."

No matter how well planned study abroad is, there remain variables that could interfere with the students' desire for an ever-growing competence. As Kinginger (2008) concluded, while study abroad is a venue that is conducive to language learning, the outcomes are not the panacea for which students and educators might hope. One important factor is what the students understand the "study-abroad experience" to be. This understanding will determine, in part, their motivation, how they choose to spend time out of class, their priorities, etc. As Kinginger (2008, p. 117) pointed out, however, another important factor is how the students interact with the host institutions and various social contexts. Some of these institutions and contexts will be open and welcoming, while others may see the students only as a source of income and, consequently, act hostilely or indifferently.

Although it appears that the tasks assist in creating lower levels of anxiety, increased linguistic fluency, and greater cultural understanding, one should interpret these results cautiously. They are not exhaustive; additional data could be analyzed. Given the relatively positive results, one might conjecture that even more than 12 tasks would result in greater linguistic and cultural gains. It could also be that a cap in terms of the number of tasks exists beyond which no additional gains occur.

Discussion Questions

1. Do you think that all students studying a language abroad would benefit from completing instructor-designed tasks? Why (not)?
2. What level of proficiency do you think students would have to have in order to complete the 12 tasks?
3. Is it reasonable to have students complete 12 tasks while abroad? Should there be more? Fewer?
4. Which additional strategies could instructors use to encourage students studying abroad to use the target language?
5. If you were designing a set of tasks for students to complete while abroad, what would you change about the tasks provided in this chapter? Why?

Resources

A Guide to Additional Resources for the Study-Abroad Experience—http://www.carla.umn.edu/maxsa/guides.html

A Study Investigating Social Interaction and Linguistic Gain during Study Abroad—http://onlinelibrary.wiley.com/doi/10.1111/j.1944–9720.2007.tb02853.x/abstract

Suggestions about Improving Oral Proficiency and Cultural Competence during Study Abroad—http://cehs.unl.edu/tlte/docs/Foreign%20Language%20certification%20students%20information.pdf

References

Archangeli, M. (1999). Study abroad and experiential learning in Salzburg, Austria. *Foreign Language Annals*, 32(1), 115–122.

Cadd, M. (2012). Encouraging students to engage with native speakers during study abroad. *Foreign Language Annals*, 45(2), 229–245.

DeKeyser, R. M. (2007). Study abroad as foreign language practice. In R. DeKeyser. (Ed.), *Practice in a second language: Perspectives from applied linguistics and cognitive psychology.* Cambridge University Press: Cambridge, England.

Kinginger, C. (2008). Language learning in study abroad: Case studies of Americans in France. *Modern Language Journal*, 92 (Winter 2008 supplement), 1–124.

Laubscher, M.R. (1994). *Encounters with difference: Student perceptions of the role of out-of-class experiences in education abroad.* Westport, CT: Greenwood Press.

Riedel, K. G. (1989). New goals for teaching language: An experience in undergraduate programs in Spain. *Hispania*, 72(3), 774–779.

Rohrlich, B. F. (1993). *Expecting the worst (or the best!). What exchange programs should know about student expectations.* Occasional Papers in Intercultural Learning 16. New York: AFS Center for the Study of Intercultural Learning. EDRS: ED 368 2891.

Wilkinson, S. (1998). Study abroad from the participants' perspective: A challenge to common beliefs. *Foreign Language Annals*, 31(1), 23–39.

26

LINKING LANGUAGE LEARNING INSIDE AND OUTSIDE THE CLASSROOM

Perspectives from Teacher Education

Maike Grau & Michael Legutke

Introduction and Overview

Even before English became the global language it is today, traditional concepts of the language classroom were criticised for placing the learning exclusively inside its four walls. Ways of opening the classroom to the world outside, including encounter or correspondence projects, have been promoted since the early 1980s (e.g., Legutke & Thomas 1991). Proponents of establishing 'living language links' have argued that tapping into the English used outside the classroom can support language learning in several ways. While contributing to learners' language competencies by giving them opportunities to communicate in the foreign language with other users of English, it can also increase the learners' motivation for language learning by showing them the relevance of the English language in society.

Thirty years on, English teachers and their learners are dealing with a language which is effectively a global language and is considered a basic competency and requirement for everyone. In Germany, all children and teenagers learn English as a core subject from primary school until they leave school at 16 or 18. For teachers of English, this means that they need to sustain students' initial enthusiasm and motivation to learn the foreign language for a long time. No past generation has had such wide out-of-school exposure to English (see, for example, Berns, de Bot, & Hasebrink, 2007). However, research carried out in German secondary schools shows that for most students this reality has still little impact on their English language classrooms (cf. Grau, 2009). This study further suggests that although there are good reasons for keeping in-school and out-of-school contacts with English separate, a majority of students are in favour of closer links between the classroom and their encounters with English elsewhere.

From the perspective of teacher education, these results are sobering. Given the increased presence of English in almost every element of our daily lives, it is not easy to understand why learning the language in school cannot be more connected with its usage outside the walls of the classroom. While factors such as students' privacy have to be taken seriously by teachers who use topics and texts from their students' free time, lack of time, or health and safety issues can play a major role in preventing teachers from organising trips. In addition, language teacher's lack of experience in organising project-based learning is another reason for a mismatch between theory and practice. In this chapter, we therefore focus on a course in a pre-service teacher education program in which student teachers get the chance to explore the teacher's role in a project which creates links between the classroom and the outside world. We first describe the structure and some of the outcomes of this course, then explain key requirements for out-of-class language projects and address some of the issues and challenges which can arise when teachers open their language classrooms. Finally, we emphasize the need to integrate out-of-class language experiences with the day-to-day work of the classroom. By using language contact opportunities outside the classroom and connecting them with their in-class work, teachers can use the everyday presence of English for making in-class learning more relevant and meaningful for children and teenagers. These opportunities should be regular features of the English language classroom and can only be so if they are included in teacher education.

Vignette

The course Interview Projects in English took place in a pre-service teacher education programme for undergraduate student teachers (ST) in their final semesters of studies. The university is located in a medium-sized German city, which is very popular with tourists from all over the world because of its old town centre and its picturesque surroundings. The central aim of the course was for participants to gain a better understanding of the complexity of such a learning arrangement by giving them the opportunity to take an active part in a project and reflect on their experiences based on theories of project-based language learning (Stoller, 2003). The course was organised in cooperation with a local secondary school, and was divided into three phases moving from university to school and back again:

1.   The objective of the first phase was three-fold: Firstly, the STs developed a rationale behind out-of-class learning through a discussion of projects documented in the literature. Secondly, they were provided with a model interview project through a documentary film of a project carried out in 1983 (Legutke, 2005, 129–31), in which learners practised their interview skills in class, then interviewed speakers of English at an international airport, and finally reported back their findings in the classroom. Obviously, the discussions of this model project had to consider changes, not only concerning the even higher accessibility of English-speaking people and international places 30 years after this film was recorded, but also in the technological

developments and their implications for the use of suitable media such a project requires. Thirdly, the STs themselves trained their interview skills and learned how to handle digital recording sets in a session lead by a professional radio broadcaster and trainer.

2. In the second phase, the STs formed two teams in order to plan for the interview projects in school. It was their responsibility to prepare and carry out a project with two groups of 15-year-old students: a regular class of 28 students, and an English after-school club consisting of 12 students. STs divided up their responsibilities in the project, such as meeting up with the teachers, developing appropriate support materials, teaching the lessons leading up to the interviews, organising the technology, and so on. The two English teachers were present throughout the whole process and supportive of the STs, helping them with the logistics and offering detailed feedback after each lesson.

The STs worked with each of the groups in a three-step process, preparing them first in the classroom through practising interview skills with a focus on linguistic aspects such as establishing and maintaining a polite conversation in English, but also including technical aspects such as working with a microphone and a digital audio recorder. The most exciting part of the projects were the interview outings, in which one group went into the town centre to find interview partners at various tourist attractions and another group went to a local campsite. In both cases, the teenagers were nervous at first and reluctant to approach strangers to ask permission for an interview. This was especially so in the town centre where some interview requests were rejected by people who were too busy for an interview, so the students had to cope with these situations, too. The fact that they were working in pairs or small groups enabled students to support each other in overcoming these difficulties.

Reflections immediately after the interviews were extremely positive and showed how proud the 15-year-old students were to see that they were able to have conversations in English, that their interview partners understood most of what they were saying and vice versa, and that most of the people they approached were willing to talk to them. Another learning point for the students was that they were able to explore the tourists' point of view on their home town by talking to visitors from different parts of the world, ranging from European countries to far-away places such as China or Brazil. Both classroom teachers who observed their students throughout this project were impressed with the participation and the enthusiasm of their groups and commented that they were particularly surprised by some of the students who participated very little in normal English lessons, but engaged in lively and quite substantial exchanges in the interviews.

The follow-up lessons in class consisted of listening to some of the recorded interviews with opportunities to give peer feedback and comment on the examples, and an evaluation of the project experience by the students. Due to time constraints in the busy school calendar other possible follow-up activities such as presentations of particularly interesting (or boring) interview partners or more in-depth explorations of the audio recordings were not possible. The students received a copy of their interview recordings, which had been digitally edited slightly by the STs to make them sound more professional.

3.   The project evaluation phase brought the STs back to the university, where they exchanged impressions of the project, discussed the learning outcomes for the teenagers based on the interview recordings and the feedback they got from the students and their English teachers, and thought about implications for themselves as future teachers of English. The resources used in this phase were again the texts, which could be read and discussed in a different light now that the students had experienced a project in action. To support the reflective process, the STs had kept a project log throughout the project. Both the discussions in the evaluation phase and the logs showed that the STs were impressed with the outcome of the project, especially concerning the students' confidence in using their English in a real-life conversation, as this extract from one of the journals shows:

> When I listened to the interviews at home afterwards, I was quite impressed I must say. The students recorded very good interviews, and I could notice that they got more and more confident with each interview. In one of the last interviews, they even inserted questions they just thought of and which fit to their interview partner, and did not only stick to the questions they prepared before. I felt quite proud when I listened to the interviews ... (M.T., p. 3).

Based on the positive feedback the STs got from the participating students and their English teachers, they felt encouraged to think about implementing similar projects in their future classrooms. Compared with the literature review in the first part of the course, discussions of the teacher role in project-based language learning were now informed by the STs' recent team-teaching experience and thus personally relevant to them: "One highly discussed topic in this session was our role as teachers. ... [T]he question was how much input and support the students needed while still having the chance to make their own experiences" (M.T., p. 1).

Principles

Within the context of the teacher education program the experience encapsulated in the vignette is significant in a number of ways, bringing to the fore at least five key principles of out-of-class learning.

Principle 1. Challenge and support learners to engage in significant encounters. Confirming findings from the research literature (Legutke & Thomas, 1991), the teenagers not only accepted the chance to test their language abilities in authentic encounters, but, once they had coped with the initial challenges, eagerly tried to perform well. No doubt, they were not only highly motivated, but they also mobilized a set of interrelated competencies and skills accounting for a high quality of the recorded texts: In addition to their linguistic skills, they had to cooperate in their teams; they had to interact with the interviewees, maintaining the flow of the interviews, and to record the event. The fact that the teachers involved were surprised by several students' active performance in English during the interviews, which differed significantly from that in the classroom, was viewed by STs as a strong indicator of the educational potential of out-of-class learning. This learning arrangement seemed to provide a new space for action in the target language.

Principle 2. Ensure that tasks are appropriate. Although STs were aware from reading the literature that such authentic encounters require careful preparation in class, it was only through working with the teachers and the students that they realized the challenges of such an approach. The interviews in the city centre and at the campsite as a core task were complex social situations, which required careful preparation, not only regarding the students' communication strategies and other factors which support oral fluency, but also regarding their knowledge about their own town and tourism in their area, their general social and intercultural strategies, their interview strategies and media competencies. Tasks had to be designed and implemented that on the one hand took into consideration what students had learned so far, and that, on the other hand, helped learners cope with the complex demands of the target task. Looking back at the experience, STs understood that it makes a lot of sense to discuss these demands with the students prior to embarking on the training in class. In view of the demands students can become aware of what they believe they can do without the help of the teacher, and where they need additional support. Furthermore, they can glean appropriate exercises from the textbook, which is reexamined from the perspective of a challenging target task.

Principle 3. Ensure that the content is appropriate and challenging. Assessing the outcomes of the experience for their professional development, STs underlined the crucial role of content to be touched upon in the interviews, and how the interview could develop into a conversation. The encounter could only yield its potential for language learning if students thought carefully, not only about the possible mindset and interests of their interviewees, but also about what the students themselves wanted to gain from the encounters. The content to be covered had to go beyond stock phrases about place of residence, hobbies or what the partners liked about the city.

Principle 4. Follow up out-of-class project work with appropriate in-class action. Looking at the data after the experience, STs realized that a number of interviews had taken the form of very interesting conversations. The partners had engaged in discourse on traffic problems, young people in the city, and surprising remarks on aspects of the city the students had not anticipated. Although STs saw the constraints the teachers were confronted with after the project (they had to return to the routines of textbook-based work), they felt that a lot of the findings the project yielded were not appreciated and used productively. The intensity of follow-up work did not match the preparation and the gains of the experience.

Principle 5. Exploit the potential of out-of-class project work to generate a variety of authentic learner texts. The teachers and STs were impressed by the quality of the recorded interviews. Not only did these learner texts differ considerably from most of the spoken texts offered by the course book, since they origi- nated from authentic encounters, they could also be read as a distinct expres- sion of an individual learner who would identify the text as his or hers. In reference to the previous issue of a lack of time for follow-up activities in the project, STs discussed a variety of learner texts which could have originated from the project, had the teacher given more room for further exploration: a portrait of the most interesting interview partner, an article for the school paper, a report for the school radio, a collage of unexpected and surprising statements about the city and its inhabitants, or collection of the most inter- esting examples of Englishes used by the interview partners from all over the world. STs agreed that out-of-class learning provides a productive environ- ment for learner texts to emerge.

Applications

Having gone through the experience of planning, teaching and supervising the projects, STs had an opportunity to assess the potential of out-of-class learning opportunities available for teachers in primary and secondary schools, such as: international airports, bus or train stations, cinemas, museums, zoos and other tourist attractions. The experience also provided a basis for STs critically review- ing reports of encounter projects studied in the first phase of the course. It was agreed that there is a wide variety of possibilities for out-of-school projects for all ages and levels of language competency, as the following three reports exemplify:

American Middle School Round the Corner (see Belova, 2013)

Compared with the experience reported in the vignette, this encounter project engages learners in more sustained contacts with English-speaking peers in their surroundings over a longer period of time. The teacher of a class of 13-year-old lower intermediate learners in a German secondary school organised a series of encounters between her class and peers at a local American middle school. Small groups consisting of pupils from each school discussed a topic they had prepared before, such as school, free time activities, and traditions. The German students researched the topics in the library and on the Internet and trained their speaking skills over a period of several weeks in order to be able to apply the key vocabulary and structures necessary to carry out a conversation with their American conversation partners.

The Teddy Bear Project (see Rau, 2009)

For several years Nathalie Rau, a primary school teacher, has run ongoing pen pal projects with her learners in their second year of English with partners in Australia, Greece, Kenya, Korea, Japan, and the United States: At the beginning of the school year, the children swap parcels containing portraits of the school, the children, the teacher, and a teddy bear. In her report, the teacher documents how the teddy bear's daily experience in the respective cultures is integrated into the elementary curriculum: talking about a particular day of the week, writing birthday letters, listening to the teddy bear introducing the school, or exploring food in the school cafeteria, to name just a few.

Meet the Author: A Virtual Encounter Through Computer-Mediated Communication (see Bühler, 2013)

Literary texts are typically used at intermediate and advanced levels of language education in secondary schools, which is not always met with enthusiasm by teenage learners. In this example, the teacher used *Greetings from Bury Park* (Manzoor, 2007), a coming-of-age story set in one of the most multicultural places of contemporary Britain and initiated a videoconferencing session with the author, whom he had contacted via his official website. The prospect of getting to meet the author in person was a driving force for the students' reading process and gave the task of keeping a reading log an authentic purpose. This way, the interview as a target task not only supported the reading process, but also helped to integrate the other language skills in a meaningful way, as the students used their written impressions of the book to initiate an oral interaction in the target language.

Payoffs and Pitfalls

As the examples clearly show, the integration of real and virtually mediated out-of-class locations adds important dimensions to learning English in an institutionalised setting. The main factor is the authenticity of the situation in which the learners interact making the use of the foreign language relevant and meaningful. Phases of systematic skills training are rendered plausible within such frameworks. In addition, spontaneous use of the foreign language may be stimulated, which is very often not achieved through language work in the classroom alone. Encounter projects can therefore have an enormous motivational potential for language learning because training and using the language are experienced as mutually supportive; they can help learners see what they can achieve in the foreign language, but also what they can still improve on. However, students will only be able to unlock the potential of out-of-class locations for learning if the core zone, the traditional classroom, displays two key functions.

First of all, it needs to be conceptualized as the location where access and approaches to the out-of-class world are prepared, where systematic support is provided, and where the experience is assessed in terms of language gains and discourse-related issues. Since computer-mediated communication projects have attracted considerable research activity over the last decade, it is worth noting that the significance of a well-organised project framework is emerging clearly from the growing research literature in this field. Even though virtual encounters using technology such as Skype, e-mail, or live chats can provide wonderful opportunities for language use and culture learning, they can also be challenging in their own ways. The published research in this field suggests that misunderstandings or even communication breakdowns are not uncommon, often caused by the very nature of computer-mediated communication (Hauck, 2010). Teachers who engage in virtual or face-to-face encounters with their classes need to be aware of these pitfalls, and of the complexity of their role, as their responsibilities include not only to set up and manage the project, but also to support their learners throughout the whole process.

Secondly, the language classroom as core location needs to be understood as an arena for learner contributions to the process of learning and its contents, as a location where learners are not only invited, but also expected to contribute topics and texts they come across in the out-of-class world. Once students have understood that there is a room where their contributions are taken seriously and used as input for learning, where the teacher's and the textbook's monopoly of providing input has been superseded, there seems to be a chance that they themselves begin to bridge the gap between their exposure to English in their free time and the world of school learning. The productive impact of these key functions on language use and learning depends on the teacher's ability to manage the complex relations between the core zone of the classroom with the out-of-class opportunities of learning. One of the teacher's major challenges is to balance the learners' need for freedom of expression with the affordances of operating in an institutional setting.

These challenges are not always adequately dealt with in the literature on project-based language learning. Therefore we argued that, in view of the global presence of English and the availability of digital technology, trainee teachers should be encouraged to understand and experience the classroom as a multilayered network of different locations, including the traditional classroom as the core zone of learning.

Discussion Questions

1. What are the main reasons for setting up encounter projects in the context of learning English in school?
2. Would you prefer to organise a face-to-face or a virtual encounter project? Why?

3. Looking at the examples given in this chapter, which one would work best in your context?
4. What kinds of practical implications would the project example you chose in question 3 have for the teacher's role? What are that teacher's main responsibilities?
5. What could be possible challenges teachers could face when organizing an encounter project, virtual or face-to-face, in your context? How would you meet them?

Resources

The Interaudio Project website provides resources in five languages for radio journalists in training as well as handouts that focus on interviewing techniques and can be used in interview projects—http://interaudio.org/cms/index.php?option=content&task=view&id=340&Itemid=37

Epals is a globally used online platform to find partners for connecting classrooms—www.epals.com

eTwinning helps European classroom teachers to find partners for collaborative project work—http://www.etwinning.net

Ideas for connecting classrooms using videoconferencing with *Skype*—https://education.skype.com/

References

Belova, M. (2013). The world next door. *Der Fremdsprachliche Unterricht Englisch*, 123, 16–19.

Berns, M., de Bot, K., & Hasebrink, U. (Eds.) (2007). *In the presence of English: Media and European youth.* New York: Springer.

Bühler, P. (2013). Greetings to Bury Park. *Der Fremdsprachliche Unterricht Englisch*, 123, 40–43.

Grau, M. (2009). Worlds apart? English in German youth cultures and in educational settings. *World Englishes,* 28(2), 160–174.

Hauck, M. (2010). Telecollaboration: At the interface between multimodal and intercultural communicative competence. In S. Guth & F. Helm (Eds.), *Telecollaboration 2.0.: Language, literacies and intercultural learning in the 21st century* (pp. 219–248). Bern: Peter Lang.

Legutke, M. (2005). Redesigning the foreign language classroom. A critical perspective on information technology and educational change. In C. Davison (Ed.), *Information technology and innovation in language education* (pp. 127–148). Hong Kong: Hong Kong University Press.

Legutke, M., & Thomas, H. (1999). *Process and experience in the language classroom*, 4th ed. Harlow, UK: Longman.

Manzoor, S. (2007). *Greeting from Bury Park. Race, religion, rock 'n' roll.* London: Bloomsbury.

Rau, N. (2009). A Teddy Bear Project. Ein Klassenkorrespondenzprojekt im Fremdsprachenunterricht der Grundschule [A correspondence project in the primary FL classroom]. *ForumSprache* 1, 88–108 (= www.forum-sprache.de).

Stoller, F. (2003). Project work. A means to promote language and content. In: J. C. Richards & W. A. Renandya (Eds.), *Methodology in language teaching: An anthology of current practice* (pp. 107–119). Cambridge: Cambridge University Press.

27

JAPANESE COMMUNITIES OF PRACTICE

Creating Opportunities for Out-of-Class Learning

Chihiro Kinoshita Thomson & Tamami Mori

Introduction and Overview

In this chapter, we describe a Japanese language program for university students in Australia, where Japanese is not spoken once the learners step out of the classroom. Nowadays learners have access to Japanese language input via the Internet and they can watch Japanese drama, read *manga*, and listen to J-pop music on their own (Northwood & Thomson, 2012). However, they still lack opportunities to have two-way communications in Japanese outside of the classroom (Spence-Brown, 2006).

One way to promote such opportunities is to design a language program so that it becomes a Community of Practice (CoP). A CoP is understood as "groups of people who share a concern or a passion for something they do and learn how to do it better as they interact regularly" (Wenger, 2006, p. 1). A language program CoP would host learners, teachers, and other target language speakers who participate in learning and using the language in a variety of shared practices. Some CoPs are made up of multiple sub-communities that network with each other. A language program CoP encompasses classrooms as sub-communities where the learner has the base affiliation and conducts regular learning activities. By designing the CoP to deliberately interconnect classrooms and other sub-communities, we can offer out-of-class learning opportunities within and around the CoP, which are authentic, meaningful, and motivational.

In the vignette, we illustrate how a learner can benefit from engaging in such a CoP through the experiences of a young man, Peter (a pseudonym as are other names in this chapter), who became an advanced-level learner of Japanese through his participation in a CoP. It is followed by a discussion on how the CoP operationalized his out-of-class learning and his development into a competent language user. We then describe how to nurture a CoP as a language program.

Vignette

This is a story about Peter, how he improved his Japanese proficiency, and developed his identity from that of a language "learner" to that of a Japanese language "user" through participating in a Japanese CoP at an Australian university.

With his interest in Japanese food, Peter enrolled in an introductory Japanese course and became a Japanese learner. While Peter was in the introductory course, he met an advanced-level learner acting as a "junior teacher," assisting the classroom teacher and supporting beginner learners in the classroom. This junior teacher became Peter's role model in learning Japanese. Peter asked him for advice in learning Japanese in and out of the classroom. This was when Peter first developed an awareness of opportunities to participate in a variety of activities outside of one's own classroom. The junior teacher was a learner in an advanced Japanese classroom, but also participated in Peter's classroom, using Japanese.

When Peter was in his second year, he entered the Australian Japanese Language Speech Contest. Suggested by his classroom teacher, he visited Japanese classes, other than his own, practiced delivering his speech countless times, and he won the first prize at the Australian National Final. This was a case in which Peter took advantage of the availability of venues and audiences within the CoP and gained experiences delivering his speech in front of various audiences. Peter then went on a student exchange at a Japanese university for six months. He had found out about the exchange opportunity in his first year from the junior teacher who had been on an exchange. The in-country experience of interacting with native speakers daily improved his proficiency greatly.

Upon returning to Australia in his final year, he enrolled in two Japanese courses: Advanced Japanese and Japanese Capstone. He chose to become a junior teacher as part of the requirement for his advanced Japanese course.

Peter was assigned to Ms. Fukatsu's introductory Japanese class. Every week he attended the class and had a 30-minute meeting with Fukatsu conducted in Japanese. The class had support members, a volunteer postgraduate student and teaching practicum students, offering various levels of interactional opportunities in Japanese to the classroom learners and to Peter.

While participating in the introductory class by answering questions of the beginner learners, taking part in pair activities, demonstrating models, and interacting with other members, Peter also enjoyed support from Fukatsu in and out of class. This had a significant impact on Peter as it gave him the legitimacy of being a junior teacher and boosted his confidence and motivation. Peter described his weekly meetings with Fukatsu as one of the most enjoyable aspects of being a junior teacher. The meetings were genuine opportunities for Peter to freely express himself in Japanese with Fukatsu. Through the class activities and the meetings, Peter learned to use Japanese as a tool for purposeful communication. This experience boosted his motivation to further improve his Japanese, while he increasingly established himself as a reliable junior teacher in the classroom community.

Peter was also involved in the Japanese Capstone, the final course for students majoring in Japanese studies at the university. Through the course, the learners were to integrate their knowledge and skills and showcase them at an out-of-class mini-conference. They organized this mini-conference themselves and gave small research presentations in Japanese to Japanese speaking audience members from the Sydney Japanese community. Peter, along with his classmates, went beyond the classroom boundary and involved themselves in the Sydney Japanese community, that is, to place advertisements in local Japanese newspapers, to issue invitations to Japan related organizations and to receive and answer enquiries. They created an official printed program, managed the whole conference program in Japanese, receiving guests at the reception, acting as emcees, making speeches, acting as the hosts of the event, and sending thank you letters. Peter synthesized his communicative skills, his experiences in Japan and his knowledge from the Japanese studies courses to actively engage and participate in the successful conference.

Peter's story illustrates how out-of-class learning opportunities within and around the CoP enhanced his Japanese. His engagement with these events and activities provided him with multiple opportunities to use Japanese for meaningful communications, enhanced his confidence and improved his Japanese proficiency. By the end of the final semester, Peter was a full member of the CoP, and firmly established his identity as a Japanese user. Peter's identity transformed in the CoP in the process of his development from being a beginner learner in the introductory course, to a junior teacher respected by introductory learners, valued by the teaching team, and who is a competent user of Japanese.

Principles

Principle 1. Encourage learner participation in Communities of Practice. Lave & Wenger (1991) regard learning as participation in a CoP, and that learning is "situated." They consider the process through which a newcomer becomes a full member in a CoP is the central process of situated learning. The process entails that the learner participates in the practices of the community, and develops an identity, which offers a sense of belonging and commitment to the community. The CoP provides a context for the learner to be engaged in the process. According to Wenger (1998), participation is not just being there for an event, but more active engagement in certain activities with certain people, in the practices of social communities, and constructing identities in relation to these communities. Identity construction in this framework is understanding who we are in the context of certain communities.

Let us illustrate how this works using our CoP to which Peter belonged in the vignette. In our CoP, learners engage in multifaceted interactions in Japanese—with their classmates, junior learners, more advanced learners, teachers, Japanese exchange students, and Japanese native speakers from the Sydney local Japanese community, in and out of classrooms and face-to-face as well as online. In this process, our "learners," initially newcomers to the Japanese-speaking CoP, gradually become full members who competently negotiate meanings in Japanese with a variety of people and identify themselves as "users" of Japanese.

Principle 2. Provide opportunities for lived experiences in Communities of Practice. Wenger's social theory of learning discredits classrooms and institutional learning as mostly irrelevant and boring, as they lack the context of our lived experiences of participation in the world (Wenger, 1998). Our approach deliberately makes classrooms and the institutional setting relevant by giving them the context in which our learners can have lived experiences. They are "learners" in their classrooms, but outside, our learners socialize, engage in community events, and through these engagements they make meanings in Japanese, which are embedded in their experiences; in other words, they become Japanese "users."

To illustrate the second principle, our Japanese CoP is set out in Figure 27.1, which includes subcommunities that seamlessly link and network with each other.

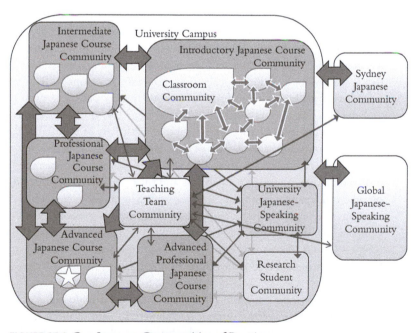

FIGURE 27.1 Our Japanese Communities of Practice.

The Japanese program at the university offers a core language sequence of Introductory, Intermediate, Advanced, Professional, and Advanced Professional Japanese. The core course communities and other subcommunities are linked with each other via joint events, projects and visits, while other relevant communities in and around the university campus are accessed regularly. These links are the keys for providing opportunities for lived experiences.

Principle 3. Promote variety and diversity through Communities of Practice. Through practices and engagement in communities, CoP members develop a shared repertoire of resources: experiences, stories, tools, ways of addressing recurring problems (Wenger, 2006). By linking the subcommunities, our CoP comprises of a variety of participants and exposes them to diverse languages used in the communities. The variety and diversity are assets for our CoP as they become integrated into the CoP as shared practices.

Peter in the vignette is shown as the star in Figure 27.1 and is located within one of the advanced Japanese classroom communities. However, his participation in this Japanese CoP is not limited to that in his classroom. He participated in the introductory Japanese course community as a junior teacher, participated in the Sydney Japanese community as a speech contest participant, as a conference presenter at the mini-conference, and was also active in the university's Japanese-speaking community in general. This exposed him to a wide variety of participants and their practices.

Peter's placement as the junior teacher in the introductory Japanese classroom, one of many sub-communities, breaks the classroom routine that Wenger called irrelevant and boring. In this new classroom community, he learned to use Japanese to attain goals set for teaching a particular lesson that is the reality in language classroom contexts. It also provides a variety that is not available in his original advanced Japanese class.

Peter was not the only one who gained from this approach. The benefit extended to the introductory learners in the classroom, as they gained access to more quantity and more variety of Japanese, provided by Fukatsu, Peter, and the teaching practicum students. The classroom learners are presented with more competent interactional partners and they are offered opportunities to observe real Japanese interactions among competent speakers, which are not available in a single teacher classroom. In addition, the introductory learners gained a role model, Peter, whom they looked up to, and benchmarked their progress against. Peter's out-of-class learning experiences enhanced in-class learning experiences of the introductory learners.

Principle 4. Establish Communities of Practice to promote commitment and collective responsibilities. Having commitment to a shared domain of interest is one of the features of CoP membership, which distinguishes it from membership of a simple group with a similar interest (Wenger, 2006). We might note here an intriguing notion of *senpai-koohai* relationship. In Japanese culture, newcomers to a CoP (such as a school, sports circle, or employment) call their seniors *senpai* with respect. In return for the respect shown by *koohai* (their juniors), a *senpai* assumes a role of mentor for their *koohai*. They develop mutual responsibilities to each other and both contribute to their learning and to the development of their CoP. This entails commitment to each other.

In our CoP example, the introductory learners, following this Japanese tradition, called Peter *senpai*. For Peter, this *senpai* role seemed to carry more emotional responsibility towards his *koohai* than just being an official junior teacher. Being a *senpai* prompted Peter to put more effort in trying to gain the introductory learners' trust by preparing for the lesson every week, and forced him to review the Japanese regularly. The presence of *koohai* also offered him a benchmark to realize how much he had progressed.

Being located within a CoP, learners participate in various practices, which may develop into certain roles, such as a role of *senpai*. Their practices influence other members and other members' practices influence them. They develop feelings of responsibility towards others, and they fulfill their responsibility by having an increasing sense of commitment.

Applications

A CoP is not something we force people to create. We create an environment that is favorable for a CoP to develop. Our CoP grew as we added links between subcommunities one by one over the years.

Junior Teacher Project

The first such link was created in 1995. The advanced course coordinator wanted to provide opportunities for advanced learners to interact with native speakers, and the large introductory course had a number of native-speaker classroom teachers. The two coordinators agreed that advanced learners would join introductory classes and assist the classroom teachers while using Japanese: the junior teacher project was born. Since then, the junior teacher project has been one of the project options for the advanced Japanese course. Both the introductory classroom teacher and the advanced Japanese course coordinator assess the junior teachers' performances; and the assessment results are counted towards the advanced Japanese course marks. Advanced learners such as Peter, who had a junior teacher in their introductory class and were inspired by them, often become junior teachers. (For more details, please see Thomson, 1998.)

Senpai Session

The *Senpai* session offers out-of-class experiences to professional-level learners and offers benefits to both professional-level and introductory-level communities.

At the end of the first semester, professional-level learners (*senpai*) visit introductory classes to have discussions in Japanese on a topic of learning Japanese. This provides the first opportunity for introductory learners to have sustained discussions in Japanese with someone they meet for the first time. While the junior teacher project is a project option, and only selects a few advanced learners to visit introductory classes, the *Senpai* session involves all professional-level and introductory-level learners and teachers. Four to five *senpai* are allocated to an introductory class of about 25 learners. It offers a number of opportunities other than the discussion itself to use Japanese. This is how it works:

First, the professional-level learners write e-mails to the assigned introductory classroom teacher to introduce themselves and seek logistic information. Upon establishing the contact, they write a letter of introduction to the introductory learners using simple Japanese, and send it to the introductory classroom teacher. The classroom teacher shows the letter to the introductory learners. They read the letter and prepare questions to be asked at the beginning of the discussion.

The professional-level learners also prepare materials to be used for the discussion on learning Japanese. The materials include flash cards they used in earlier years, a computer application, a collection of photos taken in Japan and a *manga* they love. They think about how to best present their materials in a discussion in simple Japanese.

In this activity, the professional-level learners use sophisticated Japanese with the classroom teacher, including honorifics, and simple Japanese with the introductory learners, and they have to make the distinction. With the introductory learners, they learn to use Japanese as an international language. The introductory learners gain learning tips and strategies from their *senpai* learners, understand what lies ahead of them in their second and third years of learning Japanese, and foresee what they can become in the future. (For more details, see Thomson & Masumi-So, 2009.)

Benkyou Mates Project

In our program, as in most other programs, not all learners are as brilliant as Peter. Some low-performing learners lack a solid foundation in grammar and need to review the contents of earlier years. Visiting lower-level classes and reviewing would be ideal, as the junior teachers do. However, the junior teacher project screens the learners by their previous Japanese course marks and their performance at an interview, and low-performing learners would not qualify.

The *Benkyou* Mates project offers opportunities to all learners, including low-performing learners, to attend lower-level lectures regularly and get extra credits. They attend lower-level lectures as the *Benkyou* Mates, review the lower-level content and practice Japanese, while they help out lower-level learners in their practice. This presents a win-win scenario to both upper-level and lower-level course communities. The upper-level learners get extra instruction and solidify their foundation, thus boosting the language proficiency of the lower end of the course population. The lower-level learners get practice partners who are more competent than their classmates. Although some *Benkyou* Mates are low-performing learners, they visit lectures of two levels down, and this gives them sufficient advantage to do well.

Mini-Conference

In the capstone course, learners engage in two activities. First is to form groups and present research on a topic within the discipline of Japanese studies at the Mini-conference. Second is to organize and administer the conference using the Japanese language.

The Mini-conference is open to all learners in our CoP. Lower-level learners are encouraged to come to the conference to see what they will be doing in their final semester. It is also open to the Sydney Japanese community. The capstone learners advertise the conference through local Japanese newspapers, the e-newsletter of the Consulate General, Australia–Japan Society and such. As seen in the vignette, the capstone learners manage the whole conference with support of the teaching team.

At the conference, learners use various forms of the Japanese language. They present research findings in academic language. They make speeches in formal language. They interact with visitors from the Sydney Japanese community in polite language. Lower-level learners visiting the conference can witness all these interactions.

Off-Campus Opportunities

Our learners access a number of off-campus opportunities: Annual Japanese speech contest, Japan-related events offered by a variety of organizations (e.g., Japan–Australia Multicultural Policy Exchange Program). We provide the information of the events, offer incentives, such as bonus points, and render support so that they can succeed in their participation. The entire community shares information and supports them using the well-developed network in our CoP.

The most important factor in creating a successful language program CoP is a healthy collaboration among the course coordinators and teachers. The teaching team community is the core of our CoP (see Figure 27. 1). For a learner to leap over the boundary between courses and participate in a classroom that is not his or her own, the course coordinators must have a shared understanding of what they want for the learners of both courses and create a system that allows the leap. This requires regular discussions of teaching approaches, joint creation of activities, and the alignment of event schedules and timetables for all courses in the program, which demand extra efforts of the teaching team.

Payoffs and Pitfalls

The obvious benefit of operating our language program as a CoP is the provision of real and lived interaction opportunities in the target language to our learners. By stepping out of their own classrooms and out of the traditional concept of language learning, our learners have to negotiate meanings with fellow learners, native-speaker teachers, and visitors from the Sydney Japanese community, using the Japanese language.

Course and classroom communities are seamlessly networked and the learners step in and out of the communities. This means that more competent interactions in Japanese are visible and abundant for lower-level learners to witness, copy, and learn from within the CoP, and this provides pathways for lower-level learners to transform into more capable speakers of Japanese. They have real opportunities, they have role models, and they have a sense of belonging in our CoP. They become motivated and they aim to be like the *senpai* they met and admired. The upper-level learners have native speaker members, teachers, practicum students, and those from the Sydney Japanese community with whom to interact. They also have *koohai* to mentor. They lead the community and they take pride in it.

The difficulty of the CoP approach may be discussed in two respects. One is what we already touched upon. CoPs only function well when all course coordinators communicate with each other and share similar visions. The core of the CoP, the teaching team, has to have the same level of commitment to the CoP to run the whole language program in this way. You can start small, with perhaps two courses collaborating with each other, and then grow your network and practices gradually through regular consultations and sharing of views and ideas among the teaching team members.

The other is the conflict that may arise in CoPs (Handley et al., 2006). Members of a CoP are described as starting out as a newcomer or peripheral member and develop into a core or full member. The first problem is that not everyone aspires to be a full member. In our CoP, this issue in a way resolves itself in the form of attrition. The second problem is that some members may be denied participation in certain practices, as in the case of the junior teacher project in which low-performing members are denied access. Our response was to create the *Benkyou* Mates project, which counteracts the junior teacher project. The third problem is that a shared practice in one community may be in conflict with another practice by a neighboring community and interferes with the newcomer's development. For example, a newcomer, let's say a new student, may have developed an identity as a language "learner" in the secondary school classroom community and joins our CoP. Her acculturation into our community whose members aspire to be "users" of Japanese would be challenging. We believe this challenge can most likely be dealt with in a gradual shift with plentiful support.

Discussion Questions

1. Can you think of a CoP around you? Can you describe it?
2. What are the major advantages of a language program CoP?
3. What would be some foreseeable obstacles in developing a language program CoP?
4. What roles would teachers play in nurturing a language program CoP?
5. If you were to develop a language program CoP, what mechanisms would you put in place other than those described in this chapter (e.g., junior teacher)?

Resources

> *Wenger's cite offering a guide to CoP*—http://wenger-trayner.com/map-of-resources/
>
> *CoP design guide for Higher Education*—http://net.educause.edu/ir/library/pdf/nli0531.pdf
>
> *CoP in Curriculum Development*—http://www.ibe.unesco.org/en/communities/community-of-practice-COP/about-the-community-of-practice.html
>
> *Forum for people interested in CoP*—http://cpsquare.org
>
> *Example of use of CoP at a university*—http://ctlt.ubc.ca/programs/communities-of-practice/
>
> *Examples of use of CoP in broader community*—http://sedl-3-098.sedl.org/COP/whereCOP.html
>
> *CoP in the second language learning*—http://www.jstor.org/discover/10.2307/40264309?uid=2&uid=4&sid=21102670136763

References

Handley, K., Sturdy, A., Fincham R., & Clark, T. (2006). Within and beyond communities of practice: Making sense of learning through participation, identity and practice. *Journal of Management Studies*, 43(3), 642–653.

Lave, J., & Wenger, E. (1991). *Situated learning: Legitimate peripheral participation*. Cambridge: Cambridge University Press.

Northwood, B., & Thomson, C. K. (2012). What keeps them going? Investigating ongoing learners of Japanese in Australian universities. *Japanese Studies*, 32(3), 335–355.

Spence-Brown, R. (2006). Resources and learning environment of Japanese language education: Australian data, its analysis and future issues. In *Research on Learning Environment and Learning Method in Japanese Language Education: Overseas Research Reports* (pp. 138–145). Tokyo: National Institute of Japanese Language and Linguistics. Note: Article in Japanese.

Thomson, C. K. (1998). Junior teacher internship: Promoting cooperative interaction and learner autonomy in foreign language classrooms. *Foreign Language Annals*, 31(4), 569–583.

Thomson, C. K., & Masumi-So, H. (2009). Senpai seniors are coming: Positive effects of collaboration between beginners and more advanced learners of Japanese. In C. K. Thomson (Ed.), *New pedagogies for learner agency: Japanese language education research and practice in Australia*. Tokyo: CoCoPublishing. Note: Article in Japanese.

Wenger, E. (2006). Community of practice: a brief introduction. Retrieved from http://www.ewenger.com/theory/index.htm

Wenger, E. (1998). *Community of practice: Learning, meaning, and identity*. Cambridge: Cambridge University Press.

Note

Acknowledgement is due to Lin Feng who provided part of the data. The authors are grateful, too, for the ongoing support of the Japanese studies research group and the Japanese teaching team at the University of New South Wales–Australia.

28

LEARNING ENGLISH WITH A HOME TUTOR

Meeting the Needs of Migrant Learners

Gary Barkhuizen

Introduction and Overview

Not all language teaching takes place in classrooms. One-on-one tutoring is a less formal instructional arrangement which entails a tutor and a learner working together to meet the particular language-learning needs and goals of the learner. It is different from classroom teaching in a number of respects, the most obvious being that the tutor works with only one learner. In some cases, the tutorial sessions may be tightly structured, with clearly stated objectives and detailed plans for what is to be covered and how. In other cases, the sessions can be fairly unstructured and sometimes even unplanned, and no common syllabus or curriculum is followed. There is also normally no assessment. What is of central importance in these circumstances, and what often determines the content and focus of lessons, is the immediate needs and desires of learners, as well as their longer-term goals. This low-structure context means there are minimal constraints on what tutors and learners do when they get together, and it allows space for the development of tutor–learner relationships not possible in classrooms.

In this chapter, our focus is on adult migrants learning English in ESL contexts. Although we focus on migrants, many of the principles underlying tutoring practices in such contexts are common to other tutoring situations as well. The discussion in this chapter draws on findings from a project which investigated the tutoring practices of English language tutors working one-on-one with their learners in New Zealand. The tutors are all volunteers and most have no formal training in language education. The learners are adult migrants and refugees. The tutors and learners are matched through an organization called English Language Partners New Zealand (http://englishlanguage.org.nz), which has 23 independent centres across the country. Its mission is to provide "an accessible, nationwide, community-based service that supports settlement through English for adult refugees and migrants." It offers a home-tutoring programme which involves the tutors meeting with their learners for one hour per week in the learners' homes.

We first present a vignette in the form of a narrative which tells of the experiences of one home tutor and his learner. The narrative illustrates a number of the principles associated with tutoring practices. It also presents an example of the type of tutor–learner relationship that often develops between partners in migrant contexts.

Vignette

Haolei has been Mike's learner for almost a year. He migrated to New Zealand from mainland China in 2003 with his wife. Later, his parents-in-law followed and they are now staying with him. Haolei works as a chemist in a pharmaceutical company. He studied English in China for a few years. However, he still regards his English as 'very poor': 'I can read and write some English. But my listen and speak were really bad.' When he first arrived, he faced difficulties understanding native speakers and making himself understood. A problem he now has is the inability to advance in his job. Haolei needs to improve his English skills in order to move forward in the company. However, he has little opportunity to practise English and that has become a barrier for him to improve 'because he's working only with a very small number of people at work in his laboratory situation, he doesn't get much of a chance to talk English.' Furthermore, he lives in a completely Chinese environment or what Mike terms a 'Mandarin bubble'. He speaks Mandarin to the whole family and he does not really need to interact in English outside their home. He can go to Chinese restaurants and shop at 'Asian grocery stores'. Mike believes that what Haolei actually needs is more exposure to the outside world and opportunities to speak English.

Since Haolei began working with Mike, his English has improved remarkably: 'He can read and understand quite a lot, his talking skills, after I've warmed him up, are reasonably good' and they can now have 'some quite interesting, fun conversations.' Haolei's aim in learning English is to secure his place in the company and move forward: 'He was given the hurry up at work a while ago, that if his English didn't get to a certain level, his opportunities for promotion, or maybe even continued employment with the company, may be limited.'

Mike is a retiree. He has some background in education, having taught accounting at a university. He regards himself as 'an organised sort of person' and he enjoys helping people. He believes that 'everybody has an obligation to put back into the community something that they're good at.'

When Mike first started tutoring Haolei, he always planned the lesson: 'I put a reasonable amount of time in it.' After a while, however, he found that his learner began to initiate content to work on and that often led the lesson away from the original plan. He therefore stopped making detailed lesson plans: 'I've sort of given up doing that now because he produces things and I've found that with his degree of, his current level of knowledge, I plan something and after ten minutes we've gone off track and we're doing something else that's equally important and interesting and relevant to him.' He still prepares lesson plans but keeps his preparation simple, just in case they suddenly end up with nothing to do. Mike tries to make every meeting 'fun' as well as 'practical and relevant'. For instance, in the early days, they had lessons on basic vocabulary: 'Just doing our colours and numbers and kitchen equipment and all these sorts of things." He spent some time discussing with Haolei celebrations in New Zealand such as Easter and Christmas. He also gave him opportunities to talk about China. He soon discovered Haolei's interest in fishing, and so he taught him everything about fishing: 'All the different jargon and all these things that he was mad keen to learn, it was wonderful.' Mike prepared a book in which he and Haolei write everything they do in their lessons. The book has become 'a whole encyclopaedia of lessons' which is very useful for Haolei.

Mike has a very good relationship with Haolei. He sees Haolei as 'a fun guy'. They have 'a very comfortable rapport' and Mike believes he has Haolei's 'complete confidence.' In fact, he is probably Haolei's only Kiwi friend. Sometimes Haolei treats Mike to 'ethnic dinners'. He seeks help from Mike in dealing with daily life matters: 'He brings me things, any letters he gets from work or things he doesn't understand, or any formal documents that come into the house that he can't manage, he shows me.' Mike too is very concerned about his learner. He tries to help him in every way that he can, including finding opportunities for him to get involved with the wider society in order to improve his English.

The tutoring arrangement has contributed to Mike's own development as a tutor. He finds that his own knowledge of English is improving. His goal is to work with other learners and to help them achieve proficiency in the English language so that they can integrate into the New Zealand community and become successful.

Principles

Breen et al. (2001) refer to a number of principles that guide language teachers' classroom practices; they call these *concerns*, because they are what teachers are concerned about, what they pay attention to when they plan and teach their lessons. Although the principles are focused on classroom teaching, they can be adapted to home tutoring practices beyond the classroom.

> *Principle 1. Tutors are concerned with how their learners undertake the learning process.* They choose materials and lesson content that they believe is appropriate for the learner in terms of both their needs and their level of English proficiency. They also pay attention to what their learners are interested in and what type of learning activities they prefer to do. They monitor the learning styles of the

learner and their levels of motivation. When Mike first started tutoring Haolei, for example, he always planned his lessons thoroughly. But after a while he noticed that soon after the lessons started they would drift off onto other topics which Haolei found more interesting and useful. He thus stopped making detailed lesson plans and let the sessions unfold in a more flexible manner.

Principle 2. Tutors are concerned with the particular attributes of the learner. Again, with only one learner it is possible for tutors to discover a lot about them. With regular meetings over time they focused attention on the work they do together, and the friendly personal conversations which inevitably take place, tutors are in a good position to learn about the backgrounds of their students; such as their age, personal and learning needs, their refugee/migrant status, employment issues, family circumstances and responsibilities, and their level of commitment and motivation for learning English. Consequently, they are better able to make informed decisions about what it is they do when they come together for a tutorial—decisions that address the specific needs of the individual learner. Mike knew a lot about Haolei, including his employment background and the need to improve his English in order to make progress at work, his family situation and his lack of opportunity to practise speaking English outside his Chinese community, and his interest in fishing. He constantly tried, therefore, to make the lessons relevant to Haolei's background and interests, e.g., introducing vocabulary specific to fishing.

Principle 3. Tutors are concerned with how to use the relatively short period they have with their learner effectively, efficiently and to full advantage, including being cognizant of learners' needs, desires and goals. This principle involves the effective use of the time the tutor and learner spend together. Mike, for instance, believes that Haolei needs more practice speaking English, since he doesn't get the opportunity in his community. He therefore encourages Haolei to speak as much as possible in the time they have available, offering him topics to talk about such as his life in China and fishing. They also discuss any documents or letters Haolei comes across at work that he can't understand. In a classroom situation, teachers can arrange learners into pairs or groups to work together on particular tasks. In a tutorial session, however, this is not possible. The tutor is always involved directly with the learner in one-on-one activity. Neither the tutor nor the learner can disengage with what is being done in the session—they are the only two people there!

Principle 4. Tutors are concerned with the subject matter of learning. This principle focuses very much on *what* is taught and learned. This is a priority for the tutor and critically important for the learner. They are not following a generic syllabus or one designed to meet the needs of a large number of learners (a class, a grade level). Everything they do is geared towards the needs of one particular learner. In the case of home tutors and migrants, the goal is to learn enough English to enable learners to settle and live productive lives in their new country. When Mike and Haolei get together for their weekly session, the subject matter they cover relates directly to Haolei's needs—those perceived as important by Mike and those identified by Haolei himself. The conversations may not always be about the English language or even language related but they do aim to advance settlement for Haolei and to help him interact more effectively and confidently with English speakers.

Principle 5. Tutors are concerned with the specific contributions they can make in their role as tutor. This principle is one which perhaps most significantly distinguishes the one-on-one tutor from the classroom language teacher, mainly because of the nature of the relationship tutors develop with their learners. In order for the relationship to be effectual in the learning situation, tutors need to establish a good rapport with their learner early on in their relationship. This is true for all teaching situations, of course, but especially so for one-on-one home tutors, where tutors and learners work intimately together; their focus is almost entirely on each other during the sessions. In the next section, we look more at these relationships. Here it is important to note that what the learners achieve in their English learning depends very much on the working relationship they have with their tutor.

Applications

Learning Contexts

One-on-one language learning with a tutor is an out-of-classroom learning arrangement that is designed specifically to meet the goals and needs of one particular learner. Examples of contexts in which such learning takes place include the following:

1. Young learners (pre-primary or primary, and usually because their parents want them to) take extra tuition outside of school either to reinforce the school English language curriculum or to learn additional skills.
2. Older learners at the secondary school level work with independent tutors to focus specifically on the content of the school curriculum, usually concentrating on assessment and examination preparation.
3. Learners of varying ages and for varying purposes (e.g., university entrance, immigration) work with tutors to prepare for formal proficiency tests such as TOEFL and IELTS.
4. University students take up non-credit tutoring to supplement their regular coursework. The content normally covers academic literacy.
5. Adults outside formal educational institutions take up tutoring opportunities available to them in order to learn the language of the community they are living in. This is the typical scenario in migrant contexts, and the home tutoring programme described above is a good example.

Home Tutoring Practices

Home tutoring for adult migrants works well because it primarily focuses on the life of the migrant learner. Tutors respect their learners and the experiences they bring along to their lessons. As we have emphasized in this chapter their learning is immediately relevant to their lives, and so normally learners actively collaborate with their tutors to choose and organize what they learn. These decisions are needs driven. Jitklang (2010) conducted a study to explore New Zealand home tutors' practices and how they relate to what is important in the lives of their migrant learners. The following categories describe the main areas on which the tutors and learners focus their work together. Examples illustrate how these are translated into actual tutoring-learning practices both at the time they meet and sometimes beyond in the wider community. You will notice how they reflect the tutoring principles discussed in the section above.

Wider Social Contact

Both tutors and learners are aware that learners often lack social contact with the wider English-speaking society outside of their own "ethnic bubble" (Yates, 2011). Learners are limited to their comfort zone within their own families and communities, and some do not desire or are not confident to interact with other people outside their community. Mike felt that Haolei needs "more exposure to the outside world and opportunities to speak English" and so he helped Haolei to make contact and interact with people beyond his immediate circle of family and work colleagues.

Speaking Proficiency

Proficiency in speaking English is clearly associated with wider social contact. Learners who are able to speak and understand English in their daily lives would be far more confident and willing to engage with English speakers in the workplace, in shops, schools and hospitals. With this in mind tutors encourage conversational practice in their lessons and provide the necessary vocabulary for learners to do so. Mike and Haolei, for example, were all too aware of the need to practise English—his promotion at work and possibly even his job depended on it.

Emotional Well-Being

Migrant learners go through many ups and downs as new members of an unfamiliar community and these are reflected in the varying emotional states they share with their tutors when they meet. Because of their close working relationship, expressions of emotion are easily perceived by the tutors, and so it becomes possible to address any related issues that may arise, as appropriate. Abandoning lesson plans is one way that Mike showed his willingness to adapt to Haolei's desires. He also endeavoured to make every meeting "fun" so that Haolei could relax and feel confident to engage in his learning.

Knowledge of Learning Context

In migrant learning situations, it is important for learners to have a general knowledge of the broader context in which they will use English, and more generally, live productive lives at work or while performing daily activities like shopping, banking and meeting with doctors and their children's teachers. Mike, for instance, discussed with Haolei cultural differences between people living in New Zealand and China, and he encouraged him to venture out into the broader English-speaking community to learn more about it.

Personal Needs and Goals

The most salient feature of one-on-one tutoring is that it is directed at the goals and needs of the learner. The goals may be quite explicitly stated, such as to pass an examination, get a promotion at work, sit an immigration interview, or obtain a learner driver's licence. The goals may also be rather general, such as conversational practice, acquiring cultural knowledge, or just having someone to talk to. Whatever the case may be, the goals and needs determine tutoring and learning practices.

Home Tutor Relationships

The kind of relationship that develops between tutor and learner would not be possible in a regular language classroom, where the teacher has many more students to manage. Learners in one-on-one tutoring arrangements receive undivided attention from their tutors. It is inevitable, therefore, that the role of tutor is much more easily adaptable than that of the teacher, molded by who the learners are, what their needs are, and the working relationship between the two partners. In some cases, the relationship becomes more than a "working" relationship, especially when affective or emotional factors come into play; an inter-personal, emotional dimension. O'Hara (2005) makes references to a transcendent teacher-learner relationship, a relationship in which emotions are paramount: "Caring, trust, mutual respect and love are characteristics of transcendent relationships" (p. 331).

Barkhuizen (2011) studied the different types of home tutor roles evident in the relationships tutors experienced with their migrant learners in New Zealand. Some of the more prevalent role types are as follows:

1. *Language and culture informant.* Here we have the typical tutor function, and the starting point for the development of tutor–learner relationships. This is why they come together in the first place—for tutors to teach English, and through doing so, inform the learner about life in New Zealand. This is the official "teacher" role.
2. *Visitor.* Because they meet in the home of the learner, tutors are usually welcomed as and feel like visitors. They sometimes share meals with the family of the learner, during which, no doubt, conversations in English continue.

3. *Friend.* In this role, tutors and learners begin to achieve a transcendent relationship as described by O'Hara (2005). Besides doing lessons in tutorials, they visit each other's homes, socialize together outside the home, and spend Christmas and other special occasions together—just like friends do. Often 'tutorials' are held in supermarkets, in banks, during picnics, and while walking on the beach.

4. *Social worker.* The content of what the tutors and learners do and the materials they work with are directly relevant to the learners' lives as English-learning migrants. This inevitably means going beyond a focus on grammar, vocabulary and pronunciation, and to address issues of settlement in a new country. Examples include visiting the bank to open an account, and reading and translating complicated documents such as tax forms.

Payoffs and Pitfalls

In this chapter, we have focused mainly on learner benefits associated with learning in one-on-one tutoring arrangements, paying particular attention to the home tutoring situation for adult migrants in an ESL context. To summarise (see also Bollin & Cai, 2013), they are as follows:

1. Learners receive the undivided attention of their tutors.
2. The work they do together is based on the learners' needs and goals, and so the purpose of the lessons (as evident in the content and materials used, and whether conducted in the home of the learner or outside in the community) is entirely learner centred.
3. Since the work is very much related to learners' needs and interests, they maintain a high level of motivation and notice its relevance to their lives.
4. They also enjoy their sessions because the lessons take place in an anxiety-free environment.
5. Tutors are typically native English speakers, providing a New Zealand English-speaking model many of the learners desire.
6. Tutors and learners get to know each other well and develop relationships which may go beyond the typical teacher–learner relationship. They connect emotionally, and may even become life-long friends.
7. Learners are respected and trusted. They therefore feel free to suggest lesson content and are happy to introduce their life experiences into the work they do with their tutors.

It is not always smooth sailing, however, for the learners and their tutors. One-on-one tutoring has certain limitations, and sometimes things go wrong:

1. A learner and a tutor may be a poor match. For whatever reasons, they simply do not get along.

2. Because of the close, friendly relationship that develops between learners and tutors, they might begin to pay less attention to the purpose of their meetings (i.e., to teach and learn English) and veer off into less appropriate topics and activities. This might not always be a bad thing, but it is if no further English learning takes place.
3. Tutors may take on more responsibilities for the lives of their learners than is necessary or appropriate; for example, interfering in personal employment issues, becoming too involved in a learner's family life and matchmaking with potential partners!
4. Inexperienced tutors may not be able to assess accurately the proficiency level of their learners and thus continue to teach subject matter which is too easy or difficult for the learners.
5. With one-on-one tutoring there is always only one learner during any lesson. There is no opportunity therefore to practise speaking or to work on tasks and exercises with other learners—no pair work or group work.
6. One-on-one learning may not suit the learning style of a particular learner; for example, those who would prefer to learn by communicating with other learners or would prefer to remain 'anonymous' and not actively engage with learning activities.

Discussion Questions

1. How important is teacher training or professional development for a language tutor?
2. What kind of learners would not find tutoring suitable for their learning needs?
3. What could home tutors do to sustain a high level of motivation for their learners?
4. What can learners do to ensure that they get the most out of their tutorial meetings?
5. One-on-tutoring described in this chapter is face-to-face. How could it be done online? How effective do you think it would be?

Resources

Tutoring for immigrants
The *English Language Partners New Zealand* webpage features information about home tutoring—http://englishlanguage.org.nz/esol-home-tutoring
Settlement Assistance Program in British Columbia, Canada, offers ESL tutoring—http://www.welcomebc.ca/learnenglish
The *Adult Migrant English Program (AMEP)*, Australia, is for individuals who want to become home tutors as well as learners—http://www.immi.gov.au/living-in-australia/help-with-english/amep/teaching-english/home-tutor.htm

References

Barkhuizen, G. (2011). Home tutor cognitions and the nature of tutor-learner relationships. In P. Benson & H. Reinders (Eds.), *Beyond the language classroom* (pp. 161–174). Basingstoke: Palgrave Macmillan.

Bollin, G., & Cai, W. (2013). The benefits of home tutoring of English language learners: The tutor's perspective. *International Journal of Humanities and Social Science*, 3(3), 38–44.

Breen, M., Hird, B., Milton, M., Oliver, R., & Thwaite, A. (2001). Making sense of language teaching: Teachers' principles and classroom practice. *Applied Linguistics*, 22(4), 470–501.

Jitklang, P. (2010). *Home tutor concerns and the relationship between the concerns and tutoring practices*. Unpublished master's dissertation, University of Auckland. Auckland, New Zealand.

O'Hara, H. (2005). The transcendent teacher-learner relationship: A class investigation. *Journal of Early Childhood Teacher Education*, 25, 331–337.

Yates, L. (2011). Interaction, language learning and social inclusion in early settlement. *International Journal of Bilingual Education and Bilingualism*, 14(4), 457–471.

LIST OF CONTRIBUTORS

Jane Arnold, Universidad de Sevilla, Spain

Kathleen M. Bailey, Monterey Institute of International Studies, USA

Gary Barkhuizen, University of Auckland, New Zealand

Ken Beatty, Anaheim University, USA

Julie Bytheway, Victoria University of Wellington, New Zealand

Marc Cadd, Drake University, USA

Kelley Calvert, Monterey Institute of International Studies, USA

David L. Chiesa, Beijing Normal University, People's Republic of China

Alice Chik, City University of Hong Kong, Hong Kong

Averil Coxhead, Victoria University of Wellington, New Zealand

Andy Curtis, Anaheim University, USA

Richard Day, University of Hawaii, USA

Carmen Fonseca-Mora, Universidad de Huelva, Spain

Betsy Gilliland, University of Hawaii, USA

Maike Grau, Pädagogische Hochschule Freiburg/University of Education, Germany

Jennifer Grode, Monterey Institute of International Studies, USA

Christoph A. Hafner, City University of Hong Kong, Hong Kong

Anthony Hanf, Konkuk University, South Korea

Jing Huang, Hong Kong Baptist University, Hong Kong

Erika Kerekes, Shoin University, Japan

Olga Kozar, Macquarie University, Australia

Michael Legutke, University of Giessen, Germany

Phoebe M. S. Lin, Chinese University of Hong Kong, Hong Kong ´

Nana Long, Dezhou University/Hong Kong Baptist University, Hong Kong

John Macalister, Victoria University of Wellington, New Zealand

Leonardo A. Mercado, Instituto Cultural Peruano Norteamericano (ICPNA), Peru

Lindsay Miller, City University of Hong Kong, Hong Kong

Tamami Mori, University of New South Wales, Australia

Catarina Pontes, Associação Cultura Inglesa São Paulo, Brazil

Maria do Carmo Righini, Associação Cultura Inglesa São Paulo, Brazil

Thomas Robb, Kyoto Sangyo University, Japan

Akihiko Sasaki, Kwansei Gakuin Junior High School, Japan

Marilisa Shimazumi, Associação Cultura Inglesa São Paulo, Brazil

Anna Siyanova-Chanturia, Victoria University of Wellington, New Zealand

Adrienne Stacy, Kanda University of International Studies, Japan

Phiona Stanley, University of New South Wales, Australia

Chihara Kinoshita Thomson, University of New South Wales, Australia

JoDee Walters, Yanbu University College, Saudi Arabia

Stuart Webb, Victoria University of Wellington, New Zealand

INDEX